Hadfields Cave:
Report No. 13

HADFIELDS CAVE:
A Perspective on Late Woodland Culture in Northeastern Iowa

David W. Benn

Report 13
Office of the State Archaeologist
The University of Iowa
Iowa City
1980

Hadfields Cave:
A Perspective on Late Woodland Culture
in Northeastern Iowa
By David W. Benn
*Thirteenth in a series of reports issued at intervals
by the Office of the State Archaeologist
The University of Iowa
Iowa City*

DUANE C. ANDERSON, *State Archaeologist*
DENICE RENSCHEN, *Editor*

Library of Congress Cataloging in Publication Data

Benn, David W.   1948-
    Hadfields Cave.

    (Report — Office of the State Archaeologist; 13)
    Bibliography: p.
    1. Hadfields Cave, Iowa. I. Title. II. Series:
Iowa. State Archaeologist. Report; 13.
E78.I6B46   977.7'63   79-22010
ISBN 0-87414-012-9

Table of Contents

Figures

Tables

Acknowledgments

Many dissertations are monumental undertakings requiring the cooperation and contributions of many individuals. The present work is no exception, for without the assistance of many people this dissertation could not have been completed and probably would not have been started.

My appreciation goes, first and foremost, to Dr. David A. Baerreis of the University of Wisconsin-Madison. In the capacity of graduate advisor and dissertation committee chairman, Dr. Baerreis initially molded my graduate education and subsequently provided a reservoir of criticism and support for my researches. My thanks go to Dr. James Stoltman and Dr. T. Douglas Price, also members of my dissertation committee, for their editorial contributions to this manuscript.

At least seven individuals contributed to the success of the Hadfields site excavation. David Zimmerman, formerly director of the Anamosa Neighborhood Center, provided and organized the excavation crew. Lynn and Robert Alex lent invaluable assistance in the initial stages of this project; this dissertation would not have been started without the contribution of Robert Alex. Much of the field equipment was provided by Dr. Marshall McKusick, then State Archaeologist. The cooperation of Steven Supple and other nearby landowners made access to the Hadfields site possible. Derek Marcucci assisted in the first weeks of the field season. Finally, Mr. Gene Loes, a local resident, befriended and directed me to Hadfields Cave. I continue to have a high regard for Gene Loes' interest in the cave and its contents.

The writer was assisted in the laboratory analysis by Kathy Arndt, Linda Iltis, and Bob Otis. The extensive and unselfish contributions of the former two must be stressed, for Kathy and Linda processed a phenomenal quantity of material solely in the interest of self-improvement. Stanley Riggle also warrants special appreciation for his technical assistance on the analysis of dental cementum in the teeth of white-tailed deer and for his cooperative efforts in the fabric analysis.

Six individuals participated in the production of this manuscript. My compatriot at Luther College, Clark Mallam, was a constant source of ideas and theories pertaining to the subjects of this dissertation. Clark also gave a critical reading to portions of the manuscript. Mary Housker and Dean Thompson, the laboratory assistants at Luther College, produced many of the figures and tables which appear herein. Denice Renschen was the publication editor, and Duane Anderson and Joe Tiffany assisted technically in the production of the published version.

1

Introduction

The subject of this work is the Woodland tradition of east-central and northeast Iowa—specifically those cultural horizons for the first 900 years after the birth of Christ. These discussions do not contain a comprehensive, critical survey of all data available for this tradition. Rather, a provisional configuration of the Iowa Woodland tradition is developed through a fusion of data from the Hadfields Cave site (13JN3) and observations on selected midwestern prehistoric data. Several motives for taking this approach will be made clear in the following paragraphs but the primary inducements were twofold. In the first place, 13JN3 is the first site in eastern Iowa with a relatively limited time range of occupation (ca. A.D. 300-800) where the entire material assemblage has been subjected to meticulous analysis. Thus, many of the technical details of once-extant societal institutions are exposed, offering a satisfactory data base upon which to reconstruct Woodland culture. This presupposes the second inducement: Prior to 1975 the aboriginal cultures of eastern Iowa were largely understood in terms of trait lists and a chronological sequence (the culture-historical approach). This is an unsatisfactory state of knowledge for archaeologists who profess to be engaged in the study and reconstruction of past societies (Binford 1968). This study considers the composition of Woodland societies in terms of both hard evidence and empirical propositions.

This study also utilizes a substantial bulk of evidence accumulated by previous investigations in the Midwest; the present writer is indebted to those researchers for the data and extant collections which they have produced. Comprehensive histories of archaeological investigations are detailed in several recent works (Wisconsin—Hurley 1975:11-37; Iowa—McKusick 1975 and others in preparation; Mallam 1975:33-44); therefore, a history of research is not included here. However, it is especially important to note the outstanding contribution of the Iowa Archaeological Survey and its director, Charles R. Keyes. From the 1920s through the 1940s, Keyes and his field associate, Ellison Orr, laid the groundwork for understanding Iowa prehistory by gathering a state-wide collection of artifacts from amateurs, pursuing field surveys, and testing mounds and living sites. The fruits of Keyes' intensive labors can be studied in his extensive collections at the Iowa State Historical Society, Iowa City, Iowa. Keyes also speculated on the sequence of prehistoric culture changes in Iowa (1927, 1941), but this work is clearly subordinate in significance to the sheer volume of cultural material in the Keyes collections.

The scholarly synthesis, which Keyes did not accomplish due to lack of time and professional archaeological training, was instead produced for northeast Iowa by Wilfred D. Logan (1959). Logan's work culminates a thirty-year period of survey and testing by the Iowa Archaeological Survey aimed at recovering and understanding the sequence of culture changes in Iowa. Logan's analysis follows the standard format for midwestern archaeological research in the 1930s through the 1950s—trait lists for a series of sequential cultural entities and a ceramic seriation which places these entities in chronological order.

Until very recently, our conceptions of the prehistoric peoples of eastern Iowa have stagnated at the level reached by Logan. At the onset of excavations at the Hadfields site in 1972 the available data consisted of an untested cultural sequence and numerous second-hand concepts of cultural development borrowed from the Wisconsin Effigy Mound culture and the Illinois Havana Tradition. This statement is not intended to depreciate the pioneering efforts of Keyes, Orr, Logan, and others, for their researches must be evaluated in the context of the time in which they worked. Rather, the point is that this previous knowledge has substantial shortcomings when compared to present-day standards of archaeology. One serious problem stems from the disparity between today's excavation procedures and those of the past. Modern methods of excavating involve a degree of vertical and horizontal controls and meticulous recovery techniques which were not recognized 20 or more years ago. It follows, therefore, that the stratigraphic contexts of artifacts from these pre-1960 excavations are not precise by present standards. The supposed cultural context of such artifactual evidence must be utilized with discretion. A corollary difficulty with this material is that it represents only the net portion of recoverable cultural debris, since microrecovery techniques (flotation, fine screening) were not utilized until the late 1960s in Iowa.

An additional shortcoming of the data base prior to the 1970s was the absence of comprehensive site surveys in eastern Iowa. While it is true that the Keyes collection represents many eastern Iowa sites, these sites are scattered and selective, and in most cases the extant site collections seem to be only a portion of each site's assemblage. The lack of a representative data base is just beginning to be alleviated by an organized site reporting and salvage survey effort through the Offices of Historic Preservation and the State Archaeologist. The initial moves in the direction of comprehensive site coverage came with salvage projects in the Coralville Reservoir near Iowa City (Caldwell 1961; Anderson 1971a) and are expanding with more recent surveys of the effigy mounds in northeast Iowa (Mallam 1975) and impoundment or watershed projects (Benn 1975).

Three problem-oriented studies are now available to provide some depth of understanding of Woodland societies: Clark Mallam's dissertation (1975) which develops a model for the social and subsistence activities of the people who constructed the Iowa effigy mounds; Manfred Jaehnig's dissertation (1975), a cultural ecology model for Woodland period occupations in two rock shelters about ten miles east of the Hadfields site; and this volume.

These studies have signaled a new direction for archaeology in eastern Iowa. Two broad paths of research are evident: The first is that of complete-recovery techniques of excavation and the meticulous analysis of all artifactual materials, which are of paramount importance for the reconstruction of prehistoric life systems. This method of processing archaeological data must be applied to all sites, whenever time, money, and manpower permit. We cannot continue to allow judgments of suspected significance to predetermine excavation procedures, for it is now clear that a majority of the Late Woodland period sites are small and contain relatively sparse artifact assemblages. The second and equally important path of present research is directed toward model building (for example, Mallam 1975; Jaehnig 1975).

Prehistoric Chronology

This volume deals with a period of time when culture change in eastern Iowa was fairly rapid and distinct. Evidence of these changes in material and social culture will be described throughout these pages, but it seems appropriate to provide a skeletal chronological framework at this point.

In the Midwest the most popular chronology—Early, Middle, and Late Woodland periods—has a long-established foundation in Illinois River valley researches (Cole and Deuel 1937; Griffin 1952a, 1952b). This scheme has been tested in numerous applications and receives continued support today (Griffin et al. 1970). The boundaries of these time divisions are measured relative to a cultural and chronological constant, the Illinois Havana Tradition. The Middle Woodland period is defined by the Havana Tradition, ca. 200 B.C. to A.D. 200-300 (Griffin et al. 1970:4). The Late Woodland period begins with the disappearance of the Havana Tradition type artifacts and the contiguous rise of Weaver Tradition artifacts. However, the actual "severing" from the Havana Tradition styles by Woodland peoples is not fully manifested until the advent of the Maples Mills Tradition after ca. A.D. 700 (Griffin et al. 1970). This sequence has served as the foundation for archaeological investigations and cultural reconstructions in eastern Iowa up to the present day.

4

The other out-of-state chronology relevant to this discussion was advanced by William Hurley (1970, 1975: 355-99) to structure the cultural changes in the Effigy Mound Tradition of Wisconsin. Hurley identified three periods in the evolution of this culture: Early Effigy Mound, A.D. 300-700; Middle Effigy Mound, A.D. 700-1100; and Late Effigy Mound, A.D. 1100-1642. Only the Middle ("classic") period is thoroughly dated by reliable radiocarbon assays. The latest period has radiocarbon dates for the thirteenth century only, and the earliest period is identified by seven radiocarbon dates (Hurley 1975:379-84) with questionable associations to the Effigy Mound Tradition (see chap. 3).

A basic chronology for eastern Iowa was the product of Wilfred Logan's dissertation (1959). Logan concentrated his efforts on naming a series of foci (in the Midwestern Taxonomic System) identifying cultural manifestations within the three Woodland time periods utilized in Illinois. His notions of Iowa ceramic changes follow the precedents established by Griffin (1952b). Since Logan's cultural sequence is dealt with in detail throughout this study, it will not be outlined here. But it is significant to note one difference between Logan's and Griffin's periods: ceramic types and archaeological foci assigned to the late Middle Woodland period by Logan are placed in the early Late Woodland period by Griffin, assuming a culturally equivalent context (for instance, Linn Ware and Weaver Ware, respectively). In recognizing these authors' differences, the problem of evaluating the relationships between the time span of A.D. 300-700 and the periods immediately before and after it is emphasized. In other words, our inadequate understanding of the cultural developments during the A.D. 300-700 time period in Iowa has been a major barrier to the establishment of a sound temporal framework for the Woodland sequence.

Before outlining the chronological framework utilized for this analysis, there are at least two other problems encountered in developing time sequences in Iowa and Wisconsin. First, there is an occasional tendency among some midwestern archaeologists to dilute the integrity of those Woodland cultures not identified with the Havana Tradition. That is, some Woodland cultures (often described as marginal to a culture center or focus) are viewed not as independent cultural systems with integrated bodies of beliefs and material artifacts, but as subcultures of the Havana Interaction Sphere (Struever 1964). Thus, a sequence of culture change is developed by documenting the evolutionary change which takes place throughout the Interaction Sphere. But in taking a slightly different view, there may be completely independent Woodland cultures which are participating in the Havana Interaction Sphere to different degrees. Sequence building in this case is greatly complicated because the diffusion of ideas and the recombinations of those ideas must be traced through many cultural groups across space and through time. The position taken here is that Woodland peoples in Iowa and the upper Midwest were indeed participating in many independent culture systems, albeit in dispersed settlement patterns, and that these systems can be described as entities separate from a culture system with greater visibility in the archaeological record—the Havana Tradition.

The second major problem for cultural chronologies revolves around the unwarranted use of the term *association* as it applies to the relationships of artifact types in a site midden. The small Woodland village and rock shelter sites of Wisconsin and Iowa are notorious for their lack of stratigraphy and their mixing of components. In many sites the use of arbitrary excavation levels will not produce anything close to pure assemblages. Thus, incorrect artifact associations are ingrained in the scholarly records when investigators assume that artifact types are culturally associated because they are resting within the same stratigraphic layer. Examples of this problem will be cited later in the text.

This volume will not offer an entirely new cultural sequence to compete with those already advanced. Rather, it will follow Logan's basic design of 1959, transforming portions of it into the modern taxonomy (Willey and Phillips 1958), renaming certain other parts, and suggesting slight revisions in several instances. In abstract terms this chronology will take the following form: The Middle Woodland period, including the Havana Tradition, is applied to eastern Iowa manifestations, as it is used in Illinois, for the time span of ca. 200-100 B.C. to A.D. 300. It is assumed, however, that while Iowans of this time horizon were strongly influenced by the cultures of the Illinois River valley peoples, the Iowan Havana manifestation was indigenous to the state. It is also recognized that using the term *Havana* in Iowa does *not* imply that the Hopewell burial cult was a significant component of this Woodland culture.

The time span, ca. A.D. 300-700, provides special problems. This situation is far from unique to this study, for this period has been the cause of gross confusion and the subject of problematic debate among prehistorians for decades. This period is usually prefixed onto the Late Woodland period or suffixed onto the middle Woodland period, with the result that it is then viewed as a single horizon within the larger period. To avoid such implications, this study opts for renaming the A.D. 300-650 time span and calling it the *Intermediate period*. The arguments favoring the use of Intermediate period are twofold. First, there are ceramic types which are unique to this time horizon (for example, Linn Ware), although several specific types have been described as "transitional." In fact, there is a technological change in the ceramics of this period. The second argument is that this period is identified as a time of major social change, and thus it may be defined as a transitional period from our superior perspective of hindsight. Here social change is defined as the cultural modifications which occur between the major cultural traditions which

6

precede and postdate the Intermediate period (Havana and Effigy Mound, respectively). Of course, identifying social and artifactual change as attributes of the Intermediate period suggests that the endpoints of this time period should not be permanently fixed. The absolute figures A.D. 300 and 650 are employed for convenience and may carry more than a ± 50-year error factor.

The Late Woodland period, ca. A.D. 700-1200 (the terminal date is not discussed in this study), is contemporary with the Effigy Mound Tradition in northeast Iowa and Wisconsin. The period does not include the invention of cord- (fabric-) decorated pottery such as Lane Farm Cord Impressed, but it apparently encompasses the rapid spread and development of the fabric-decorated pottery known as Madison Fabric Impressed and Minotts Cord Impressed. The coterminous relationship between the Late Woodland period and the Effigy Mound Tradition is especially important, since the construction of effigy mounds indicates that a particular complex of integrated beliefs and behaviors was being widely practiced by Woodland peoples. It is the cultural system of the peoples who built effigy mounds that should be bracketed by the Late Woodland period.

The Data Base

Hadfields Cave was excavated during the summer of 1972 by this writer with the assistance of laborers provided by the Youth Work Corps program through the Neighborhood Center in Anamosa, Iowa. This site was selected for excavation because it appeared that it would contain a deep midden with a long cultural sequence. In reality the midden was shallow and the intensive occupation had taken place only between ca. A.D. 300 and 800. The focus of this study was therefore shifted to the reconstruction of man's culture and paleoecology for that time span. To attain these goals in the most complete and satisfactory manner, the artifactual material was processed through a wide range of analytical procedures. These included fine screening of selected soil samples from the midden, identification of the floral and faunal remains, a butchering analysis of selected faunal remains, age and seasonal determinations on cementum growth rings from the teeth of the white-tailed deer (*Odocoileus virginianus*), reconstruction of the inhabitants' diet, and rubber latex casting of pottery sherd surfaces for a fabric analysis of Madison Ware vessels. The complex analysis of this material provides an in-depth view of life patterns at one site. The site is utilized in this volume as the data base for organizing a discussion of the cultures of Intermediate and Late Woodland peoples in eastern Iowa. The ultimate results of this discussion are stated in a series of informal hypotheses which describe and explain the patterns of Woodland culture for this time span.

A series of appendices, containing detailed artifact descriptions and an analysis of the faunal assemblage, accompanies the text. These can be found on microfiche in the back pocket of the book.

2

Hadfields Cave

Hadfields Cave (13JN3), located in the heavily forested North Maquoketa River valley in northeastern Jones County, Iowa, is accessible only on foot. The cave's mouth opens on the property of Mr. Steven Supple, the owner at the time of excavation (Figs. 1-2). The cave opening is situated at the summit of the bluff talus slope with approximately 50 vertical feet of bedrock exposed as a cliff face above the opening. The entrance faces the northeast. The cave is located roughly 300 feet west of the North Maquoketa River bank on the north bluff face of a deep gully which empties into the Maquoketa River. This gully is approximately one-half mile in length, about 150 feet at its greatest depth, and runs in a westerly direction from the west side of the river trench. The gully is heavily forested along nearly its entire length and supports an ephemeral stream.

The Hadfields site is positioned on the western border of the Driftless Zone, a highly dissected region of northeast Iowa and the three adjacent states. Erosional forces have removed much of the glacial till mantle in this part of the state, thus accounting for the earlier interpretation that this area was untouched by the glaciers. All of the four major Pleistocene glaciations passed into Iowa, but only two of these affected the northeastern section (Fig. 3). The first two episodes, the Nebraskan and Kansan, passed through the state. The Illinoian glaciation crossed only the southeastern corner of the state. The final glaciation, the Wisconsin, spread over the northern half of central Iowa. Jones County was crossed by narrow fingers of the Iowan Erosional Surface, but large portions of the county's northeast quarter remained unaffected. The North and South forks of the Maquoketa River flow through areas covered only by Kansan and Nebraskan ice (Trowbridge 1966; Ruhe et al. 1968).

The region of Kansan drift where 13JN3 is situated has been called the Drift Border Area by McGee (1891:382-92). This is an area 8-20 miles wide which extends along the western edge of the Driftless Zone. McGee characterized the Drift Border Area as a mixture of features found in the depositional topography of recently glaciated central Iowa and the Driftless Zone. While nearly all of the Kansan till has been removed by erosion from the Drift Border Area, the topographic pattern typically

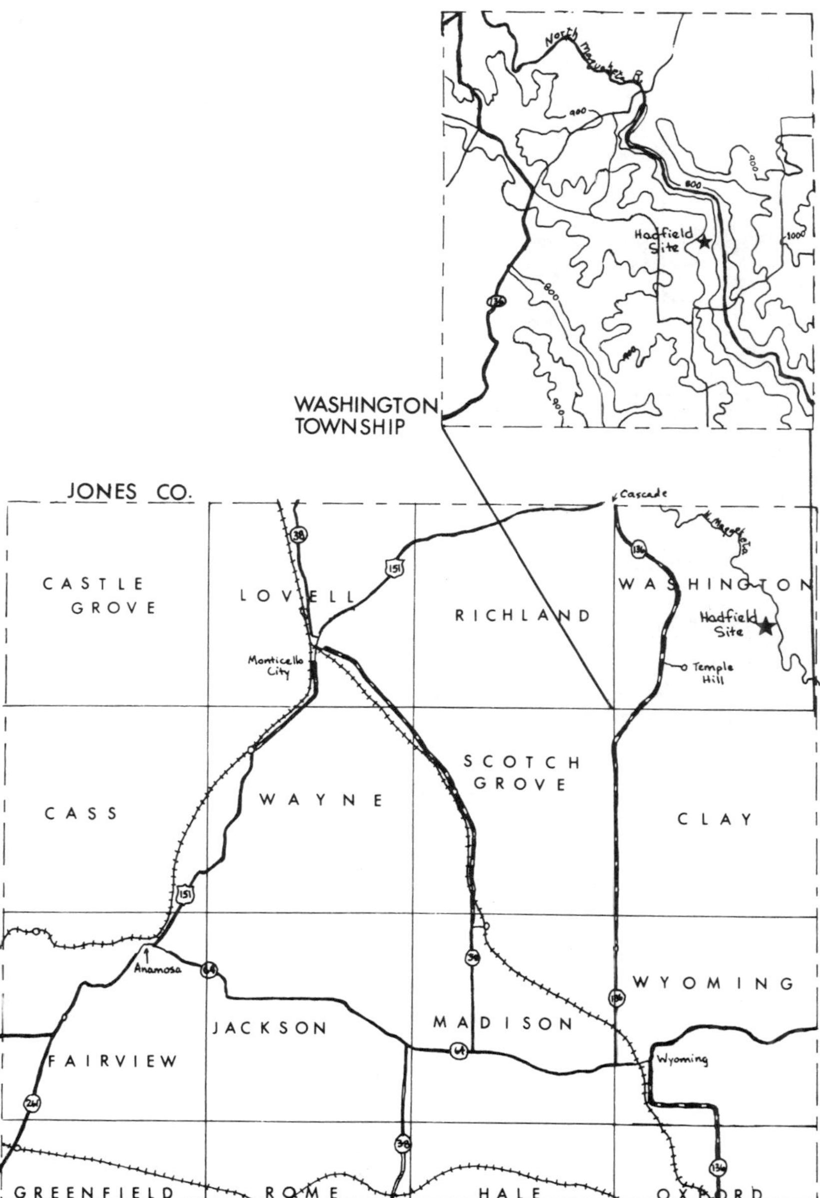

Fig. 1. Location of Hadfields Cave (13JN3) in Jones County, Iowa.

10

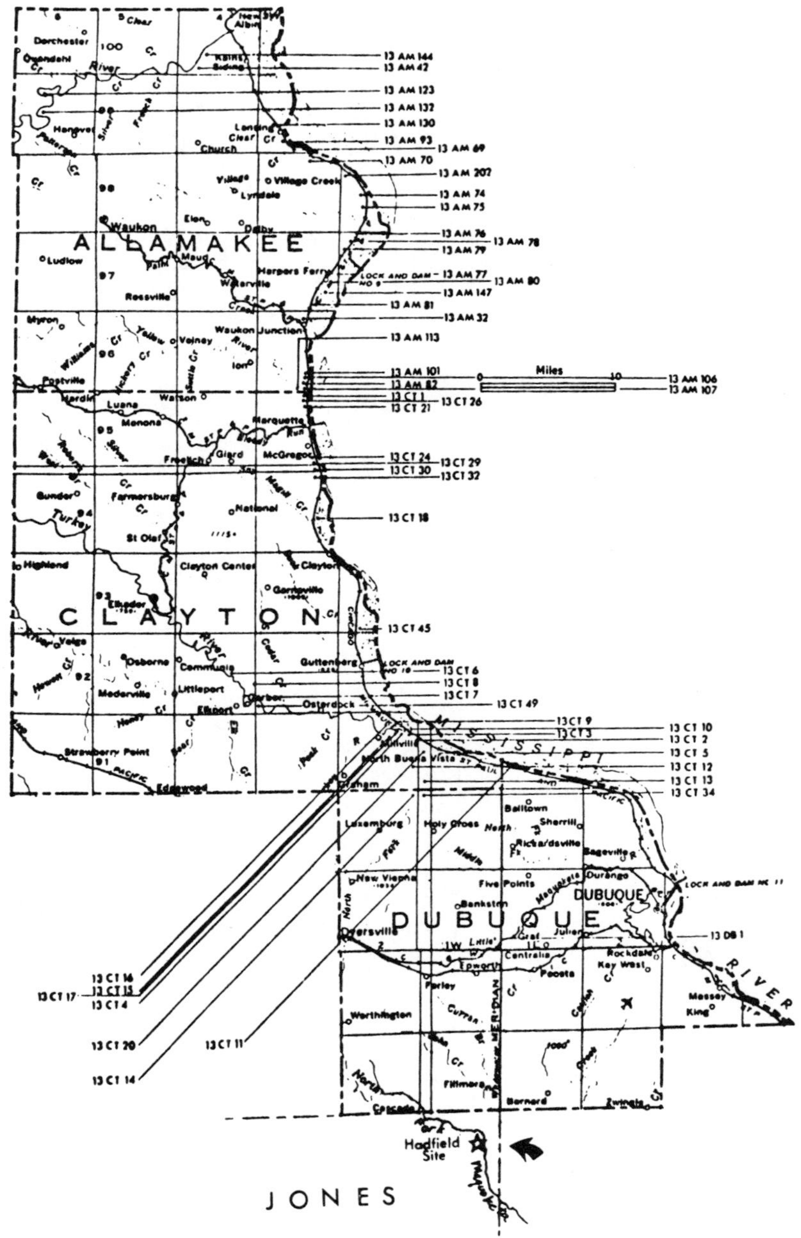

Fig. 2. Distribution of the Effigy Mounds in Iowa.

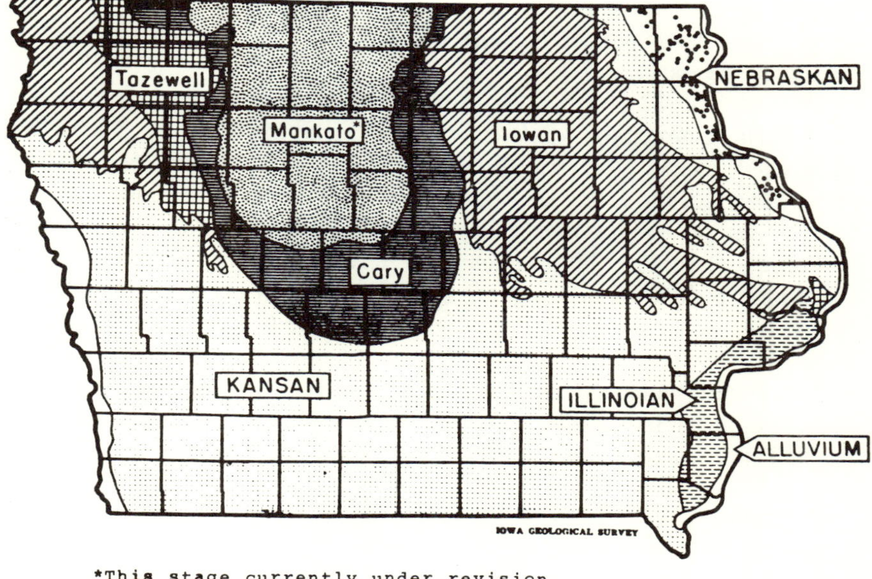

*This stage currently under revision.

Fig. 3. Surface glacial deposits in Iowa.

consists of rolling hills interrupted by deep gullies, entrenched streams, and deep river gorges. This drainage network is well developed, although it is not as mature nor as deeply entrenched as the drainage system of the Driftless Zone, the region of Nebraskan age immediately to the east. Approximately 4,400 square miles are contained in the Drift Border Area, and about 4,000 square miles comprise the Driftless Zone of Iowa.

Ten miles southwest of Hadfields Cave the landscape is gently rolling with broad, shallow river valleys. At this point the Iowa erosional surface (Ruhe et al. 1968) is the dominant landform. The Iowan surface is an eroded till of the Tazewell substage of the Wisconsin glaciation and continues across Iowa to the central portion of the state. In central Iowa the Iowan surface is overlain by till of the Cary substage of the Wisconsin glaciation (Ruhe et al. 1968).

In the past the dissected topography of northeast Iowa was considered to be morphologically and temporally identical to the Driftless Zone of southwest Wisconsin, southeast Minnesota, and northwest Illinois (Martin 1932). Indeed, all four regions are similar in that they have mature, dentritic networks of streams and rivers delineated by precipitous cliffs and bluffs, sharp ridges, and towering buttes. Recent authors (Hedges and Darland 1963; Trowbridge 1966) have recognized that the major river systems of northeast Iowa were formed in preglacial periods, and were subsequently buried by Nebraskan and Kansan glacial till. Due to the

12

absence of Illinoian and Wisconsin drift deposits, these preglacial river valleys have been partially resurrected by the reoccupation of buried courses by rivers.

The valley of the North Maquoketa River in the immediate vicinity of 13JN3 is little more than 1,500 feet wide and about 250 feet deep. The river trench is V-shaped with nearly vertical walls up to 200 feet high. The vertical faces of the valley walls are broken at intervals of several hundred feet by lateral gullies and valleys containing intermittent run-off or spring-fed streams. This portion of the valley is entrenched in the Hopkinton Formation, a Niagaran (middle Silurian) age dolomite (Rose 1967). Two other dolomite formations, Kankakee (upper Alexandrian— lower Silurian age) and Edgewood (lower Alexandrian age), underlie the Hopkinton unit but are buried by the valley wall talus slope. The former of these two buried formations contains interbedded layers of chert and may be the source of all of the local cherts utilized by the inhabitants of the site.

Hadfields Cave is basically composed of three contiguous rooms separated by passages only slightly smaller than the dimensions of the rooms. The first and largest room immediately inside the entrance contains the site (Figs. 4-6). It is roughly 100 feet in the north-south dimension and 40 feet in the east-west dimension. The two remaining rooms each decrease in size by about one-third toward the back of the cave, giving the entire cave an approximate length of 200 feet. A number of smaller passages and domes adjoin the larger rooms; however, these are largely clogged with breakdown and soil deposits.

The cave was probably formed by solution at or immediately below the water table during the early Pleistocene. Since its formation there has been considerable modification of the walls and ceiling due to the corrosive actions of percolating ground water and thermoclastic fracturing. The former weathering pattern is found primarily more than 50 feet from the entrance, while the latter is most intense at or near the entrance. At present, travertine formations are not well developed, as the movement of ground water through the cave is slow and sporadic.

In one of the few studies relevant to the morphological origin and age of the Maquoketa River caves, Hedges and Darland (1963) suggest an Aftonian age for cave development. They also indicate that these caves were formed at or slightly below the water table ("shallow-phreatic" caves) "during periods of water-table stability coinciding with periods of graded condition in surface streams" (Hedges and Darland 1963:300-302). The sequence of cave floor deposits which they present (reproduced below) is morphologically similar to that exposed in the excavation of Squares 113, 112, and 121 at 13JN3 (Fig. 7).

    5)   (uppermost) sub-aqueously deposited calcite; also, sub-aerially deposited calcite and argonite; also, (at entrance) talus.

4a) unconformity.
4) lacustrine silts and clays; also, sub-aqueously deposited calcite.
3) fluvial sands and silts.
2) sub-aerially deposited calcite.
1) (lowermost) breakdown.
[Hedges and Darland 1963:302]

In this stratigraphic sequence, levels 3 and 4 represent deposits of pre-Kansan age. At 13JN3 the deposit in Square 113, only 20 feet inside the entrance, contained fluvial and lacustrine deposits analogous to levels 3 and 4 at 42-50 inches in depth. However, if we are to assume that only 42 inches of soil and breakdown has been deposited in the cave since the close of the Kansan glaciation, then the rate of natural deposition at Hadfields Cave has been incredibly slow for the last several hundred thousand years. Seemingly, this reconstructed rate of filling is too slow considering that the entrance is very large (ca. 3x40 feet) and well ventilated.

Recognizing this problem, this report will assume the tentative position that Hadfields Cave has been inundated to some extent during more recent glacial episodes, possibly as late as the Tazewell substage of the Wisconsin stadial. Modest fluvial deposits, such as those between 42 and 50 inches, could have been deposited in shallow standing water. Accumulation of water on the cave floor would have resulted if the floor deposits became saturated and drainage was blocked by the higher talus below the drip-line of the entrance.

Excavation

Hadfields Cave has been known to a small number of local residents for almost a century. The location is frequently visited by picnickers and has been the object of attention by area Boy Scout troops for as long as 50 years. A 1-2 inch thick deposit of soil and modern charcoal covers portions of the cave floor. The majority of this material has accumulated as a result of this modern activity. This uppermost layer was easily separated from the aboriginal midden.

The extent of previous excavation is undocumented, but a limited amount of amateur disturbance was revealed during the 1972 excavations. One rectangular "pothole" approximately 9 inches in depth was present in Squares 100-101. Backdirt from this intrusive pit had been thinly scattered over adjacent squares. Another probable pothole was located along the line separating Squares 134 and 135. The identity of this latter undocumented excavation was realized when Features 40 and 43 from this area were reconstructed in vertical and horizontal profiles in the laboratory. This disturbance may have been 3 to 4 feet in diameter with a pointed bottom.

14

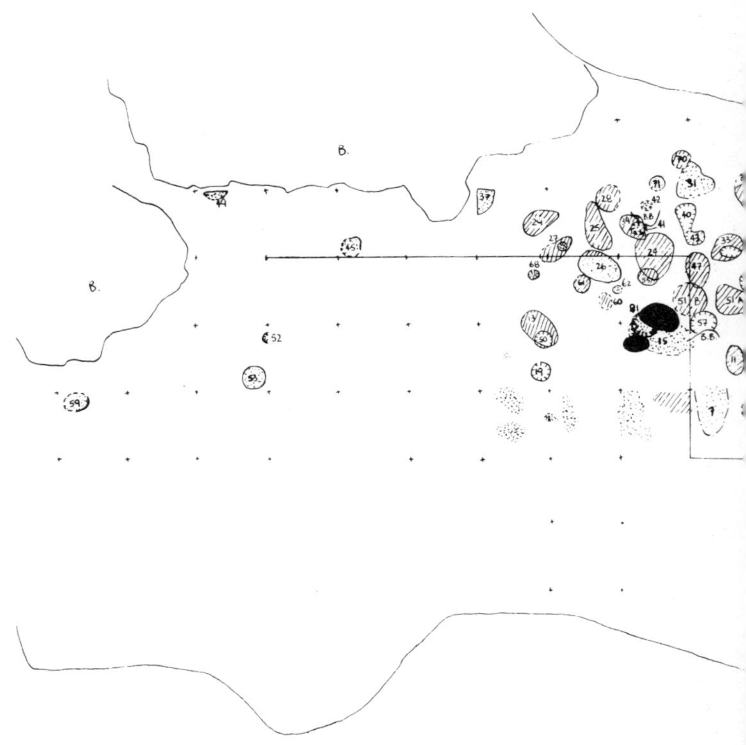

Fig. 4. Plan map of the Hadfields site (13JN3).

During the course of the 1972 field season it was necessary to change the excavation strategy. Initially, the cave deposits were believed to have considerable depth. The floor was extremely flat, the walls and ceiling were smoothed by weathering and fire blackened, the talus slope at the entrance drip-line was several feet higher than the interior cave floor, and the cave walls were expanding as they disappeared below the cave floor. Easy access was afforded by the wide entrance, yet a relatively constant temperature was obviously maintained in the first room year-round. For these reasons it was anticipated that we would encounter a considerable time depth in the cultural deposits, and that several feet of stratified midden would be exposed.

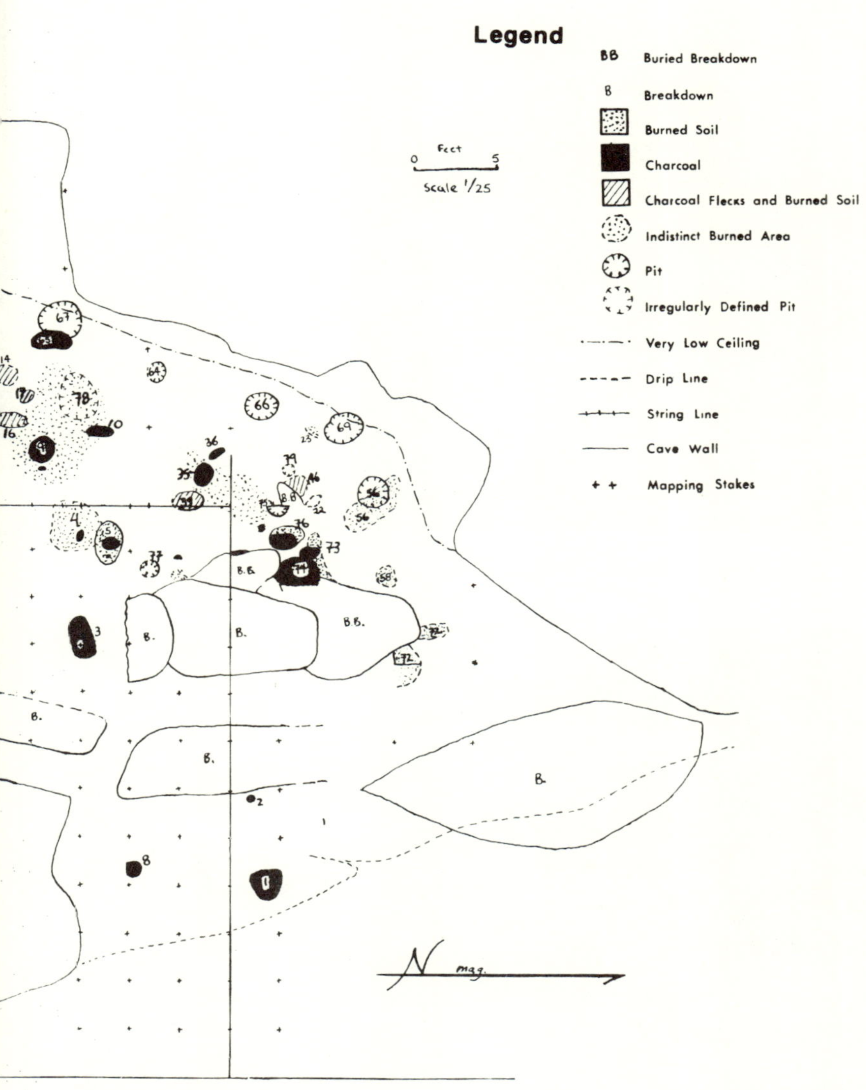

The first four weeks of the field season were given to excavating deposits at the entrance and developing the initial trenches across the interior cave floor. Arbitrary 3-inch levels were maintained throughout the season as the only vertical excavation unit. The steep talus slope at the cave's entrance and the first 18 feet immediately inside the entrance were divided into 3x3 feet control squares (Fig. 4). It was believed that this relatively small control square would facilitate the excavating of this portion of the site,

Fig. 5. View of Hadfields Cave entrance.

Fig. 6. View of interior of cave.

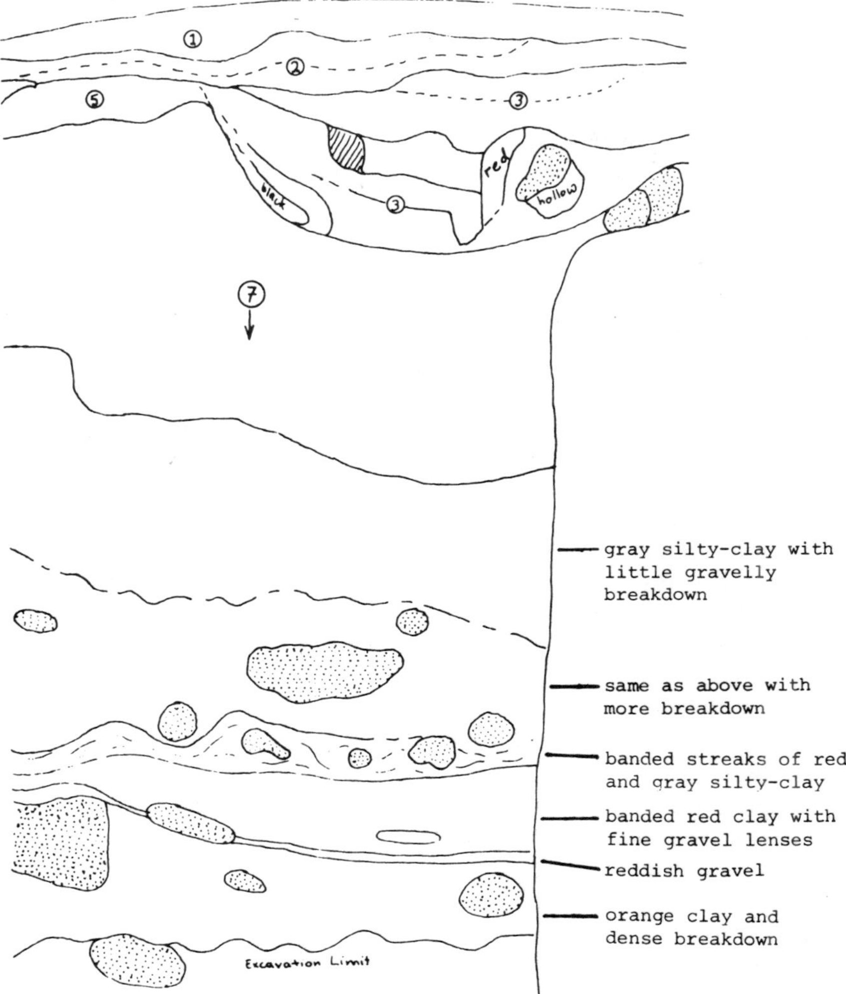

Fig. 7. North wall profile of Square 113.

since squares were excavated according to their natural surface angle, and a number of large, immovable blocks of ceiling fall clogged the entrance. A section at the entrance, 18x12 feet, was the first to be excavated. Removal of this section provided an opportunity for training the inexperienced crew and for increasing the height of the walkway to the first room. The entrance was excavated to a depth of about 2 feet, although a control trench (Squares 8-14) eventually went to a depth of 5 feet. Exceedingly little cultural material was located in these operations, and during the second week the focus of work proceeded to the area of 3x3 feet squares (9x18 feet) immediately inside the entrance. Three large features (fired areas, Features 3, 4, 5) and a substantial amount of cultural debris were located here. However, large, blocky ceiling fall was encountered at a depth of ca. 12 inches inside the entrance, preventing deeper investigations without an enormous input of labor.

The remainder of the site was staked out in 5x5 feet control squares. By the third week efforts were being directed toward developing a north-south trench in these 5 feet squares across the entire floor of the first room. Initially Squares 101-104 were excavated for this purpose, but again, large breakdown was exposed after only 1 foot of midden had been removed. Several of these fallen blocks were more than 4 feet in length, and all were securely wedged in an impenetrable mass. The trenching operation was then shifted to the adjacent line of squares, numbers 113-121. Large breakdown was encountered between 12 and 20 inches here as well, but Squares 113 and 121 were carried to a depth of 60 and 48 inches respectively. By the end of the fourth week a large portion of this longest trench had been opened, and the deepest squares had been completed.

The stratigraphic exposure in Square 113 demonstrated that the occupational strata in the cave were relegated roughly to the topmost 15 inches (Fig. 7). A zone of breakdown approximately 36 inches thick lay below the cultural horizon. This layer of breakdown was composed of a heterogeneous mixture of angular blocks, pebbles, gravels, and coarse soil particles. Below the breakdown was a 6-9 inch wide zone of gray and red lacustrine clays and silts. This deposit was clearly developed in stagnant water and appeared to predate the Holocene. After the lacustrine deposits were removed another layer of breakdown was encountered, but only about 9 inches of this level were excavated. This breakdown was so compact that our best efforts with the pick mattock were largely repelled, and the pit was abandoned at a depth of ca. 60 inches.

Due to the sterile condition of the deeper deposits in Squares 113 and 121, the excavation plan was altered in the fifth week. The decision was made to attempt to remove nearly all of the site, recovering as many of the artifactual remains as possible. Following completion of the initial trench (Squares 113-121), new areas were opened on the north and south ends of this trench (Squares 112-85, 100-98, 304, 305, 320). Subsequently another line of squares was opened (numbers 157-307). One row (numbers 124-132) was left unexcavated pending completion of the bordering rows of squares. The standing walls of this unexcavated line of squares provided the vertical profiles for mapping three-fourths of the site midden (Figs. 8-10). Squares 124-132 were then excavated with the additional aid of vertical profiles as references. Among the last squares to be excavated were numbers 105-108, 94-96, 91, 88, and 211. This series provided added insight concerning the horizontal distribution of cultural remains, as several squares produced relatively little evidence of human activity. With the exception of a very small portion of midden under and around several large blocks of fall at the entrance, the entire site was investigated and essentially all of the artifactual debris was recovered.

During the course of these excavations, the focus of our endeavors was toward the most complete recovery of the artifactual record. Soil which was not bagged as soil samples was put through one-quarter inch mesh screens. Approximately 2,800 cubic feet of soil were excavated and screened in this manner. Another 800 liters of soil were returned to the laboratory in the form of over 100 soil samples. Eighty-nine samples (550 liters) represent culture bearing strata and have been processed by flotation and fine screening with number 40 mesh screens. These 89 soil samples were taken from two types of contexts. Forty-one samples were composed of soil taken at random from specified (3 inch) arbitrary excavation levels of the control squares. To ensure that these 41 general soil samples were representative of the midden, a sample was taken at every level of odd-numbered squares in the first trench across the site (Squares 113-121). In addition, several general level samples were taken where rich midden deposits were encountered. The second context from which soil samples were removed was the feature. A total of 48 locations were sampled from the most clearly defined of the 81 features at the site. In some cases the entire feature's contents were bagged as a unit.

Nature of the Cultural Deposit

Hadfields Cave, like many other cave and rock shelter sites, is spatially limited in inhabitable floor area. For this reason the human deposit shows the effects of extensive mixing of stratigraphic zones due to the seasonal reuse of living floors and aboriginal earth moving.

The culture bearing zone is composed of loamy-silt soil with relatively low but variable amounts of clay. Soil deposited more than about 50 feet from the entrance tends to be high in clay content. Interspersed with this soil is a substantial amount of coarser sand-sized particles, fine gravels (2-10 mm. diameter), and fist-sized breakdown. This coarse component represents both natural ceiling fall and rotting limestone. The cultural strata contain small, variable amounts of breakdown. Because the cave was a locus of extended occupation by man, the topmost soil layers are essentially a midden. The natural accumulation of soil on the cave floor has been drastically modified by extensive digging activities, the incorporation of large amounts of organic wastes, and alteration of the cave "atmosphere." The obvious effects of man's presence are somewhat obscured near the entrance, as the mouth of the cave functions as a trap for large quantities of leaves and other organic forest debris. These natural organic materials have contributed quantities of humus to the soil at the entrance and have, in turn, diffused several of the distinct outlines of the cultural features.

20

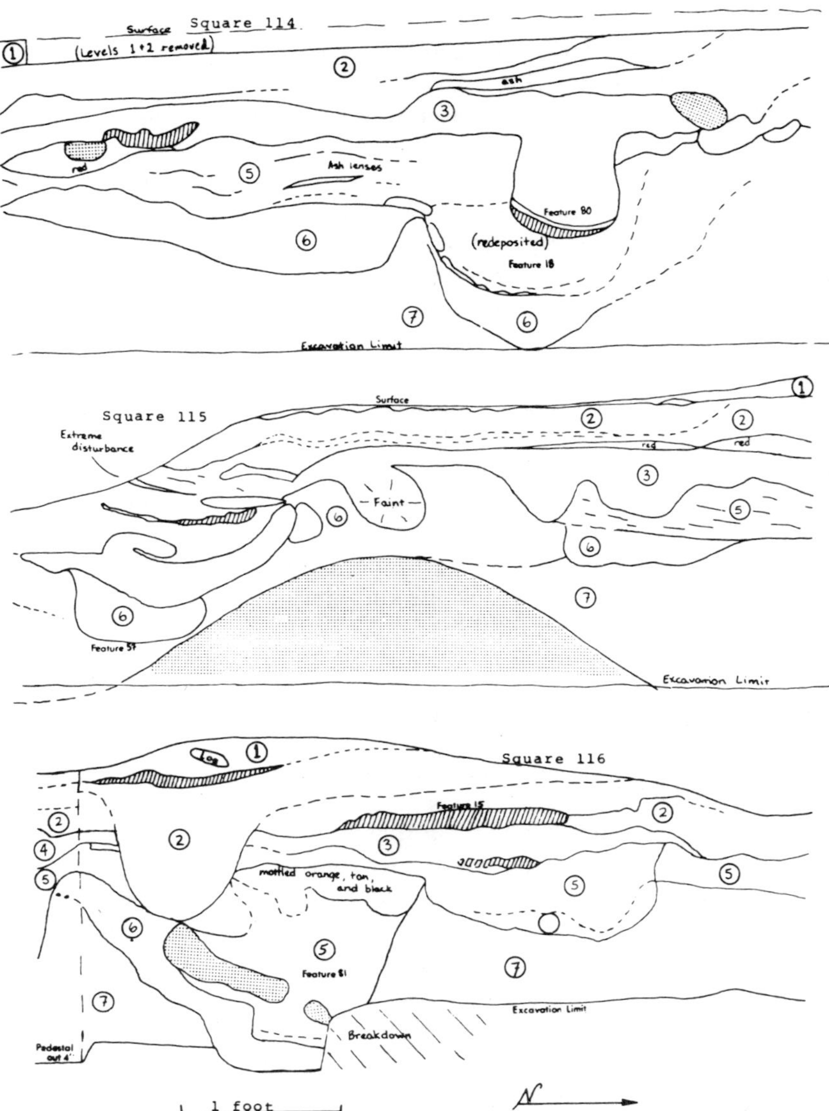

Fig. 8. West wall profiles of Squares 114-119.

Key for Figs. 7, 8, 9, and 10

strata no.   Description

1   Brown (10 YR 5/4) silt-loam with a layer and flecks of modern charcoal.

2   Light brown (10 YR 5/4) silt-loam with flecks of charcoal and streaks and spots of darker and lighter colors; little or no gravel included.

3   Mottled tan and brown (7.5 YR 5/4) silt-loam with much streaking and banding; includes a small amount of gravelly breakdown, numerous charcoal flecks, and a great deal of cultural debris.

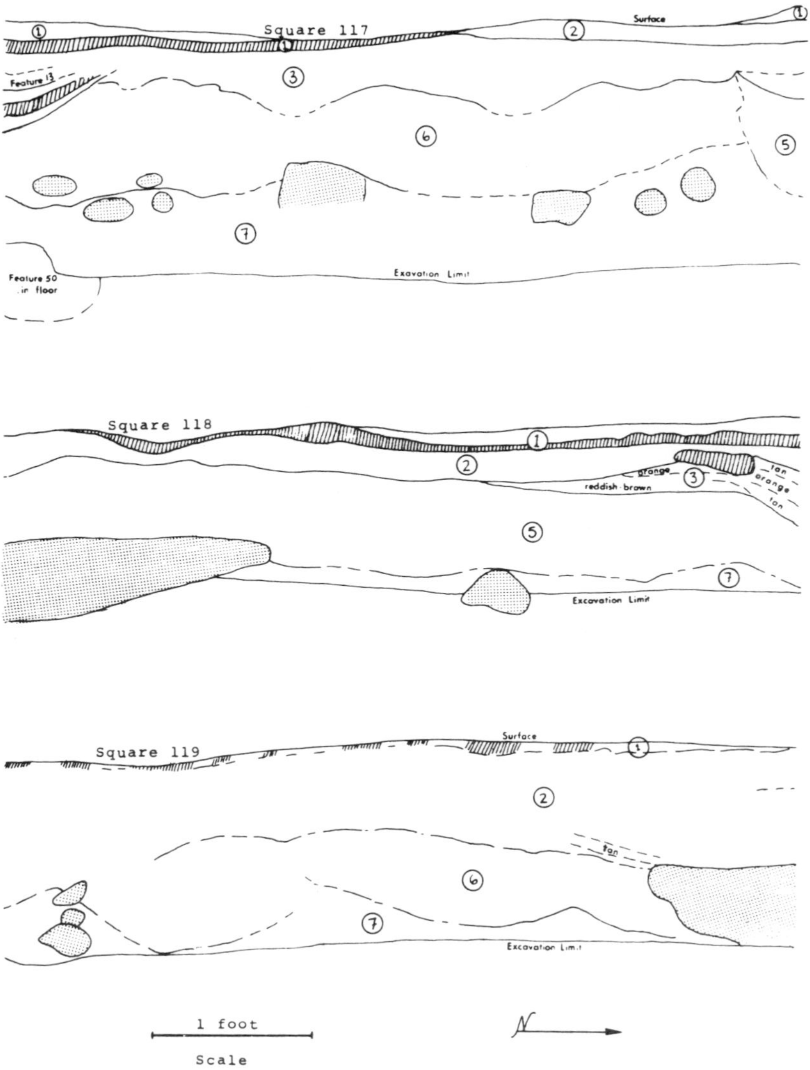

4   Extremely mottled silt-loam; probably *redeposited* culture bearing strata.

5   Homogeneous zone of brown (10 YR 4/4 and lighter) silt-loam with little or no gravelly breakdown, but may include ashy lenses.

6   Homogeneous zone of brown (10 YR 4/3-4/4) silty clay-loam with little to moderate amounts of gravelly breakdown; no streaks or mottles.

7   Homogeneous light brown (10 YR 5/6), silty clay-loam subsoil with moderate to large amounts of gravelly breakdown and large breakdown.

 Cobble or breakdown   Charcoal concentration

22

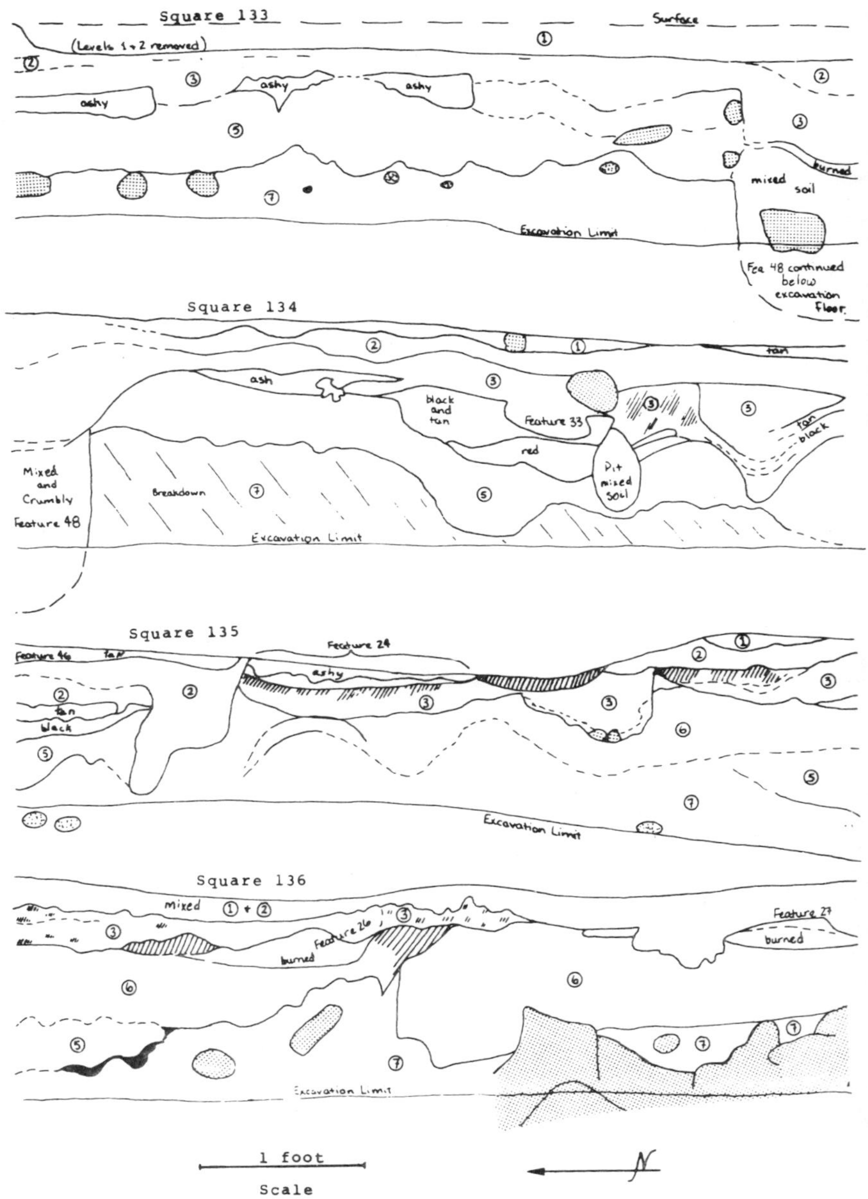

Fig. 9. East wall profiles of Squares 133-136.

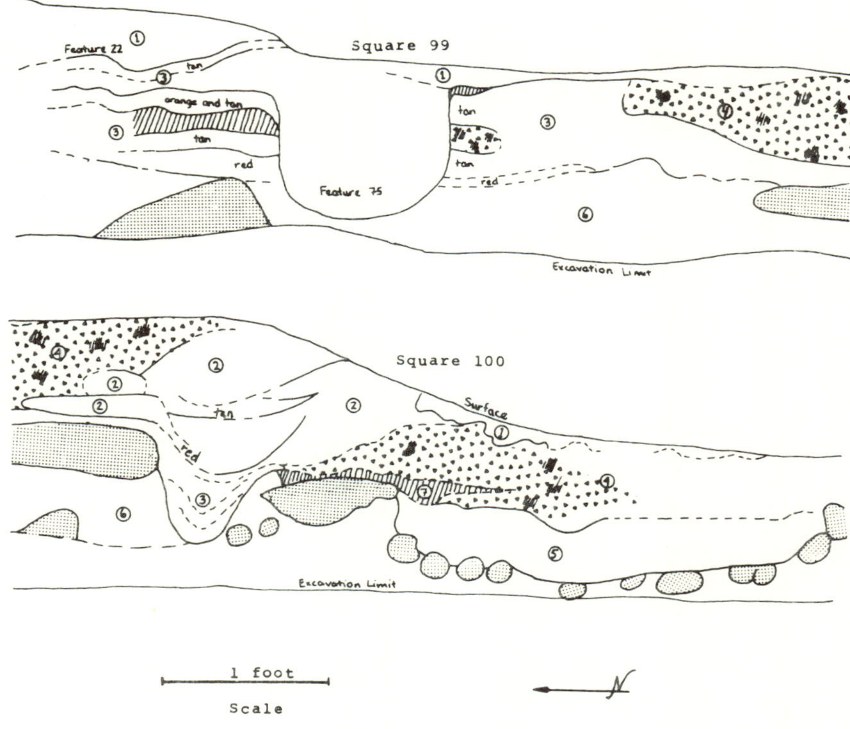

Fig. 10. East wall profiles of Squares 99-100.

Eighty-one cultural features were identified by number as they were exposed during excavation. These are described here in Table 1 and identified by location on the site grid (Fig. 4). All of the following were identified as features at 13JN3: pits—typically round, shallow excavations filled with mixed soil and cultural debris; fired areas—shallow, localized concentrations of charcoal and brightly colored, burned soil; and unusual concentrations of bone or carbon (Figs. 12-13). Features on the whole were difficult to define and excavate. The fired areas had not been prepared or shaped in any fashion prior to kindling a campfire. The still-burning coals of most fires were not immediately covered; therefore, combustion in hearths left only a thin layer of ash and a great deal of fire-reddened soil. These factors made fired areas difficult to define vertically and horizontally. At some locations the degree of firing apparent was minimal, and loci, which had initially received numbers, failed to materialize into definitive features upon excavation.

Pits were characteristically small, the largest being ca. 30 inches in diameter. Because many of the soil colors were pale shades of brown and

TABLE 1
13JN3 Feature Description

Feature no.	Location Square no(s).	Stratigraphic depth (in.)	Size horizontal / vertical (in.)	Fill Type	Samples˙	Comments
1	11,12	1-2	18X20 / 1	charcoal and ash	S	hearth; dark brown soil; *Miscellaneous side-notched* projectile point associated
2	13	11	dia. 5 / 1	charcoal	—	—
3	49, 45	3-6	28X18 / 3	fired soil and charcoal	C	—
4	41, 47	2-6	36X36 / 4	fired soil and charcoal	C	charcoal concentration and vague area of fired soil
5	41, 40	6-10	34X19 / 4	fired soil and charcoal	C S	hearth superimposed by Feature 4
6	103, 104 114, 115	7-10	41X34 / 3	fired soil and charcoal	C S	heavy firing over wide area with vague edges and charcoal flecks
7	104, 115	7-9	44X27 / 2	fired soil	S	hearth with vague edges
8	26	24-27	dia. 10 / 1	charcoal	—	poorly defined hearth with sparse charcoal
9	102	6-8	20X16 / 1-2	charcoal	C	wide fired area around small charcoal concentration
10	101	7-8	12X8 / 1	charcoal and bones	S	grinder resting over debris of a small hearth
11	115	3-6	25X15 / 2	fired soil and bones	—	hearth

12	114-115	6-7	dia. 16 / 1	fired soil, bones, charcoal	—	thin and poorly defined hearth
13	117, 118 128, 129	2-4	36X24 / 2	fired soil and charcoal	S	firepit at center of large, vague fired area
14	113	8-9	16X15 / 1	fired soil and charcoal	—	vaguely defined hearth
15	116-127	3-5	34X35 / 2	fired soil and charcoal	S S	soil sample from both squares; two carbon concentrations within large fired area
16	113	9-12	23X13 / ?	fired soil and charcoal	S	pit not recognized until 9″ depth; 3″ deep from 9″ level
17	113	9-12	ca. 6″ long	charcoal and fired soil	—	probably a remnant of a disturbed feature
18	114	9-12	36X31 / 2	fired soil	S	fired area with vague edges
19	118	12-18	dia. 15 / +6	tan soil	S	pit recognized at 12″ depth
20	numbered in the field, but not recognized as a true feature					
21	114, 115 125, 126	3-6	20X13 / 2	charcoal	S	light colored soil with a con-centration of burned nutshell
22	99	3-6	ca. 6″ dia.	fired soil and charcoal	—	shallow and vague spot
23	99	3-6	ca. 6″ dia.	fired soil and charcoal	—	shallow and vague spot
24	127, 135	1-4	39X32 / 3	fired soil and charcoal	S	heavily fired area with vague edges; truncated on north by modern disturbance
25	136	2-5	42X19 / 3	fired soil	S	extensive area of fired soil— possibly two major fired areas

26	128, 136	3-9	36X24 / 6	fired soil and charcoal	S	extensive area of fired soil; 6″ deep only at west edge
27	128, 129 136, 137	3-6	24X18/2 dia. 10 4	fired soil, charcoal, bones	S S	fired area superimposed by a pit; both features soil samples; pit 4″ total depth
28	136	6-10	dia. 20 / 4	tan soil and charcoal	—	irregular fired area with faint coloring
29	136, 137	3-6	31X22 / 3	tan soil and charcoal	—	irregular fired area with faint coloring and vague edges
30	133, 134 141, 142	3-6	30X25 / 2	fired soil, charcoal, bones	S S	extensive bone concentration, faint coloring, irregular edges; two soil samples
31	134, 135 142, 143	3	31X24 / 1	ash and bone	—	bone concentration with faint colors and irregular edges
32	133, 134	3	17X14 / 1	fired soil and charcoal	S	small fired area disturbed on north edge
33	126, 134	3-9	27X25/6 7 dia./5	fired soil, charcoal, bones	S S	pit superimposed on center of hearth; fired area sharply defined and thick; soil samples from both features
34	135	3-6	21X21 / 2	fired soil and charcoal	S	vague fired area near Feature 24 and superimposed on Feature 41
35	100	3-5	dia. 12 / 2	fired soil and charcoal	S	fired area with concentration of charcoal
36	100	5-6	12X2 / 1	charcoal and bone	—	irregular concentration of debris
37	137	3-6	22X16 / 2	tan soil and bones	—	faint coloring, irregular edges, produced all bone in square
38	133, 157	3-4	25X16 / 1	tan soil, ash, charcoal	S	slightly fired area with faint edges

39	96, 100	9-12	22X12 / 4	fired soil and charcoal	S	fired area with vague edges
40	134, 135	6-15	27X17 / ca. 19	mixed soil	S	this feature and Feature 43 probably are lower portions of a pit which superceded *all* aboriginal features
41	135	6-12	dia. 9 / 6	mixed soil and bones	—	pit recognized near bottom
42	135	6-9	dia. 8 / +3	mixed soil and bones	—	pit recognized near bottom
43	134, 135	6-10	16X10 / ca. 10	mixed soil	S	pit; see Feature 40
44	133	6	dia. 18 / 1	fired soil	S	fired area irregular and poorly defined
45	139	3-6	dia. 13 / 1	fired soil	S	fired area irregular and poorly defined; *diminutive side-notched* projectile point associated
46	99	12	dia. 18 / 1	faint stains and charcoal	C	fired area with very faint coloring
47	126	1-2	29X15 / 1	fired soil	—	hearth; depression of the feature visible on the surface
48	125, 126 133, 134	4-20	18X15 / 16	mixed soil, bone, charcoal	S S	pit filled with bones and mixed soil; two soil samples—one taken after feature was profiled
49	307	3	20X8 / 1	tan soil	—	very faint fired area
50	118	12-18	dia. 16 / +6	brown soil	S	pit identified below the probable orifice
51a	126	6-10	38X25 / 4	fired soil and charcoal	—	extensive fired area, probably representing several hearths

51b	127, 127	6-10	dia. 30 / 4	fired soil and charcoal	—	extensive fired area
52	305, (121)	6-15	dia. 10 / 9	brown soil	S	pit; recognized after Square 121 was excavated
53	305	4-6	dia. 19 / 2	fired soil	S	fired area with faint coloring
54	126	9-18	14X11 / 8	mixed soil	S	pit recognized at 9″ depth
55	127	6-9	dia. 16 / 1	fired soil	S	fired area superimposed by Feature 24
56a	94-98	3-18	48X20 / 15	ash and tan soil	S C	hearth filled with tan soil; extensive area covered, depression at center
56b	98	9-14	dia. 23 / +7	mixed soil and bones	S	large pit superimposed by Feature 51a; Feature 51a probably used immediately after 51b was filled
57	115, 126	15-21	dia. 20 / 6	mixed soil and charcoal	S	pit recognized at 15″ depth
58	94	3-6	dia. 15 / 1	fired soil	—	faint, irregular fired spot
59	320	3-6	dia. 13 / 1	fired soil	—	faint fired spot with traces of ash and charcoal
60	128	0-3	15X9 / 2	fired soil	S	irregular fired area
61	128	3-6	16X13 / 1	fired soil	S	fired area adjacent to Feature 26
62	128	11	dia. 6 / 1/2	tan soil	—	small lens noted in excavation wall
63	numbered in field; now parts of Features 73 and 74					

64	111	3-7	dia. 13 / 4	mixed soil	S	poorly defined it
65	124	4-5	28X16 / 1	tan soil and charcoal	S	hearth superimposed over edge of Feature 67
66	86	9-16	23X21 / +7	mixed soil and bones	S	pit with orifice poorly defined in loose, disturbed soil
67	123, 124	9-24	dia. 30 / 15	mixed soil and bones	C	pit with orifice poorly defined in loose, disturbed soil
68	129	6-12	dia. 7 / 6	tan soil and charcoal	—	small pit with poorly defined orifice
69	85, 98	9-24	dia. 28 / +15	mixed soil and bones	—	large pit with poorly defined orifice; much of bone from Squares 85 and 98 came from this feature
70	143	3-4	dia. 14 / 1	fired soil and charcoal	S	well-defined fired area
71	143	3-6	dia. 10 / 1	tan soil and charcoal	—	faint fired area
72	91	6-8	20X8/1 / 20X12/2	fired soil and ash	S	extensive, irregular area of burned soil; became two distinct features with excavation
73	95	6-9	14X11 / 2	fired soil and charcoal	—	irregular burned area probably associated with Feature 74
74	95	5-7	dia. 28 / 2	tan soil and charcoal	S	tan, fired soil surrounding heavy charcoal concentration
75	95, (99)	3-15	dia. 14 / 9	mixed soil	S	pit identified in vertical profile; excavated in Square 95 only
76	95	9-10	24X16 / 1	fired soil and charcoal	—	well-defined fired area

77	96	10-18	dia. 13/8	mixed soil, bones, charcoal	—	pit originating in upper stratum
78	112, 113	8-25	dia. 35/17	tan soil and charcoal	S	large, basin-shaped depression originating in lower stratum
79	99	9-13	dia. 8/4	mixed soil and bones	—	very small, indistinct pit
80	114, 125	7-15	dia. 7/8	mixed soil, charcoal on bottom	S	pit recognized in vertical profile (Square 114 west) and samples from Square 125; orifice originated in lower part of upper stratum.
81	116, 127	10-23	22X19/13	mixed soil and ceiling fall	—	irregular pit with upper stratum imposed on it, truncating upper portions of the pit

*S=soil sample; C=carbon sample

buff, the orifices of pits were virtually impossible to define on the horizontal plane among the numerous cultural disturbances. The majority were recognized at depths of 9 or 12 inches. Four small pits (numbers 48, 75, 77, 80) were discovered in vertical profiles, and their entire contents were sampled accordingly.

This report places relatively little emphasis on the associations and superpositions of features in the midden for the reasons apparent in the previous two paragraphs. In addition, fired areas contained only small amounts of pottery and stone, and the stratigraphic level at which most pits originated could not be clearly defined. Mention will be made of features with special characteristics at appropriate points throughout the report.

Despite the mixing of features and living floors, there are two distinguishable strata in the midden (Figs. 9-12). The lower stratum is uniformly tan or light brown in color and varies in thickness from 1-2 to 3-4 inches. This stratum contains noticeably fewer features and less cultural material than the upper stratum. It is quite clear that a considerable proportion of the lower stratum became incorporated into the upper stratum while the latter was being accumulated. The lower stratum was developed at the time Linn Ware ceramics were brought to the cave, probably A.D. 300-400. The upper stratum, varying from 6 to 9 inches in average thickness, contains the majority of cultural artifacts and features. It is composed of multiple lenses of burned soil, ash, and redeposited soil. Pit digging activities have interrupted the lateral uniformity of these lenses to such an extent that no single lens (that is, living floor) can be traced entirely across this stratum. The upper stratum represents a greater time span of occupation, ca. A.D. 500-800, incorporating most of the Linn and Madison Ware pottery. A thin (ca. 1-2 inch) layer of recently deposited soil covers the aboriginal midden at present.

A small number of unidentifiable longbone splinters (mammal) were located at the entrance immediately below the drip-line (Squares 10 and 11) at a depth of 42-45 inches. No other cultural evidence was found in that trench (Squares 8-13), and two squares (numbers 112 and 113) inside the cave failed to show evidence of occupation at that depth. It was concluded that insufficient evidence existed to justify searching for a deep component at 13JN3.

While the midden has a significant degree of vertical stratification, the horizontal distributions of artifactual remains are not clearly segregated into activity areas or zones of temporally specific occupation. However, there are a number of general statements which describe the scatter of features and cultural debris. Occupations of every period were limited to the interior of the cave and to the first room. Practically all of the living debris and features were found in an area of that room which is lighted by sunlight from the entrance and maintains a relatively stable temperature (ca. 50° F).

32

The primary occupational scatter was oval in shape with the longitudinal axis of this area paralleling and abutting the northwest cave wall. Fired areas usually occurred more than 5 feet away from the cave wall in areas where there was more than 4 feet of head room (Figs. 15-16). The remainder of the first room contained only scattered evidence of occupation. Other rooms in the cave's deeper recesses showed no evidence of occupational midden, and a test square likewise failed to produce cultural evidence.

The major proportion of bone remains was found in the control squares immediately adjacent to and including the "crawl space" under the northwest cave wall. This area apparently served as the repository for habitation garbage, as the very low ceiling renders this area useless for any other purposes. Bone remains from animal foods were found in relatively sporadic concentrations throughout the rest of the midden.

Features in the oval occupational area were roughly grouped into three zones. An intense concentration of relatively clearly defined features was centered in Squares 126, 127, and 134-136 (Figs. 13-14). Nearly all of the features at this location were associated with the upper stratum. Another group of features in Squares 101-104, 113, and 114 were very difficult to define. They were in the walk-way across this section of the first room (maximum clearance, ca. 4.5 feet), and undoubtedly were subjected to intensive trampling throughout .the aboriginal occupation. The third concentration of features was scattered among several large blocks of ceiling breakdown at the north end of the occupation area. The boundaries of individual features and upper and lower strata were somewhat confused at this end of the site due to extensive aboriginal pit digging. The initial occupation in the cave centered at the north end of the first room. Because there was subsequent activity in this area, many of the earliest features were destroyed or diffused.

It has been stated that most of the features are located within 10-20 feet of the cave's northwest wall. The floor area enclosed by this wall and the fired features appears to have been the preferred living area. Over three-quarters of the projectile points were found in this region of the site. In addition, nearly 90% of the bone tools and the vast majority of lithic waste materials were recovered from this area. This would have been the preferred location for special activity areas—skin working, stone chipping, socializing, and so on—as radiated heat from the hearth would be reflected from the wall. On the other hand, sherds from individual ceramic vessels tended to cluster around specific locations, usually among the fired features but not necessarily in the activity area along the northwest wall.

Fig. 11. View of rear of the first room.

Fig. 12. Features in Square 136 at 3 inches depth.

Fig. 13. Feature 33 at 6 inches depth.

Fig. 14. Stratigraphy of the cave as seen in Square 114.

Radiocarbon Dates

Six radiocarbon dates (Bender et al. 1973:615) were obtained for 13JN3 through the kind cooperation of David A. Baerreis and the Center for Climatic Research of the University of Wisconsin, Madison. All six dates fall within the time range anticipated and are accepted here without qualification. The precise context for each assay is given below, although in a form slightly amended from the descriptions in *Radiocarbon* (Bender et al. 1973). The descriptions were published prior to making a thorough analysis of the field notes, and discrepancies realized subsequently are considered below.

Wis-594 A.D. 420 (1530 ± 55 years)
> Provenience: Feature 46, Square 99, Level 5 (9-12 inches)
> This date represents an undisturbed charcoal concentration in the lower stratum.

Wis-589 A.D. 295 (1655 ± 65 years)
> Provenience: Feature 9, Square 102, Level 4 (6-9 inches)
> This date was taken on dispersed charcoal gathered from an area of fired soil stratigraphically situated in the lower stratum.

Wis-588 A.D. 660 (1290 ± 55 years)
> Provenience: Square 104, Level 3 (3-6 inches)
> This date is on nutshell fragments from in and around the area of Feature 6 in the upper stratum. This and the previous date represent areas of the midden where there was uniform horizontal layering and no pit digging.

Wis-599 A.D. 555 (1395 ± 55 years)
> Provenience: Feature 65, Square 124 (4 inches depth)
> Nutshell fragments and a very small amount of charcoal were processed for this date. Feature 65 was an area of fired soil and concentrated carbon in the upper stratum. The west edge of this feature was imposed over the east edge of Feature 67, dated in the following sample.

Wis-596 A.D. 730 (1220 ± 60 years)
> Provenience: Feature 67, Square 124
> The date was run on charcoal fragments collected throughout this cylindrical pit. The orifice of Feature 67 was not determined because of the loose, dry nature of the soil in this area of the site. It is certain, however, that the orifice originated in the upper stratum and may have been superimposed by Feature 65. This radiocarbon date is probably the least definitive of the six, since the feature's association and context were partially obscured by a rodent-run over the northwest edge.

36

Wis-597 A.D. 800 (1150 ± 55 years)
Provenience: Feature 16, Square 113, Level 5 (9-12 inches)
Laboratory analysis revealed that this date was taken on charcoal from an upper stratum feature which intruded into the lower stratum.

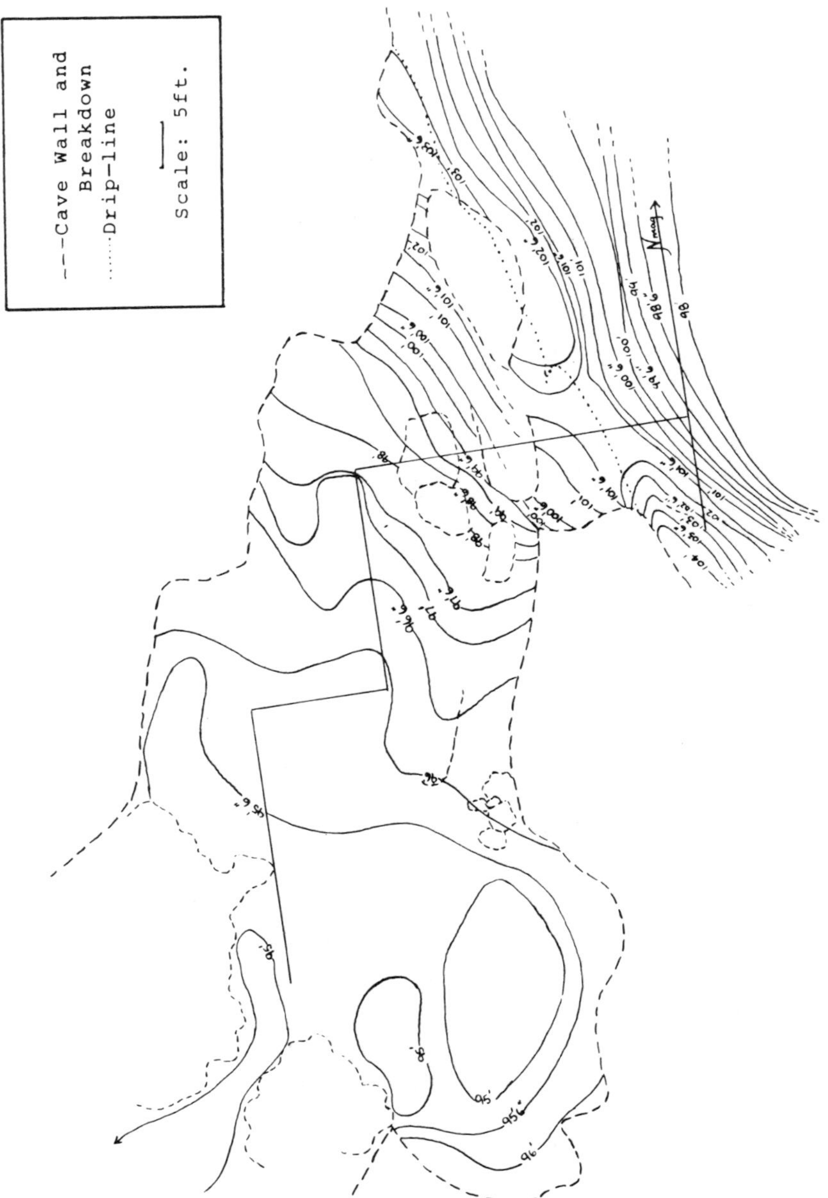

Fig. 15. Hadfields Cave floor contours.

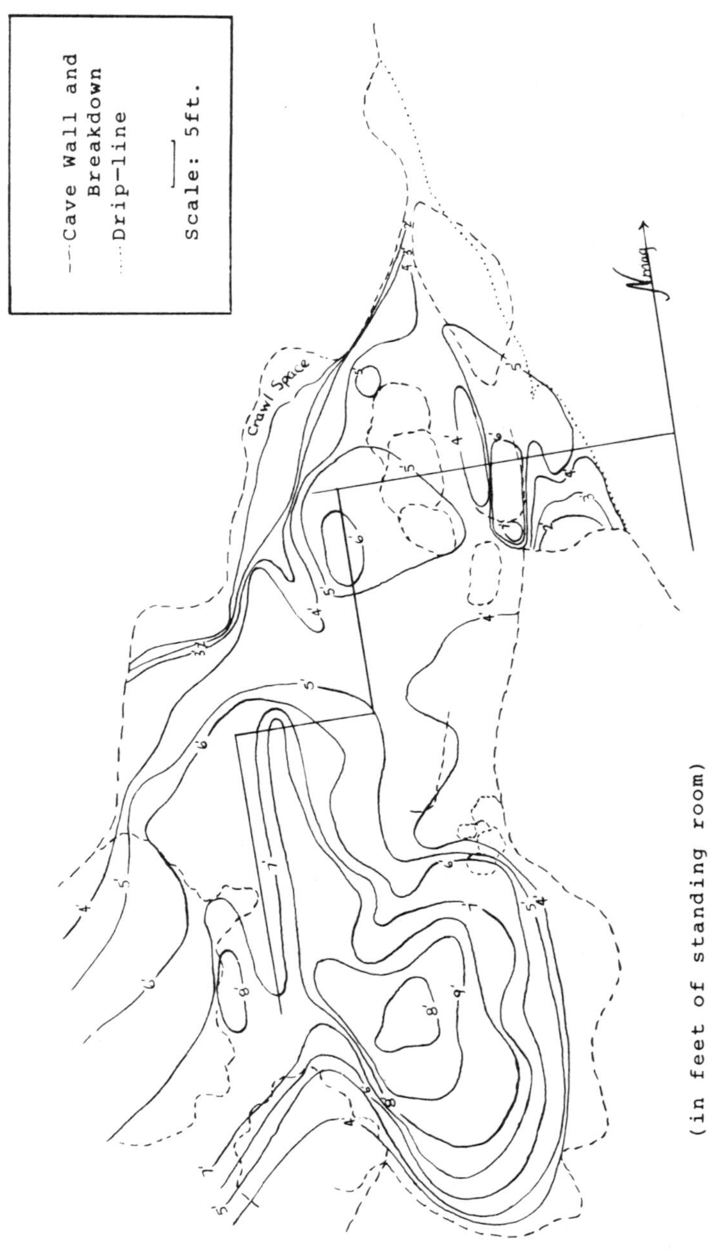

Fig. 16. Hadfields Cave ceiling contours.

3

Ceramics

The excavations at Hadfields Cave resulted in the recovery of 2,413 pottery sherds (Table 2). This number includes 103 sherds too damaged to be analytically useful, 132 rims, 197 decorated sherds (apart from rims and cord-roughened body sherds), and 1,981 body fragments. By many standards this is a smaller-than-average sample for a ceramic bearing site. However, the size of the sample rendered vessel reconstruction a manageable undertaking.

The decision to work with vessels rather than with individual rims was made because a significant number of vessels had been decorated with fabrics—25 of the total of 46 vessels. The recent recognition of the prolific use of fabric decoration in Madison Ware by William Hurley (1966, 1970) has emphasized the need for the analysis of corded decorations found on the pottery of Woodland time periods. Hurley's work demonstrated that a fabric structure can be reconstructed from its impression on the vessel rim. Analysis of vessels from 13JN3 will further show that such fabrics were not produced merely as appliques for pottery. Rather, in many cases the fabric decoration covers the entire rim and shoulder surface of the vessel as a single, nonrepeating unit, apparently representing a collar or bag structure. This conclusion will be dealt with in greater detail in the following pages. For the moment it should be noted that a precise investigation of the structure and technological use of fabrics impressed on ceramic vessels requires that a significant portion of the vessel be available for study—a complete shoulder-to-lip section is indispensable.

Individual vessels are described in terms of their peculiar decorative characteristics. The focus of this analysis centers on decoration, especially in the applications of fabrics, since the cords and fabrics impressed on these vessels vary to the extreme of being individualistic. The descriptions of manufacturing attributes and paste follow the terminology of Anna Shepard (1961), while Wheeler (1952) is referred to for the nomenclature of vessel form. Mineral rocks (Mohs scale) were employed to determine the hardness of vessel paste. The Munsell colors are also provided, the colors being determined while sherds were dry. Fabric description has only recently been made available to the archaeologist with the publicaton of

38

Irene Emery's *The Primary Structure of Fabrics* (1966). Much of the present analysis draws upon information contained in Emery's book and the findings of Hurley (1966, 1970, 1975). The cord and fabric impressions on vessels were studied with the familiar procedure of casting these designs in plasticine and latex rubber (Rachlin 1955). Such a cast renders an exact copy of the cords used to produce the vessel's design. The cast, however, represents only one face of a fabric, often only partially, while the task of analysis involves detecting the structure and position of all elements in the fabric.

The definitions of four terms used in these discussions should be made clear at this point. Paste, the tempered plastic material from which vessels were made, is composed of two ingredients. The first is temper, the nonplastic inclusions. The other is clay, a plastic material which makes up the larger portion of the paste. The clay in 13JN3 vessels typically has a substantial amount of silt-sized particles and in some cases probably contained a considerable volume of organic matter in humic and macrofossil form. In matters pertaining to cord analysis, the term ply refers to the number of times elements of a cord are interacted. For example, four elements may be twined in pairs to produce two single-ply cords, and two single-ply cords may be twined together to produce one double-ply cord.

The Hadfields Cave ceramics have been fitted into the scheme of wares and types originally developed by Logan (1959) in his definitive study of the Woodland pottery of northeast Iowa. Although this sample is probably not sufficiently large to permit a redefinition of all his types, this writer has yet to encounter any insurmountable problems with Logan's basic typology. His remains the first and only comprehensive modern work to deal with the prehistoric cultures of this region, and the ceramic sequences and typology remain, with but a few changes in terminology and emphasis, apropos today.

The following paragraphs contain discussions of the ceramic ware groups evidenced at 13JN3 and of Havana Ware, which is not. Individual vessel descriptions have been appended to these discussions (Appendices A, B, and C) to allow for continuity in the text. These three appendices provide the data base alluded to in the more general discussion of vessel types and ware groups.

Havana Ware

One trait which typifies Havana Ware is the coarseness of the paste. The Iowa material is usually heavily tempered, giving the wall cross-section a blocky structure. Iowa Havana vessels are deep, conoidal jars with nearly straight rims and slightly expanding shoulders. Vessel walls are almost always thick, ca. 6-10 mm. or more. Decoration consists of zones of punctating, incising, and stamping, with the latter being far more common

TABLE 2
13JN3 Pottery Sherd Counts

	Vessel no.	No. of Rims	No. of Other Decorated*	No. of Body Sherds
Linn Ware	1	1	2	0
	2	3	0	4
	3	1	1	4
	4	1	0	20
	5	4	2	65
	6c	1	0	23
	7	2	0	9
	10a	4	0	0
	10b	1	0	96
	11	2	3	8
	12	5	4	31
	13	4	2	57
	14	1	0	2
	24	1	1	11
	25	1	0	22
	26	3	0	11
Linn Ware Subtotals		35	15	323
Miscellaneous	6a	3	0	0
	6b	1	0	0
	8	2	2	15
	9	6	0	9
Miscellaneous Subtotals		12	2	24
Madison Ware	15	7	16	1
	16	2	2	0
	17	5	5	0
	18	5	13	5
	19	1	6	7
	20	8	25	178
	21	6	6	1
	22	14	26	14
	23	4	11	3
	27	3	4	0
	28	8	7	18
	29	1	5	0
	30	0	5	3
	31	1	1	0
	32	1	5	0
	33	1	4	0
	34	1	3	0
	35	0	7	0
	36	5	1	0
	37	1	1	0
	38	4	2	0
	39	3	3	0
	40	1	0	0
	41	1	0	0
	42	1	0	0
	43	1	0	0
	Miscellaneous	0	22	0

Madison Ware Subtotals		85	180	230
Type 1 Body Sherds		(probably Vessel 19)		35
Type 2 Body Sherds		(Linn Ware)		
		6 plain		
		2 polished plain		
		6 smoothed-over cord-marked		
		51 cord-roughened		65
Type 3 Body Sherds		(Madison Ware)		1304
Exfoliated Sherds				103

Totals	Rims	Other Decorated	Body Sherds	Destroyed
	132	197	1981	103

TOTAL (all categories) 2,413 sherds

*includes perforated sherds

than the other two. Logan (1959:153, 206) has stated that the Iowa Havana ceramics are so similar to Illinois types that both should remain in the same ware group. More recent excavations of Havana ceramics have shown that, while it is presently convenient to continue this relationship, there are some grounds for giving it renewed scrutiny. Perhaps Havana pottery from the Mississippi River trench should be typologically separated from that of the interior.

It is important to emphasize that the Iowa Havana is indigenous to the state. Very little material of Iowan provenience can be traced to manufacture in Illinois (the Havana Tradition), and the few Hopewellian objects found west of the Mississippi River in Iowa were probably traded from Havana villages located in that river's trench (cf. Wolfe site, 13DM1, Straffin 1971). Havana-like sherds from the interior of eastern Iowa often conform to the Illinois types in form, decoration, paste, and general quality of manufacture. However, a numerical attribute analysis comparing individual Illinois types with their Iowa counterparts would probably reveal that moderate differences exist in the motifs and amount of stamp applications, combinations of design motifs, zonation, and surface finish (cf. Benn and Thompson 1977). Such variations might be explained by the phenomenon of culture drift, the tendency for styles to change as they diffuse from an area of origin to outlying districts. Another factor which identifies Iowa Havana Ware as an indigenous product is the persistent appearance of local clays in the paste. This has yet to be demonstrated through petrographic analysis of vessel wall thin sections, but it seems a fairly reasonable inference. To gain some perspective on this use of local clays, one can study the surface collections from a single area such as the Coralville Reservoir in Johnson County, Iowa. Sherds from this area representing all time horizons—Early to Late Woodland—generally have rather sandy pastes, although rims from different time periods usually evidence variations in color, temper, surface treatment, and wall thickness.

Sites in the dissected topography of northeastern Iowa evidence even greater individuality of paste compositions, often varying more between valleys than among the wares from a single multi-component site.

Linn Ware

For the archaeologist, the Linn Ware category represents a stylistic complex in the difficult position of occurring temporally between two highly visible manifestations, Havana and Effigy Mound. Linn Ware ceramic types show heavy influence from the earlier Havana Tradition and contain many of the same attributes found in Madison Ware types. The initial type descriptions of Linn Ware were developed by Logan (1959) and assumed to be roughly coterminous with the time span of Weaver Ware in Illinois. The similarities between Weaver and Linn Ware types are striking indeed, although the latter group contains a number of design elements which are strictly indigenous to eastern Iowa.

According to Logan's criteria (1959:206) the definitive characters of Linn Ware are found in paste, vessel form, and decoration. The paste is typically finer than Havana Ware, and temper is smaller and less conspicuous. Linn Ware vessels are more globular than the often bag-shaped Havana Ware vessels, walls are somewhat thinner, and the shoulders and rims of Linn vessels are more sharply defined than in Havana types. Linn Ware decorations consist of punctating, stamping, and incising in zoned patterns similar to those of Havana Ware.

A total of 16 vessels from 13JN3 fall into the Linn Ware ceramic category. This group has been separated into two divisions: Variant I with vessels illustrating all of the definitive characters of the Linn Ware type definition (Figs. 17-20) and Variant II which includes vessels with characteristics more peripheral to the type definition (Figs. 21-22). The division of the site's Linn Ware into two variants will assist in demonstrating the apparent affinities of Variant I vessels with Weaver and Havana Wares and Variant II vessels with Madison Ware.

In the Variant I group Vessel 12, a Spring Hollow Plain type, and Vessel 13, Levsen Punctated (Fig. 19), are especially similar in paste color, vessel form, and surface treatment. Both vessels have cord-roughened bodies and plain shoulders and rims. This cord roughening was applied with a cord-wrapped paddle and is characterized by very fine, widely spaced, single-ply S-cords. The paste of these vessels is very compact, and the interior and exterior surfaces have been worked with tools. Deep, vertical upper rim notches give the lips a scalloped appearance. In short, the technological treatment of both vessels is extraordinarily similar to Griffin's type definition of Weaver Plain (1952b:121). Vessels 12 and 13 have more abruptly everted rims than do Illinois Weaver vessels. Their forms, however, correspond more closely to a few of the recurved rim profiles illustrated by Logan (1959: Figs. 5o, 6).

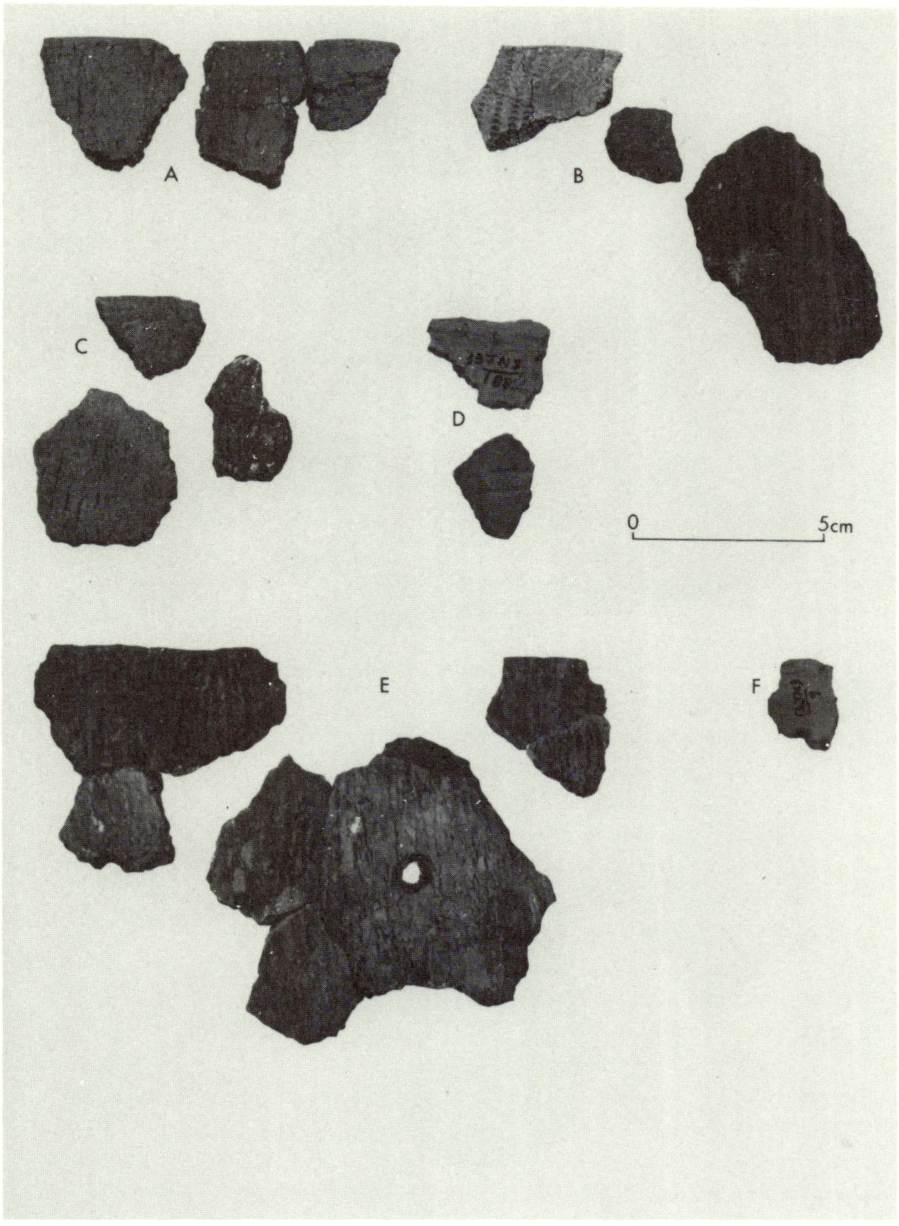

Fig. 17. Linn Ware Variant I. A, Vessel 1; B, Vessel 2; C, Vessel 4; D, Vessel 24; E, Vessel 5; F, Vessel 25.

44

Fig. 18. Linn Ware Variant I. A, Vessel 11; B, Vessel 3; C, Vessel 6c.

Fig. 19. Linn Ware Variant I. A, Vessel 13; B, Vessel 12.

The presence of a geometric decoration on Vessel 13 necessarily places it in a different type category from Vessel 12. This decoration is a squared zigzag motif executed in small punctates on the shoulder of Vessel 13. Although this specific design was not found by Logan in eastern Iowa, it is fundamentally like other geometric punctated designs on Levsen Punctated vessels in his report (1959: Fig. 5). This writer is aware of a small number of punctated decorations which appear on Late Woodland period pottery, exclusive of Levsen Punctated, in the region of northeast Iowa and Wisconsin. The most numerous examples of punctate designs occur in Hurley's ceramic type, Madison Punctate (1970), but several other examples occur on very small sherds, usually numbering only one or two in each site collection. The incidence of exclusively punctated designs on Late Woodland period vessels is probably very low, and such specimens should be recognized as variants of some major ceramic type.

The Variant I group also includes nine other vessels of varying types (Figs. 17-18). Vessel 3 has a plain surface and at least three horizontal rows of oblique dentate stamps. This decorative combination is especially reminiscent of Naples Stamped types in Illinois, although the expanding shoulder and compact paste of this vessel conform to the criteria for Linn Ware. Vessel 1, a Levsen rim with groups of at least four vertical cord-wrapped stick stamps, has a straight rim and flat lip. Four vessels, numbers 2, 4, 6c, and 25, are placed in the Spring Hollow Plain type. Only one of these, Vessel 6c, is decorated with lip notches. Two vessels, numbers 5 and 11, have been typed Spring Hollow Cord Marked. Both have been cord roughened on the exterior (Z§ and Z§ cords) up to the lip, and the high points of the cord roughening have been partially smoothed over to give a glossy finish. Vessel 5 is decorated with exterior lip notches. Decoration on Vessel 11 consists of fine lip notches and a possible cord design (ladder-like, perhaps) on the upper rim exterior. This last character is quite problematical as only a very small portion of it is present on the broken edge of the rim sherd. The potential presence of a geometric corded decoration on a Spring Hollow Cord Marked vessel is incongruous with Logan's type definition, but this design element is the only attribute on Vessel 11 which is not in accordance with the definition. Iowa prehistoric ceramics often possess combinations of attributes which make it difficult to pigeonhole them in mutually exclusive typological categories. This problem will be brought into clearer perspective in the discussion at the end of this chapter. The remaining vessel, number 24, lacks the exterior surface, but has an interior channel and inwardly bevelled lip.

The Variant II group contains five vessels. The paste characteristics (color, texture, structure, ingredients) of many vessels in this group are essentially the same as those on some of the Madison Fabric Impressed vessels. However, the exterior surfaces on all Variant II rims are plain, with no corded decorations of any sort. These vessels are also quite small (orifices probably less than ca. 12 cm. in diameter), not being comparable in size to the other vessels in both Linn and Madison Ware categories. Variant II has been placed in Linn Ware because the surface treatment and decoration on these vessels conform to the type definition. Variant II has not been placed in Madison Ware in order not to compromise the typological concept of this ware group. Madison Ware (previously Lake Michigan Ware) was originally defined in Wisconsin, where no provision has been made for a type or variant with a plain exterior surface. Thus, it would seem presumptuous to name an Iowa ceramic type, which has a very small geographic distribution, as an inclusion in Madison Ware.

A more careful look at the Variant II vessels will provide more depth to this discussion (Figs. 21-22). Vessel 26, a miniature Spring Hollow Plain pot, is undecorated and has a compact paste which feels slightly chalky to the touch. A cross-section of this vessel's wall shows the paste to be laminated and contorted. Vessel 10a has characters essentially like those of Vessel 26. It is more uniformly gray or charcoal in color, has a slightly blockier texture, and is generally similar in paste characters to Madison Fabric Impressed Vessel 19. Vessel 7 also has a blockier paste than Vessel 26, and the organic content of the clay was apparently much greater. The colors of Vessel 7 vary from charcoal rim surfaces and reddish brown cores to shades of bright buff throughout the body sherds. The paste of this vessel is much more similar to that of the Madison Fabric Impressed vessels in color, texture, and ingredients, although the exterior surface is finished with smoothed-over cord roughening and the lip is tooled flat. Vessel 10b is represented by a single rim sherd which was considered too incomplete for reliable typing. This rim has a punctate design, notched lip, and plain exterior surface, all apparently conforming to the Levsen Punctated type. However, the color, paste characteristics, and thickness of the walls on Vessel 10b lie within the ranges for Madison Ware vessels. The final vessel, number 14, has a Madison Ware paste and rim shape. Its exterior surface is plain, and the lip is flat with oblique tool gashes on the exterior edge. More than any other vessel in the Variant II group, Vessel 14 exhibits attributes which are identifiable with both Madison and Linn Wares. The other four vessels illustrate specific traits which are typical of the thin, compact walls and dark reddish brown to charcoal colors characteristic of Madison Ware.

The temporal position of Linn Ware at 13JN3 can be roughly estimated to the span of A.D. 295 ± 65 (Wis-589) to 660 ± 55 (Wis-588). These are the radiocarbon limits to the site's lower stratum where the initial occupation of the site is contained, and to the lower level 3 of the upper stratum where a great deal of the Linn Ware was found. The presence of Madison Ware in the upper stratum and the apparent affinities of Linn Ware Variant II vessels with Madison Ware indicate that vessels from both ware groups were deposited either as contemporaries or immediately following one another.

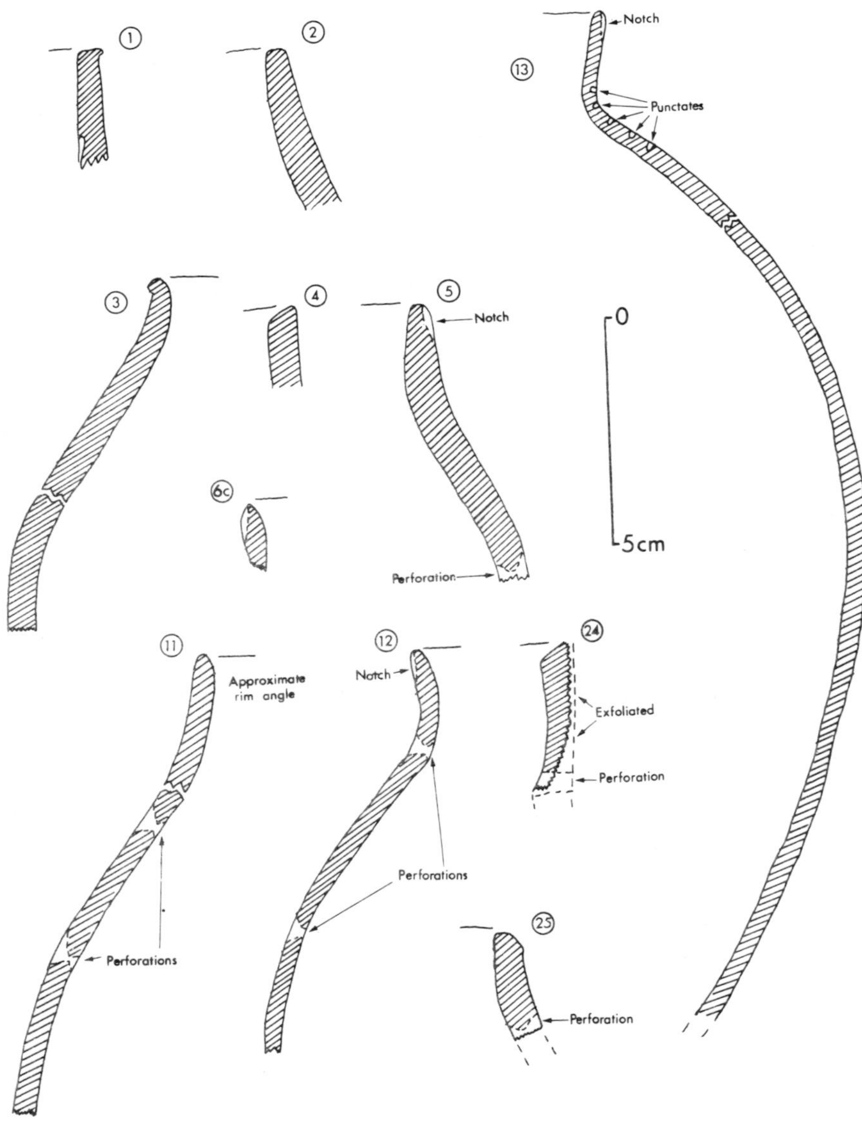

Fig. 20. Linn Ware Variant I rim profiles.

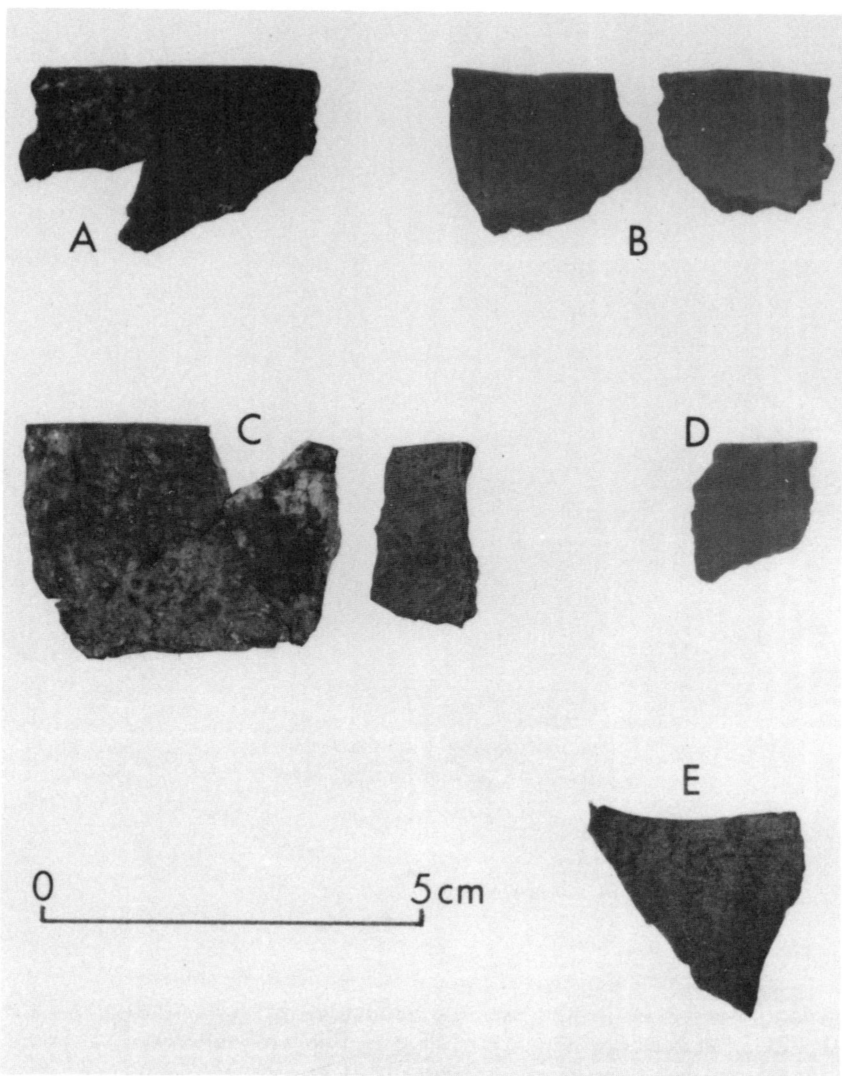

Fig. 21. Linn Ware Variant II. A, Vessel 7; B, Vessel 14; C, Vessel 10a; D, Vessel 26; E, Vessel 10b.

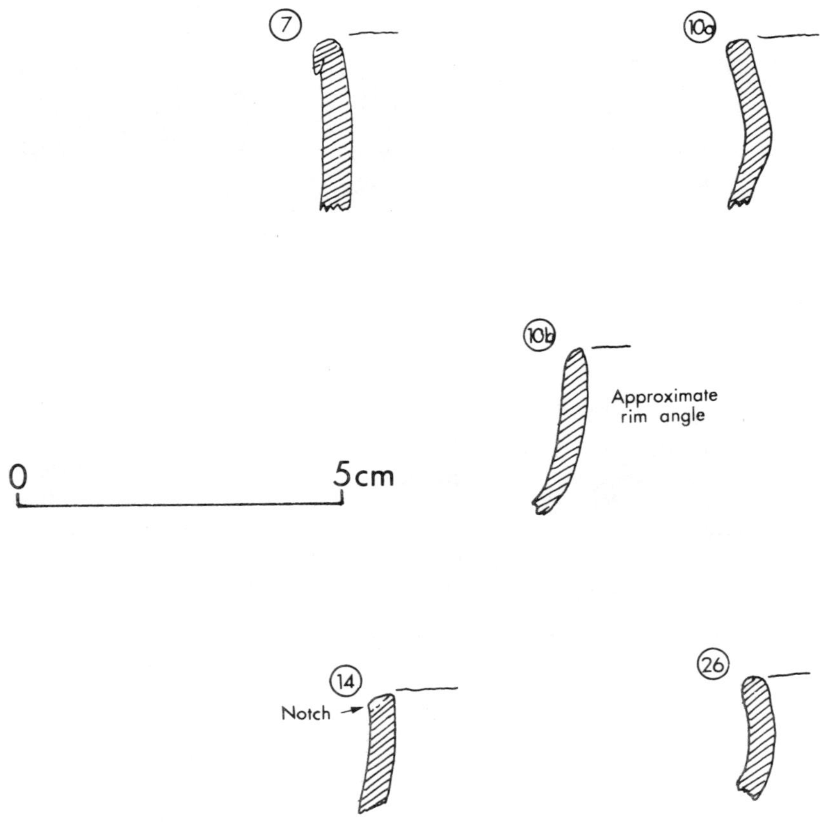

Fig. 22. Linn Ware Variant II rim profiles.

A temporal scheme, such as the one just outlined, is consistent with the general consensus of the ceramic sequence for the Middle to Late Woodland period transition. Linn Ware is closely related to Weaver Ware in Illinois; indeed, many Spring Hollow Plain vessels nearly duplicate some Weaver Plain and Cord Marked vessels (cf. Wray and MacNeish 1961:56-60). It would be consistent with what is presently known about the temporal developments of ceramic types in Illinois and Iowa to predict that Linn and Weaver Wares were contemporaries throughout almost the entire time span of each. However, it is important to maintain that Linn Ware pottery types have many attributes which are strictly limited to the region of eastern Iowa. Linn Ware contains a greater variety of decorative styles, many of which are holdovers as well as modifications of the earlier Havana styles. The application or absence of decorative motifs on Linn Ware ceramic types is undoubtedly related to both temporal and geographic factors. For example, the distribution of Levsen Punctated is generally limited to Allamakee, Clayton, and Jackson Counties, Levsen Stamped to these three counties and Linn County as well, and Spring Hollow Plain and Cord Marked to eastern Iowa (Logan 1959). After perusing many collections from sites in eastern Iowa, it is this writer's impression that in the central portion of the state (roughly west and south of the Driftless Zone) styles of zoned stamped or punctated decoration faded out of use as Havana-like ware disappeared and Linn Ware came into popularity. This does not appear to be true for the area of the Driftless Zone, where one is likely to encounter almost any combination of decorative styles on vessels purported to be Linn Ware.

As for the several Linn Ware pottery types, Logan's discussion of comparisons between types is the most comprehensive analysis presently available. His conclusions can only be supplemented to a minor extent by the relatively small collection from Hadfields Cave. It is somewhat informative that Spring Hollow Incised and Brushed do not appear in this sample. If the former type was derived in any way from the Early Woodland Black Sand Incised pottery, then its absence at 13JN3 would seem to indicate that it belongs to the Early or Middle Woodland time period in Iowa. Levsen Punctated and Stamped are types of the Intermediate period. They are curious conglomerates of Weaver-like paste and vessel form, Havana-like stamped and punctated decorations, and locally invented styles of zoned, geometric design motifs. It is also difficult to measure how much difference there is between the two Levsen types and Spring Hollow Plain and Cord Marked. Decoration, or the absence of it, seems to be the central factor subdividing Linn Ware into Spring Hollow and Levsen categories. In general, the condition of eastern Iowa ceramics during the Intermediate period seems to have been one of widespread technological change blended with the conservative retention of popular decorative styles, suffused with a high degree of individualistic variation. Technological change here refers to the advent of finer grained, more compacted pastes which are the hallmark of Weaver, Linn, and Madison Wares.

It seems appropriate at this point to recognize that Lane Farm Cord Impressed pottery has many aspects in common with Linn Ware. Logan (1959:169, 171) pointed this out, but tentatively placed this type in Madison Ware (Lake Michigan Ware) because of its corded decorations and globular shaped vessel forms. However, the few Lane Farm vessels in the Keyes collection from the Lane Farm Mounds in Allamakee County have Linn Ware paste, plain surfaces, only slightly expanding shoulders, and conoidal bases. The Quandahl rock shelter in Winneshiek County produced a large quantity of Lane Farm sherds with similar attributes. From an aesthetic standpoint such vessels appear to be the Spring Hollow Plain type with corded and rocker stamped decorations. Ceramic typology certainly should not be allowed to drift into the study of aesthetics or evolutionary genetics, for pots do not mate and foster mixed offspring. Rather, it is man as an innovator of new techniques and conservator of traditions who blends the old and new into his handmade artifacts. The ceramic type Lane Farm Cord Impressed appears to be just such a blend. Lane Farm Cord Impressed and Stamped types should be placed in the Linn Ware group because of their technological similarity to other types in this ware category. Inclusion of the Lane Farm types—particularly the former—in Linn Ware signifies that this ware group is a truly transitional one, one which incorporates many traits found in the two major wares immediately preceding and postdating Linn Ware in time. At the same time this approach also preserves the integrity of the term *ware* by recognizing the consistency of technological attributes common to Linn Ware types: plain surfaces, decorations impressed on plain surfaces, and compact paste.

The archaeologist frequently finds it difficult to impose an abstract typology over these artifactual remains, particularly when they take the form of highly variable conglomerates of attributes. Peoples of the Driftless region of Iowa are no different from other peoples of the world in fostering several ceramic forms which are apparently transitional between sharply delineated ceramic types and traditions. Ceramics of the Driftless region are distinguished by the large numbers of individual vessels within each transitional type. Thus, our definitions of types and ware groups for eastern Iowa must be elastic enough to permit the inclusion of a wide range of major variations while still maintaining a thread of continuity which is useful for cultural recognition and reconstruction. At some future time the eastern Iowa ceramic types may be subjected to modern statistical analyses using attribute clustering (for example, Johnson and Johnson 1975). This would assist in assessing the temporal and typological variability within ceramic categories so that their potential sensitivity as indicators of culture content could be more judiciously appraised.

Madison Ware

Ceramic types associated with the Late Woodland period in northeastern Iowa were initially placed under the heading of Lake Michigan Ware by Logan (1959). His conceptual scheme of wares and types has been preserved for this investigation but the earlier term has been replaced by that of Madison Ware. Hurley (1970) has made the same substitution for his Effigy Mound study in Wisconsin (see also Baerreis 1966:126). The now antiquated term, Lake Michigan Ware, was coined by McKern (1930:469) in his pioneering work with the Effigy Mound culture of Wisconsin, but in the more than 40 years since its inception the extensive variety of ceramic types included with Lake Michigan Ware has been reworked into more than three ware categories.

The application of a Wisconsin ceramic category, Madison Ware, in Iowa would seem to need justification. It is important to recognize that utilizing Madison Ware in Iowa would extend its distribution from roughly Green Bay, Wisconsin to Cedar Rapids, Iowa, a distance of 300 miles! This is an extraordinary range for a single Late Woodland ware when one considers that it crosscuts several major river drainages. The employment of Madison Ware in this discussion is intended to reflect the fact that the majority of Late Woodland period ceramics in southern Wisconsin and northeast Iowa are substantially alike in both technological and decorative attributes. Some of the most recognizable similarities in the ceramics of both regions can be found in the attributes which reflect the techniques of manufacture. Coloring of the paste suggests that a low temperature, rapid combustion firing was employed, producing hues predominantly in the Munsell 5YR- to 7.5YR- range—charcoal black to reddish brown, or dark grays to dull tan. Vessels often have firing clouds and exterior surfaces impregnated with soot, indicating differential heating. The clay usually contains a significant amount of silt-sized particles and has a relatively high organic content. These materials, whether human additives or natural inclusions in the clay, endow the fired paste with a gritty surface texture. Another striking characteristic of the majority of Madison Ware vessels is the thinness and uniformity of rims and body walls. The Hadfields sample has a range of 2.5-6 mm. and an average of 3-4 mm. thickness for rim and body sherd walls. These values are in significant contrast to the range of 6-9 mm. and average of ca. 7 mm. for the walls of Havana ceramics at other sites. However, the sample of vessels from which these values were taken is statistically small. If sufficient time had been available for measuring the hundreds of Madison and Havana Ware sherds in the Keyes collection, nearly identical results would undoubtedly have been obtained.

A final character, one essential in defining Madison Ware, is a cord and/or fabric-roughened exterior surface with the rim usually impressed with a decorative fabric. Many of the vessels from Wisconsin and Iowa seen by this writer show no evidence of surface preparation (such as tool smoothing or wiping) which preceded fabric impressing. This statement is especially applicable to the type Madison Fabric Impressed (Logan 1959). Fabric roughening as a single treatment applied to the exterior of vessels under construction should not be confused with the much more widespread use of a cord-wrapped paddle to malleate the pliable walls of newly formed vessels. One purpose of this discussion is to show that fabric impressing is the end product of a hypothetical method for producing pottery vessels which is distinctly different from the paddle and anvil technique. The new technique involves forming at least the rim and shoulder portions of the vessel by pressing the plastic paste on the inside of a fabric "collar." Thus, a soft vessel is enclosed by a supportive fabric structure, and large vessels with exceptionally thin walls can be successfully formed and dried (cf. Tolstoy 1953:26-30). The fabric structure and its decorative cords in this way become indelibly recorded on the exterior surface of the vessel. The structure of the fabrics gives additional indications that these are more than simple decorative elements on pots. A thorough description of the Hadfields Cave sample of fabric impressions on vessels will demonstrate the fabrics' functional use in pottery production. First, however, the pioneering work of Hurley (1970) will be reviewed, as some of his findings are contradictory to conclusions based on the Hadfields fabrics.

Hurley has been the first archaeologist to investigate the forms and structures of the cord impressions found on Late Woodland period ceramics in Wisconsin. His provocative insight has opened to archaeological analysis a new set of previously unrecognized decorative attributes and has made possible access to a record of prehistoric fabrics, the art of which had gradually disappeared after European contact with the New World. Hurley has partially reviewed the rather small number of existing textile studies of prehistoric ceramics from the eastern United States (1970:611-15), but he has excluded from discussion at least two significant analyses of prehistoric fabrics (Orchard 1920; Willoughby 1952) and a body of ethnographic data on bag making by Wisconsin tribes. These references are especially useful for illuminating the cultural contexts of the fabrics which are impressed on Madison Ware vessels. It is this examination of the cultural context and purpose of fabrics which is absent from Hurley's analyses. Also absent are precise explanations of fabric structures, such as descriptions of the directional movement of interworked elements, the associations between plain-faced fabrics (body cord roughening) and patterned fabrics (rim designs), and the superposition of cords. Lack of consideration for these aspects ultimately resulted in misidentification of a few of the fabrics as well as misrepresentations in several of the line-drawn fabric reconstructions (cf. Hurley 1970:623-50, Figs. 111-121).

Some of these problems have not been entirely resolved in this analysis of the Hadfields fabrics. This is because many of the fabric impressions on vessel surfaces are shallow or poorly preserved, and in some cases, there was insufficient information for a complete reconstruction. This problem is compounded because archaeologists, for the most part, are novices in fabric analysis (cf. Quimby 1961).

Before discussing the fabrics on Madison Ware vessels, it should be noted that two small rims from two Madison Plain vessels were recovered at 13JN3. Unfortunately, both are too fragmentary for a satisfactory reconstruction of vessel form or even lip profile. We are also precluded from distinguishing whether the exterior surfaces are simply cord roughened or are fabric impressed.

Madison Plain is a category coined by Keslin (1958) to identify a small number of vessels which conformed to all of the characteristics for Madison Ware but were cord roughened over the entire exterior surface and lacked corded designs. The two specimens from 13JN3 exhibit every character typical of the other Madison Ware sherds at the site, except that they also lack corded decorations. Similar rims with very thin walls and cord-roughened exterior surfaces appear in almost every northeast Iowa site collection where a substantial number of Late Woodland rims are found. Madison Plain rims never seem to appear in large numbers in these collections, but only as one or two elements at a time. Adding to the confusion surrounding this type is the established presence of Spring Hollow Cord Marked in Iowa. Chronologically, the Spring Hollow type should have been made earlier than Madison Plain, and the possibility exists that the former grades imperceptibly into the latter. Differences between the two may be found in paste characters, the steps involved in finishing surfaces, lip treatments, and the possibility that Madison Plain is usually fabric roughened while Spring Hollow Cord Marked is malleated with a cord-wrapped paddle. Evidence for this last character may be seen in several of the Madison Plain rims from the Bigelow site (47PT29), Wisconsin (Hurley 1970). Rubber latex casts of five rims from this site revealed to this writer that all were probably impressed with fabric-like structures, that is, undecorated warp-twined fabrics, although none of the sherds provided enough surface area to absolutely confirm this assertion.

All of the fabrics on the Hadfields site's Madison Ware vessels fall into the general category of twined structures. Twined fabrics are present when "... pairs (or larger groups) of adjacent elements of one set spiral or turn about each other in their passage through a fabric, enclosing successive elements of the other set in each turn or half-turn ..." (Emery 1966:196). For our purposes, either or both of the two elements can be twined: warp-twining, or the vertical cords, and weft-twining, the horizontal and sometimes oblique cords. One structural-functional distinction between these two types of twining is important for these prehistoric fabrics.

> ... There is an important additional possibility of effective structural variation which occurs in *weft-twining* alone, namely, the possibility of 'spacing' the twining groups and thereby exposing the non-twining elements to view. While *warp-twining* is consistently compact, or 'close-twined', concealing the non-twining elements, *weft-twining* can be either correspondingly 'compact' or it can be 'spaced'....The warps then assume visual importance and provide further possibilities of variation. [Emery 1966:196; emphasis hers]

It can be added that it is this spacing of weft cords which provides the decorative patterning (or selvage) found on nearly all fabric-impressed rims.

The Hadfields Cave site contained 24 vessels which had been decorated with fabrics and, of these, 14 were sufficiently reconstructed so that an entire rim and shoulder section could be studied (Figs. 23-26). Two

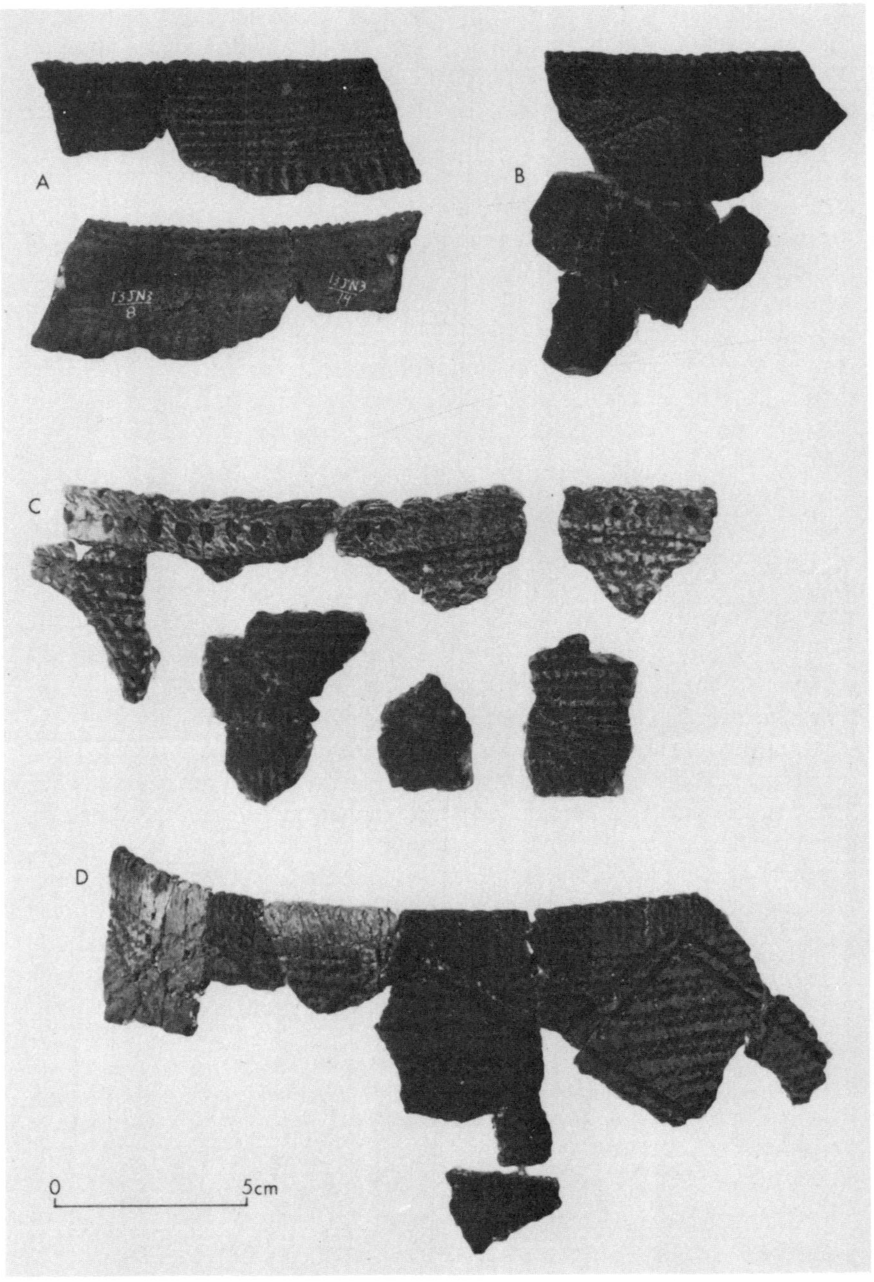

Fig. 23. Madison Ware. A, Vessel 16; B, Vessel 22; C, Vessel 20; D, Vessel 21.

Fig. 24. Madison Ware. A, Vessel 18; B, Vessel 28; C, Vessel 29.

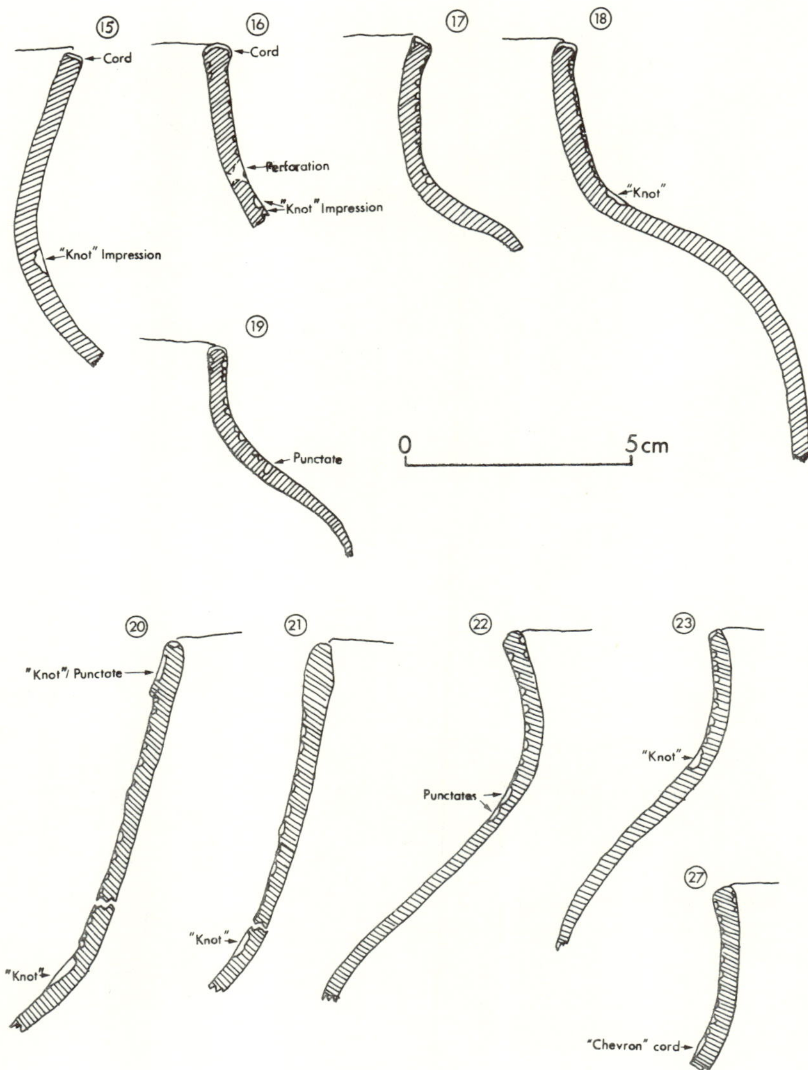

Fig. 25. Madison Ware rim profiles.

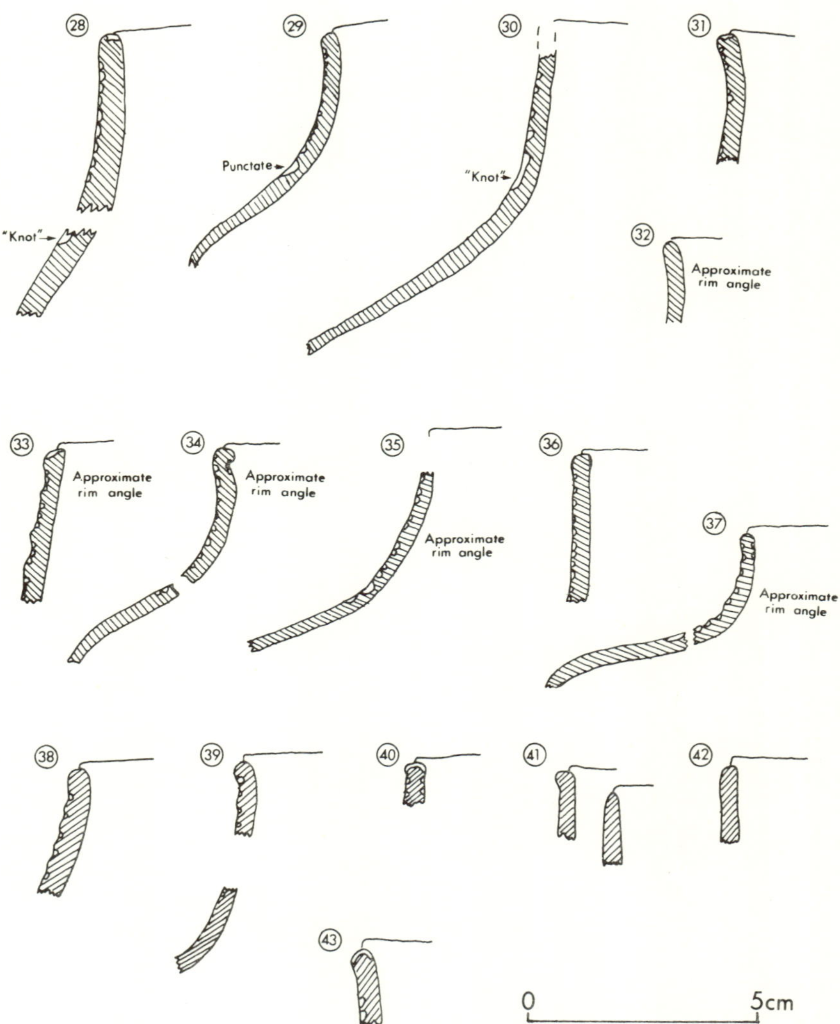

Fig. 26. Madison Ware rim profiles.

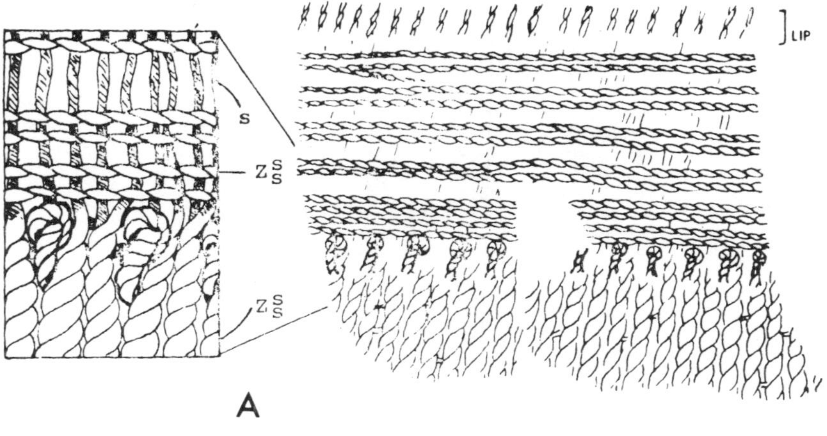

A

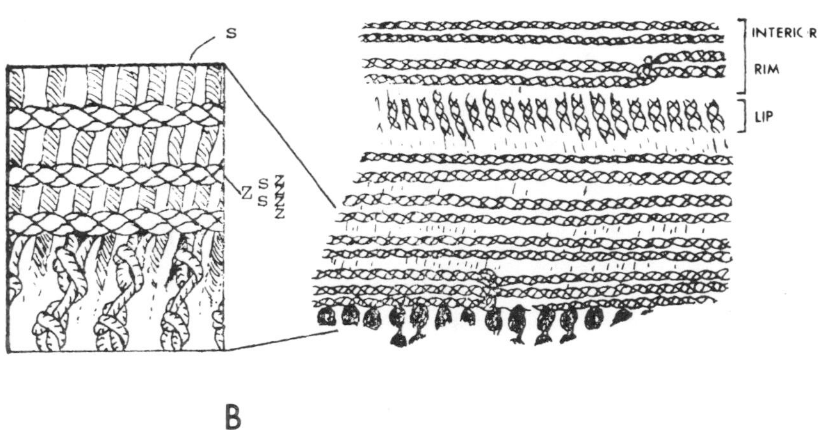

B

Fig. 27. Fabric renderings. A, Vessel 15; B, Vessel 16.

differing structural variations were noted in the fabrics of all 14 vessels: shoulders had impressions of warp-twined structures while rims were impressed with varying kinds of spaced weft-twined structures. However, the rim and shoulder impressions represented a *single* fabric sheet with the structural change usually placed at the rim/shoulder juncture. Similar dual-structured fabrics are intuitively evident in many of the line-drawn reconstructions by Hurley, but they may have gone unrecognized because few of the rims in that very large sample could be fitted to body sherds.

The nature of the warp-twined fabrics on the bodies of vessels at 13JN3 was found to be highly uniform. All of these fabrics were warp-faced; that is, the weft elements were entirely obscured by the compacting of warp cords. The fact that wefts were hidden points to the first major problem encountered in this analysis. Lacking visible, repetitive evidence for wefts, it is difficult to distinguish between compact warp-twining and interlinking. The latter structure involves only a single set of parallel elements, each linking (crossing) with an adjacent or nearly adjacent element (Emery 1966:61). Interlinking, however, tends to produce a fabric face with rows of horizontal wales or lines of continuous diagonal spirals (Emery 1966), neither of which was evident in the Hadfields fabrics. Rather, rare breaks in the warp which occasionally exposed weft elements indicate that these body fabrics are in all likelihood warp-twined structures. It has been more difficult to establish the exact number of elements which form individual cords for each vessel. The warps are loosely twisted and apparently quite soft. In general, the patterns of warp impressions in the past have a distinctive vertically furrowed appearance rather than that of horizontal rows. This vertical furrowing is characteristic of single-ply warp cords with three or four component elements.

There are no decorative patterns built into these warp-twined structures, nor are the bodies of Madison Ware vessels ordinarily decorated beyond the application of this same fabric roughening. Emery, in discussing warp-twined fabrics, indicates that designs are largely restricted to varying the direction of cord twists, varying the colors of individual elements in the warp cord, or occasionally spacing the warp cords. All of the vessels at 13JN3 and all of the Madison Ware vessels familiar to this author show but one twist direction (Z—counterclockwise, or S—clockwise) in the fabric structure on each vessel. Hurley has pictured a single sherd (1970: Fig. 112b) with an interlinked body fabric, but the remainder of his sample shows sherds which probably have warp-twined fabric impressions.

Moving to the rims of vessels in the Hadfields collection, the fabric structure present on all specimens is composed of some variation of weft-twining. The transition from shoulder, warp-twining, to rim, weft-twining, required that the artisan drop the single element wefts and employ multiple-strand weft-twining. In many specimens the warp was not twined through the rim design but remained as individual elements enclosed by the twining weft elements. The patterns of spaced horizontal and oblique cords, "knots," and geometric zones of cord impressions are usually composed of weft cords. The almost exclusive use of wefts as design elements is in contrast to many of Hurley's reconstructions, which show decorative elements frequently arising from warp cords only. One of his examples (1970:650, Fig. 121b), showing warp cords giving rise to a horizontal "suspended" design cord, is in itself contradictory, for the individual elements and ply of the warps have twists which are opposite those of the design structure. In this example the warps cannot logically give rise to the design element; instead the design is probably composed of bands of alternately "floating" and "obscured" wefts. Likewise, many of the "warp-derived" designs in Hurley's reconstructions are probably more properly attributable to variations in weft movements or to superimposed cord stamps.

The 24 fabric-impressed vessels at 13JN3 evidence two major variations of weft-twining: simple and compound (Figs. 27-33). Seventeen vessels have simple weft-twining with single sets of warp element and weft cords. Decorative patterns on these vessels result from varying the weft design—combinations of Z- and S-twists, spacing or pairing of cords, and alternate floating and obscuring of cords. The warp of these fabrics is uniform and probably was not intended to contribute significantly to the design impression in the clay. Eleven of the 17 vessels have two-strand warp-twining in addition to the decorative weft-twining, while the remaining six have single element warps. To enhance the aesthetic quality of the corded impression the artisans in most cases twined weft cords so that they were raised above the plane of the warp elements. This was accomplished by any combination of four methods: (a) warp elements were enclosed by the twining action of weft cords; (b) if both warp- and weft-twining were used, only one element of both warp and weft cords was linked (resulting in a "faced" fabric of which we see only the weft-face); (c) wefts were made thicker than the warp by multiple-plying of the weft cords; (d) each passage of the weft cord enclosed two or more warp elements in the twining process (resulting in a floating weft). All 17 vessel fabrics have spaced wefts, a character which is virtually always present in the type Madison Fabric Impressed. Slightly less than one-third of the 13JN3 rims have grouped, spaced wefts, usually in pairs or triplicates. Countering, a structural variation which also lends a grouping effect to horizontal wefts, is present on four rims. Countering involves twisting adjacent cords in opposite directions and gives a chaining effect to the cord pair.

An additional design variation is present in simple weft-twined fabrics (one compound fabric, Vessel 23, is also considered here for this structural trait). Ten of the 12 vessels with the shoulder/rim juncture present have a single row of decorative impressions immediately below the horizontal wefts. Eight of these ten are cord structures (the remaining two are tool impressions). Two examples (Vessels 16 and 37) have knots created by looping and tying a section of weft cord which emerges from a ground of compact warp twining. Another (Vessel 17) has two horizontal wefts which are alternately enclosed in the compact warp twining and float over a pair of warp cords. The floating wefts create an illusion of knot impressions finishing off the base of the rim design. A third group of five fabrics (Vessels 15, 18, 23, 30, and 35) has a row of decorative cord twists probably produced by the technique of weft wrapping (Emery 1966:214-15). (In the case of this structure a positive identification cannot be assured due to the poor quality of the majority of these twist impressions.) To create these structures a weft was alternately hidden by warp-twining and wrapped once or twice around a single warp cord. The product of this wrapping technique is a short section of what appears to be a two-ply twisted cord, but is in reality two passes of a single element around a warp. One possible variation on this structure may be present on Vessel 30 where two weft cords are twisted together three times in a vertical direction. Another structural variation which is employed to create this vertical cord or "knot" has been observed on a single rim fragment (accession no. 172-434) from the Rock Run rock shelter (13CD10; Alex 1968) and on a few Lane Farm Cord Impressed sherds from Allamakee County. This technique involves doubling a single warp cord back on itself and twisting this doubled cord such that a short, thick, two-ply cord is formed. This new element is allowed to float over the warp-faced fabric surface. The final variation observed by this author is found on a fabric-impressed Minotts Cord Impressed rim from the type site (accession no. Ln-2838). At the base of this rim design the illusion of short, oblique cords is created with twilled-twining. Although this structure appears to be an oblique, Z-twisted, two-ply cord, it is in fact the S-twisted, two-ply warp cords being twilled with the wefts.

The second major variation of weft-twining, that of compound fabrics, is found in seven of the 24 fabric-impressed vessels at 13JN3. These differ from the 17 simple fabrics described in the previous paragraphs in that they have three sets of structural members. The three members consist of the basic warp and weft as well as additional cords for weft patterning. Emery (1966:140) described two types of extra-weft patterning: *supplementary* and *complementary* cords. The latter are cords which are structurally coequal with the elements of either the warp or weft (only the weft at 13JN3), while the former are clearly additions to the basic warp-weft foundation. Complementary cords are twined into the fabric foundation as it is produced, while supplementary cords (in the two Hadfields examples) are additions to the warp and weft of a *completed* fabric.

Four of the seven compound fabrics probably have complementary weft patterning. Three of these have horizontal paired wefts similar to those found on simple fabrics, but additional sets of oblique weft cords have been imposed in the fabric structure in the same structural plane as the horizontal wefts. Two of these fabrics (Vessels 20 and 23) have groups of oblique weft patterning downward from right to left around the rim. These extra wefts are probably short sections of cord added to the primary warp-weft structure while the fabric was being made. This design also could have been achieved by a process of supplementary weft patterning.

64

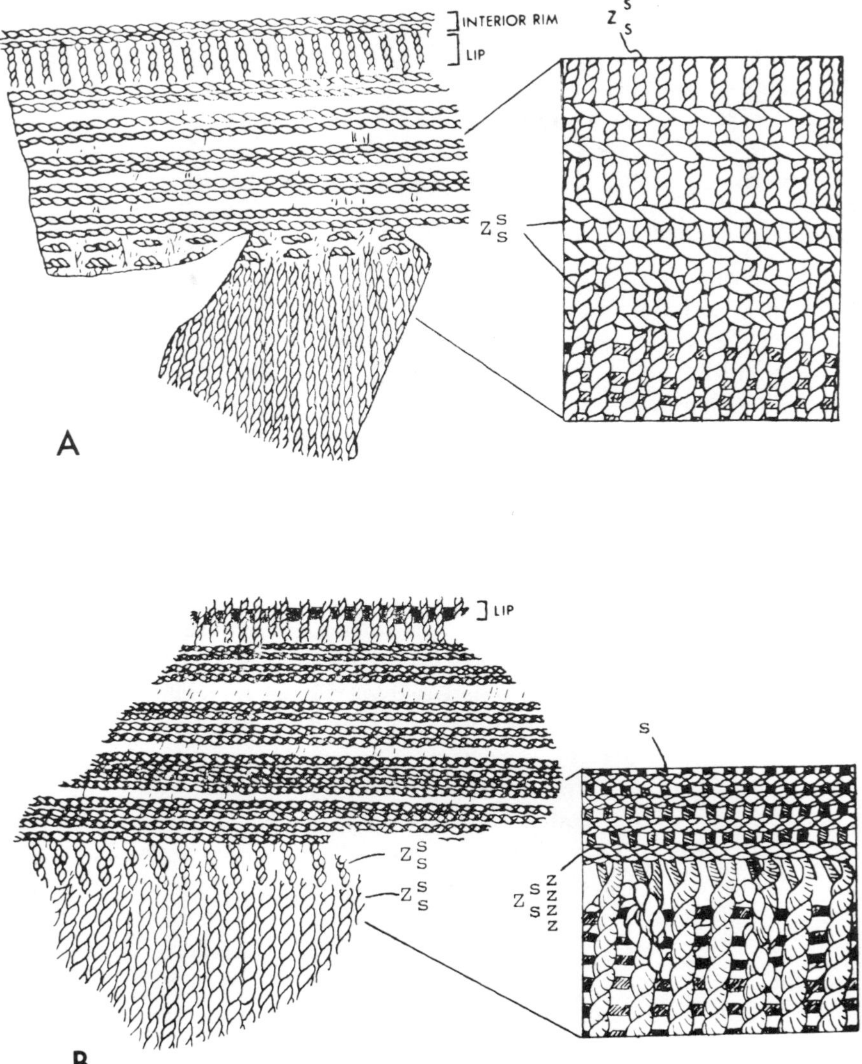

Fig. 28. Fabric renderings. A, Vessel 17; B, Vessel 18.

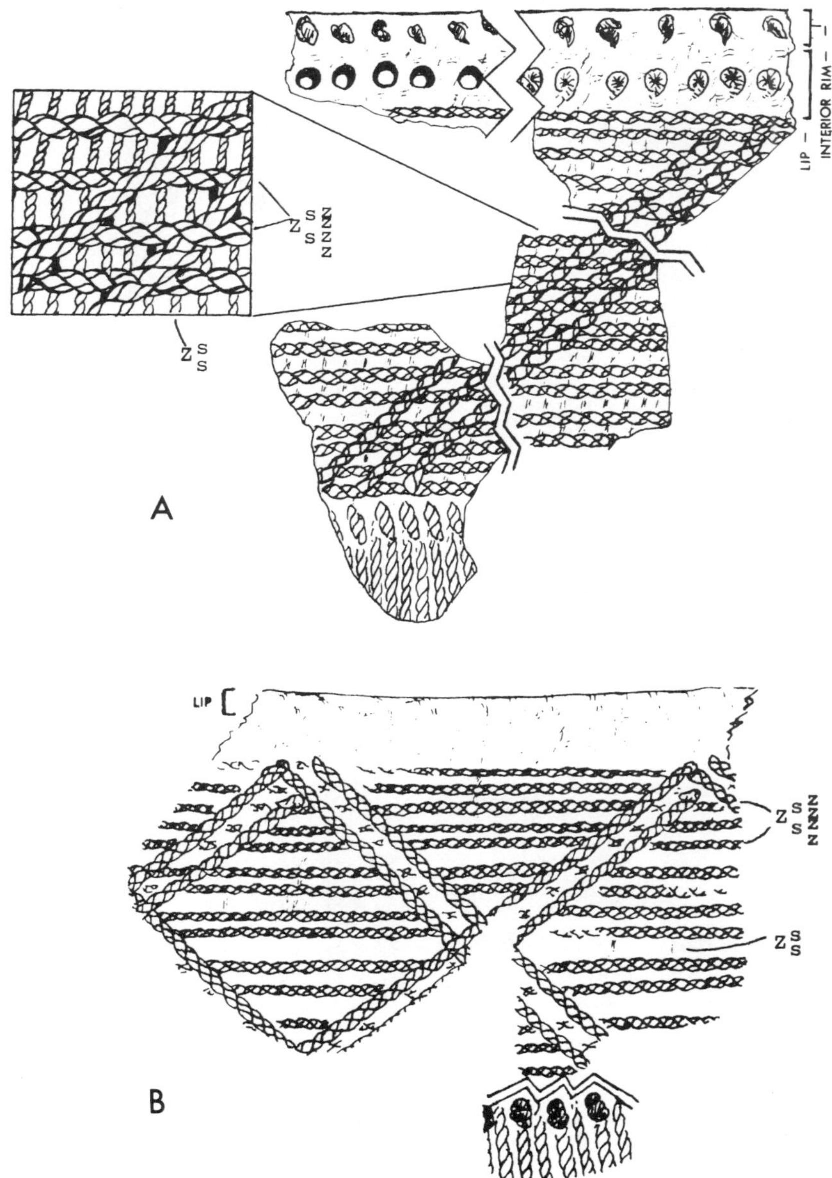

Fig. 29. Fabric renderings. A, Vessel 20; B, Vessel 21.

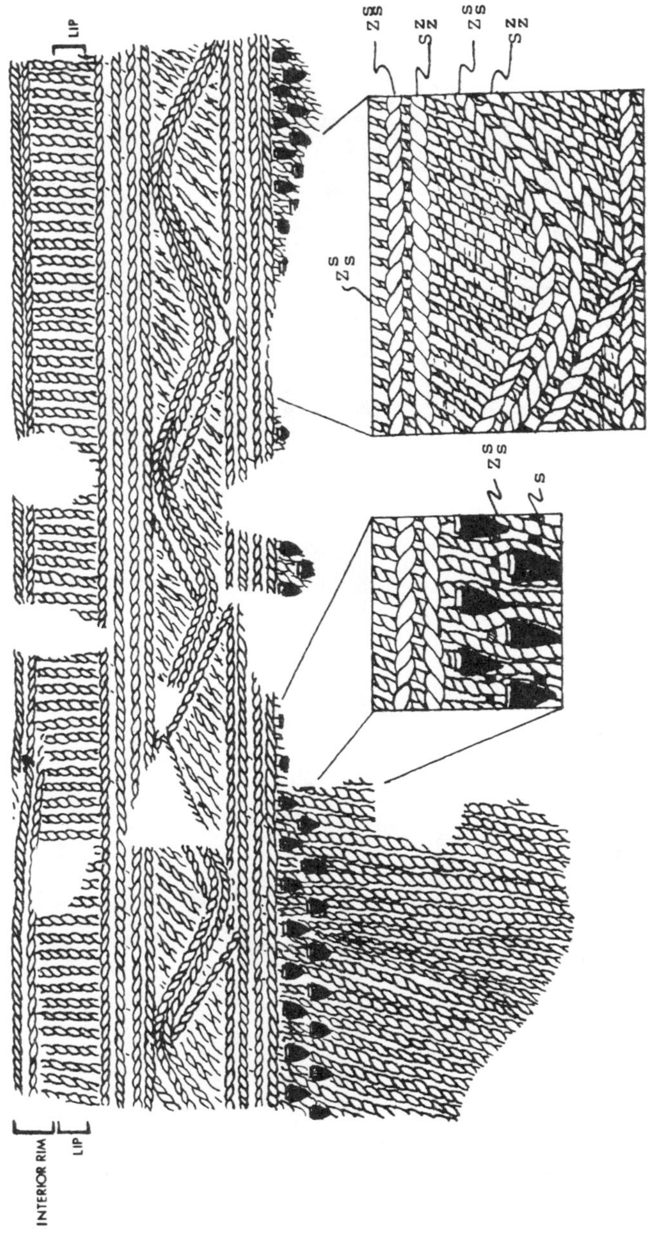

Fig. 30. Fabric rendering, Vessel 22.

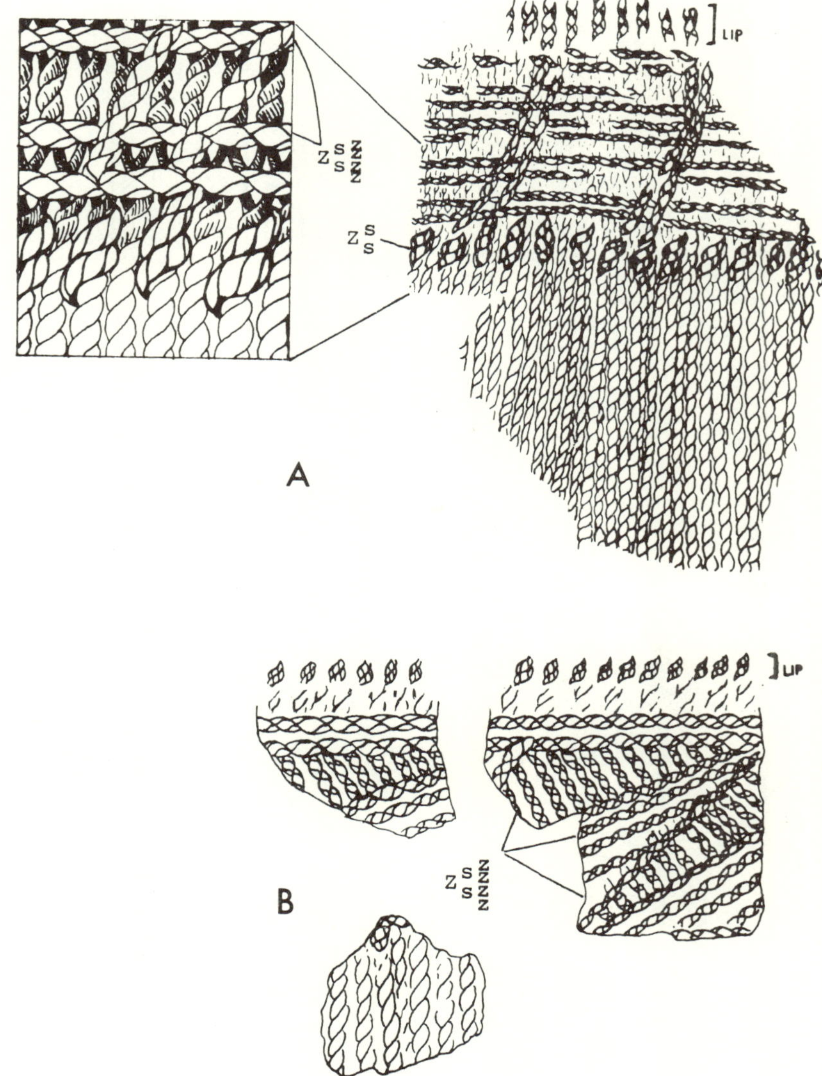

Fig. 31. Fabric renderings. A, Vessel 23; B, Vessel 28.

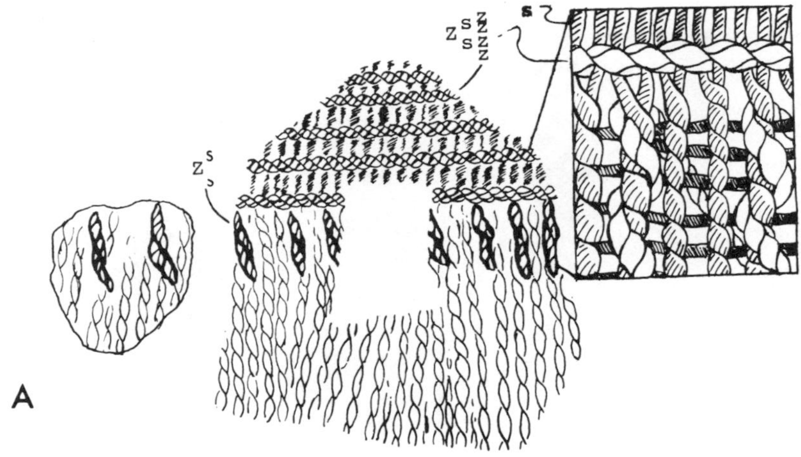

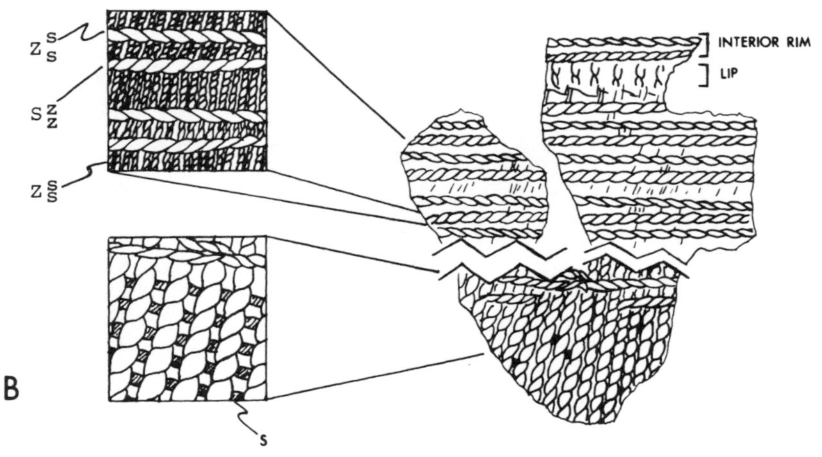

Fig. 32. Fabric renderings. A, Vessel 30; B, Vessel 34.

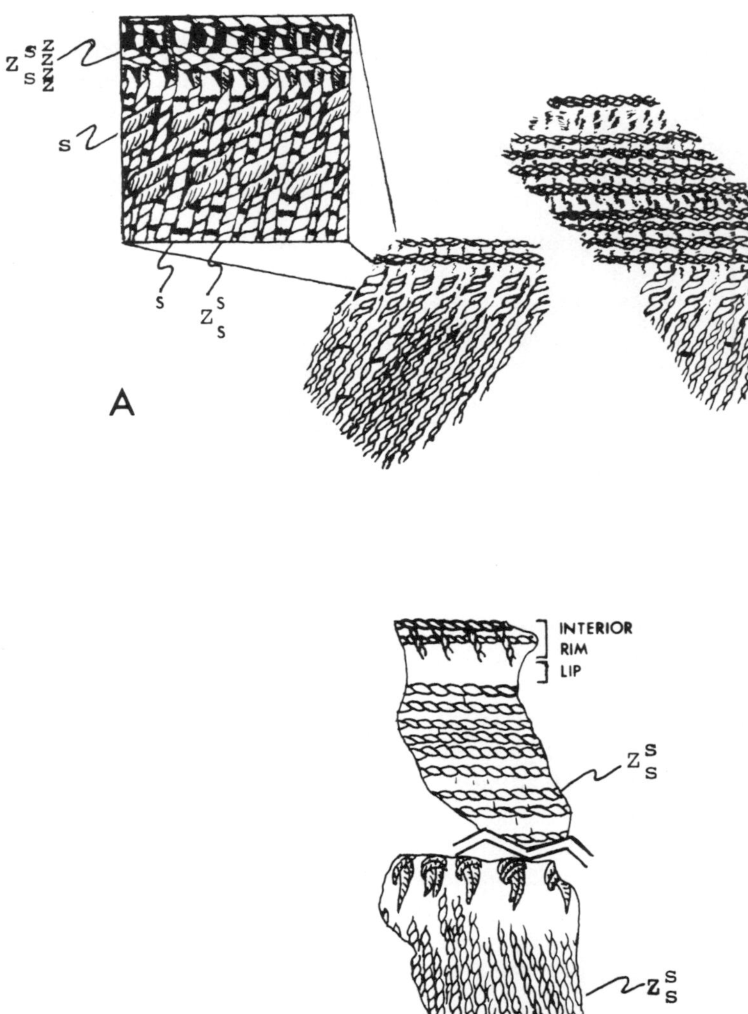

Fig. 33. Fabric renderings. A, Vessel 35; B, Vessel 37.

A procedure of this type would involve twining a group of wefts in a zigzag pattern around the zone of design, and switching the oblique wefts to the opposite face of the fabric at each turn in the pattern. (Such a procedure would necessarily have to be done on a completed fabric.) Thus, one face of the fabric would show wefts of one slant, the "zigs," and the opposite face would show wefts of the alternate slant, the "zags." Vessel 27 appears to have just such a pattern in a single weft twined in a zigzag pattern below two horizontal wefts, but in this case the zigzag cord remained on the impression face only.

The third compound fabric with complementary weft-patterning (Vessel 28) has two sets of perpendicular oblique wefts and one set of horizontal wefts. The geometric pattern on this rim consists of at least two horizontal cord rows bordering a continuous band of (obtuse) triangle-shaped zones of corded designs. The weft cords, which are the components of the design, effectively cover the entire surface of the rim, obscuring the warp elements except immediately below the lip. This weft-patterning has been achieved through the structural mechanism of floating, twining each component of a weft cord over two or more warps at a time, and by employing thick, two-ply weft cords. The effect of cord-filled zones of obtuse triangles has been accomplished by utilizing two perpendicular sets of angled wefts and floating these sets on alternating faces of the fabric to produce zones of parallel cords. One other vessel (number 31) with complementary weft patterning has a weft structure similar to that on Vessel 28. The shape of the triangular zones is slightly different, and several of the zones are not decorated with oblique, floating weft-patterning. The absence of weft cords in some zones has allowed the background warp elements to be impressed in the clay as well, but not sufficiently to identify them properly.

Compound fabrics with supplementary weft-patterning are found on three vessels (numbers 21, 22, and 27). These fabrics have two sets of weft cords—a set of horizontal, paired wefts composing the majority of the design, to which has been added a series of oblique, weft-patterning cords. All of the weft cords in this series of compound fabrics are floating. Vessel 21 has a rim covered with pairs of floating, two-ply, horizontal wefts, which are superimposed by two pairs of supplementary wefts twined on one face of the fabric. These supplementary wefts were superimposed on the completed fabric by intertwining with all of the warp and weft components in that fabric. The cord pairs of this supplemental weft-patterning are twined in continuous zigzag patterns, offset from one another to produce a diamond pattern.

The remaining compound fabric with supplementary weft-patterning is not only the most structurally complicated design at 13JN3, but was impressed on a vessel with exceptionally thin walls. The fabric on Vessel 22 was executed with single-ply, countered wefts floating on a background of warp twining. The design is composed of upper- and lower-rim bands of horizontal paired and countered wefts bordering a central decorative band. This central band is decorated with zigzag wefts which outline isosceles triangles of warp-faced fabric. The central band was probably structured in the following manner: single-element wefts were enclosed in compact warp twining for the foundation fabric; the entire fabric was completed prior to adding the supplementary zigzag cords; weft-patterning was twined in zigzag patterns on the faces of the completed foundation fabric. A total of six cords contributes to the zigzag weft-patterning; two cords were twined on one face within the boundaries of the central band, while four cords were twined from top to bottom of the entire rim design, switching faces to contribute appropriately to the central band's pattern of opposing triangles. The artisan was careful to intertwine the supplementary cords (zigzags) with the same relief as the horizontal weft pairs bordering the central band; thus, the entire rim design has a uniform relief despite having been produced in two stages.

The final aspect to be considered concerns the cord impressions which invariably appear on the lips or upper rim interiors of Madison Fabric Impressed vessels. Cord structures on the lips of vessels are never like those found on the rim, whereas those located on the interior rim are usually similar to those on the exterior surface. Thirteen vessels from 13JN3 have sufficient portions of the rim present to determine the origin of cord structures on the lip. Nine of these 13 have spaced, one-ply or two-ply cords which are continuations of the warp elements in the exterior rim fabric. These cords are crudely impressed over the lip from exterior to interior surfaces and show no evidence of being intertwined along the lip by weft elements. Three additional rims have lip cord impressions with the same general structure, but these cords are like the exterior rim wefts only. The last vessel (number 21) has a very poor impression of what appears to be braiding on the lip.

The discussion thus far has focused on the nature of individual structures within fabrics. It should be recognized that each fabric-impressed vessel at 13JN3 has been decorated with a single fabric sheet, regardless of the number of structural variations incorporated into the fabric. The shoulders of vessels are impressed with an unbroken sheet of warp-faced fabric which is superimposed by paddled cord roughening below the shoulder/body juncture. The warp cords are usually vertical and only occasionally may be slightly oblique from the vertical. It is plain from the record of cord impressions that the fibrous components of this warp become intertwined with the wefts in the rim design. The rim fabrics on many vessels are structurally linked to the corded constructions found on the lips and interior rims of these same vessels. Thus, there is conclusive evidence for fabrics which were impressed on vessel rims and shoulders as a single unit. It should be clear with the considerable recurving present in most of the Madison Ware rims and shoulders that rolling as the technique of cord application can be rejected. There is no evidence of overlapping cord impressions on any of the vessels, thus precluding the use of fabric stamps. In short, the continuous fabric evidenced by these impressions indicates that a fabric collar was employed to produce the cord impressions. It is reasonable to speculate that such a structure was used in the production of vessels. A vessel may have been shaped by pressing the paste on the interior of a fabric, shaping the base with the aid of a cord-wrapped paddle and anvil, and allowing the vessel to air-dry with the fabric as a support (Fig. 34). The walls of many Hadfields vessels are extraordinarily thin, and a technology of these methods may have produced such results.

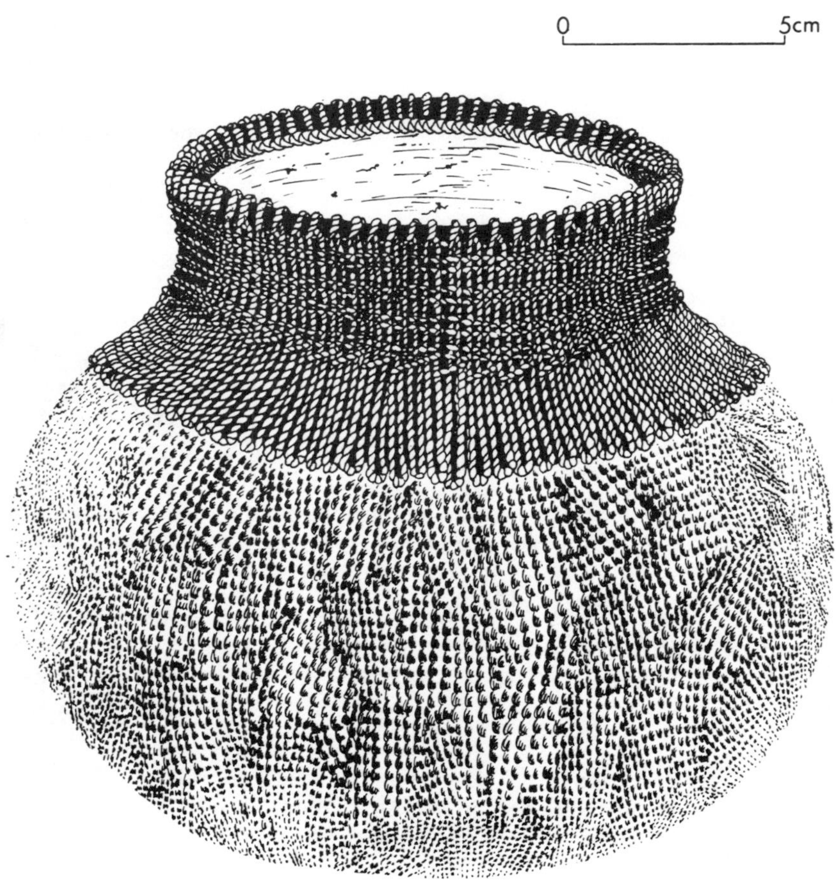

Fig. 34. Reconstructed fabric collar.

Intersite Comparison

A broader perspective of the structure and functions of fabrics impressed on the Hadfields vessels can be gained by considering some descriptions of fabrics in ethnographic accounts and in analysis of prehistoric remains. A point made in many of these investigations (for example, Skinner 1921:231; Willoughby 1952:108) is that a great deal of the aboriginal material culture of fabrics was lost in the disintegration of Indian communities after European contact. A potential inventory of this loss for current anthropological researchers is probably only partially documented in the many variations to be found in the fabrics on Madison Ware vessels. It seems fairly clear that the fabric-impressed vessels of the Late Woodland time period in the upper Midwest carry one of the most substantial records of aboriginal fabrics in North America.

W. H. Holmes (1896, 1903) was one of a very few authors to grant more than passing attention to fabric-impressed pottery in the eastern United States. Holmes studied plasticine impressions of sherds to identify the movements of elements in fabrics and described the structures he found in fragments of cloth taken from Ohio (Hopewell) burial mounds. In addition, he attempted to duplicate aboriginal methods of applying cord impressions to the surfaces of vessels. He attributed the application of corded designs on Madison Ware vessels to paddling or rocking with cord- or fabric-covered tools (1903:196).

A review of the sources cited here shows that there are no described fabrics which are structurally like those from 13JN3. However, the majority of individual fabric structures found at 13JN3 can be duplicated in at least one of these sources. Warp-faced, warp-twined fabrics, such as are found on practically all of the bodies of 13JN3 vessels, are described and pictured by Holmes (1896:35-36; Fig. 10, Plates VI, VII, VIII) as weft-faced. Another, a "blanket" with 6-8 element single-ply wefts, is described by Orchard (1920:17, Plate V). Whether these fragmentary examples were actually warp- or weft-faced is probably debatable, but the structural similarity is unequivocal. Those described by Holmes have notably fine, tightly packed cords, similar to the majority of body fabrics at Hadfields Cave. The size and firmness of cordage in the sample vary considerably, and the body fabric of at least one vessel (number 15) is similar to that described by Orchard. It is perhaps a significant indicator of the historic changes in material culture that none of the corded bags described in the ethnographic sources have warp-faced twining like that at 13JN3.

The corded designs which are twined in relief on the rims of Hadfields ceramics have only a few sequels in historic period fabrics. Most of the bags pictured or described have widely spaced weft-twining over warp-twining, the latter often being patterned by grouping elements for each weft twist (for example, Radin 1923: Plate 37; Skinner 1926:286, Plate XLIX, Fig.

74

1). A bag with this structure collected by Skinner (1921:236, Plate LVIa) from the Menomini has colored geometric patterning developed in the warp. Three others (Skinner 1921:234-36, Plates LIVa and LV; 1952b: Plate XXI) have from three to six variations of twined and diagonal-twined twining in a single fabric plane. The artisan employed several colors of cordage in producing these two bags, and the variations of twining were necessary to bring specific colors to the face of the fabric. None of these bags, however, has what could be referred to as both "rim," or selvage, and "body" fabrics; all of them are either decorated or undecorated from orifice to base. A single example of a prehistoric "bag" from the Spiro Mound in Oklahoma has such a selvage design (Willoughby 1952:118, Plate 152). In this example the body fabric has spaced weft-twining over warp-twining, and the selvage has two bands of weft-faced weft-twining over the same warp. Examples of oblique, extra-weft patterning, such as those found at 13JN3, are not pictured or described by any of the sources referenced here.

The structure employed to finish many bag edges just described is strikingly similar to the patterns of cord impressions on the lips of vessels at 13JN3. Historic period bags made of twined cordage were usually finished at the orifice by gathering the warp elements into larger cords and binding these in a horizontal, braided cord (for example, Holmes 1896:34; Skinner 1921: Plate LIV; Radin 1923: Plate 37). A prehistoric bag from an unknown Kentucky cave has an identical border (Orchard 1920: Plate VI). An equivalent structure seems to be impressed on at least nine Hadfields vessels. Spaced warps, which are always found on or immediately below the lip of such a vessel, were clearly intended to be placed at this point on the vessel. Furthermore, such spaced warps only occur immediately above the fabric design of the rim. However, the absence of clear cord impressions on the rim interior, presumably cords which intertwine with the spaced warps on the lip, precludes making firm judgments about these structures.

Turning to the region of eastern Iowa, there are large numbers of cord-decorated, prehistoric ceramics available for study. The greatest portion of this material is contained in the Keyes collection. Some of this material was donated by amateur collectors, but much of it was excavated or salvaged from the many sites investigated by Keyes and Orr. All of the artifact assemblages compiled by Keyes and Orr are treated here as surface collections. The stratigraphic controls employed by these pioneer investigators do not conform to modern methods, and there has been considerable mixing of the boxes in the collections. Excepting Logan's (1959) work with a portion of this collection, a substantial amount of this material has yet to be studied.

This discussion will not attempt to cover all of the cord-decorated ceramics available in the Keyes collection. Rather, a nonrandom sample of 44 vessel fabrics, preserved on latex rubber casts, has been gathered by this author from the Keyes collection and the Luther College repository.

Comparisons between this small sample and the Hadfields fabrics seem to provide an initial view of the range of variation present in Iowa fabrics.

The 44 vessel fabrics come from four Iowa counties: 5—Allamakee, 10—Winneshiek, 9—Jones (excluding Hadfields Cave), and 20—Linn County. A tabulation of these fabrics according to simple and compound structures is presented in Table 3 to clarify their distribution. In this nonrandom sample the fabrics from Allamakee and Winneshiek Counties are predominantly simple structured (77%), while those from Linn County are almost equally divided between simple and compound structures (56% and 44% respectively). Simple structures are always composed of spaced or paired horizontal wefts and vertical warps. Compound structures, on the other hand, are developed from vertical warps and two or three sets of coequal wefts, one or more of which are oblique. When one or more sets of oblique wefts are employed in compound fabrics, the decorative fabric patterns often take the form of triangular cord-filled zones of alternating cord directions (see Vessel 28, Fig. 31). Comparing fabric structures from Winneshiek and Allamakee Counties in the northeast corner of Iowa with those from Linn County in the east-central portion of the state, we find a higher proportion of structurally compound fabrics in the latter region. This greater use of compound structures may have been necessitated by the  artisans' more frequent use of the triangular design motif in their fabrics. Logan (1959:333-34) initially noted the high incidence of triangular cord design motifs in east-central Iowa, and this attribute became one of the major factors distinguishing Minotts Focus of this region from an unnamed focus in northeast Iowa.

TABLE 3
Simple and Compound Fabrics Impressed
on Eastern Iowa Rims

Area Sites	Nos. of Fabrics			Site Total
	simple	compound	indeter.	
Northeast				
13WH35/-79	7	1	2	10
*Allamakee Co. sites	3	2	—	5
Subtotals	10 (77%)	3 (23%)	2	15
Jones Co.				
*Fuller I rock shelter	3	3	—	6
*Rattlesnake rock shelter	2	—	—	2
*Ely rock shelter	—	1	—	1
Subtotals	5 (56%)	4 (44%)	—	9
Linn Co.				
13LN133/-135	1	2	—	3
*Spring Hollow rock shelter	3	2	—	5
*Minotts rock shelter	6	4	2	12
Subtotals	10 (56%)	8 (44%)	2	20
13JN3	17 (71%)	7 (29%)	—	24

*sherds from the Keyes collection

Although 13JN3 is in the county immediately east of Linn County, the proportions of simple and compound fabrics, 71% and 29% respectively, are more similar to those of the northeast corner of the state. Of the seven compound fabrics at 13JN3, only three have triangular, cord-patterned zones in their decorative motifs. In contrast to 13JN3, three other sites in central Jones County—Fuller I, Rattlesnake, and Ely rock shelters—have combined proportions of 56% simple and 44% compound fabric structures (Table 3). Two sites (13JK20 and 13JK21) in Jackson County about five miles east of Hadfields Cave have produced fabric structures with approximately equal numbers of simple and compound structures (cf. Jaehnig 1975).

Unfortunately, this is the limit of the number of excavated sites which have produced substantial numbers of fabric-decorated ceramics. It would be unreasonable to advance any positive arguments to explain the variations in proportions of fabric structures described here, for this sample is small and nonrandom. In addition, the sample has been presented without regard for temporal control, a factor which is considerably more difficult to deal with than geography. However, a number of observations and speculations are relevant to this dicussion and have the potential for developing into viable inferences through a comprehensive analysis of the extant collections in Iowa, Wisconsin, and Illinois.

Lane Farm Cord Impressed has been designated by Logan (1959) as the temporally pivotal cord-decorated pottery type in northeast Iowa. This opinion has been widely encouraged by many of those interested in the origins and development of cord- and fabric-impressed pottery. However, a thorough study of this type has yet to be undertaken, and no sites containing large quantities of Lane Farm sherds have been excavated with current scientific methods. Thus, any discussion of this type must proceed without the desired analytical controls of ceramic analysis.

The Lane Farm pottery type is usually characterized by relatively thick vessel walls (ca. 5-10 mm.), straight to slightly flaring lips, slightly expanding shoulders, flat lips, and scraped (tooled) and smoothed (sometimes lustrous) surfaces. The corded design is usually relegated to the vessel's exterior rim, while the exterior shoulders and body of the vessel are covered with dentate or rocker-dentate stamping. The paste is generally hard, coarse textured, and tempered with large angular grit. The impression of this writer is that Lane Farm vessels are very similar in technological attributes to the Linn Ware ceramic types from eastern Iowa and probably belong to that ware group. Rocker-dentate stamping, which has been the single most distinguishing feature of this type, is a trait belonging exclusively to the Middle Woodland period in Illinois. Cord decorating on Lane Farm rims is the one aberrant feature which creates problems for ceramic typologists. This decorative trait is associated with the Late Woodland period in the Midwest but not exclusive of the Weaver or Havana Wares of Illinois.

The cord decorations on Lane Farm Cord Impressed seem to have been applied as fabrics. This statement is intentionally tentative. The fabric impressions on more than three-quarters of the rims are so shallow that the warp was not impressed at any point in the paste. A few rims, however, have been impressed sufficiently to show the warp. Perhaps this occurred when mistakes in twining were made by the artisan and a hidden element's weave was exposed in the impression. The largest available collection of Lane Farm ceramics came from the Quandahl rock shelter (13WH35), a site in eastern Winneshiek County on North Bear Creek which was looted by others between 1920 and 1950 and partially reported (Mallam n.d.). The extant collection, now at the Luther College Archaeological Research Center, was salvaged from the backdirt of the pothunters. From the selective sample of sherds in this collection it can be estimated that the site contained several dozen vessels of which nearly all were Lane Farm Cord Impressed and Madison Ware types. Latex rubber impressions were taken of nine large Lane Farm rims. Of these, seven are simple structured fabrics with a band of four to ten spaced, horizontal wefts bordered at the top and bottom of the rim by a horizontal band of short, spaced, vertical cords. This design is the most common one on Madison Fabric Impressed vessels in Wisconsin and Iowa. An eighth simple structured fabric at Quandahl has four horizontal rows of spaced, vertical cords as the sole design element. The single compound structured fabric in this Lane Farm group is represented by a small neck fragment with a corded triangular motif. The warp elements are visible on only four of nine rims described here. It is evident in all four examples that the warp elements are completely enclosed by the weft-twining, causing the fabric to be effectively weft-faced when lightly impressed on the vessel surface. A tenth cast was also taken of a Madison Fabric Impressed rim. This specimen has a Madison Ware paste, unlike the Lane Farm vessels, and the fabric impressions are deep and clear in the clay. This vessel's fabric is a compound structure with ten paired and spaced, horizontal wefts and a zigzag weft superimposed over the bottom weft pair. The design's warp is single Z-elements, while the body fabric is unclear due to the small sherd size.

Other sherds present at Quandahl include small portions of two Madison Fabric Impressed vessels, plain miniature vessels, and one cord-roughened and undecorated rim similar to Madison Plain rims at 13JN3. One S-shaped rim reminiscent of the style of Levsen ceramic types is also present. It has a deep inner rim channel, a narrow band of impressed cords on the exterior rim near the lip, and technological attributes identical to the Lane Farm rims.

A perusal of the Lane Farm and Madison Fabric Impressed rims in the Keyes collection and from Quandahl should make it clear that these two types generally differ in technological and design attributes and are similar in fabric structure. Lane Farm vessels apparently were produced by the same techniques as Havana vessels. The surfaces on Lane Farm sherds are compact and occasionally lustrous, having been scraped and smoothed prior to the applications of designs. Both the dentate stamping and fabric designs were applied over this prepared surface, and typically only the design (weft) cords of the fabric were pressed into the clay. In contrast, the surfaces of (Iowa) Madison Fabric Impressed vessels are almost completely covered with the individual cord impressions of a fabric. There is virtually no evidence on *most* of these vessels for prior surface preparation (for an exception see Vessel 21 from 13JN3). In many cases the wet paste on the vessel surface has penetrated between the fibers and cords of the fabric, and the vessel walls are covered with dents and undulations resulting from the human hands which applied the paste and shaped the vessel. In short, there seems to be good evidence that rims and shoulders of Madison Fabric Impressed vessels were formed by pressing wet clay onto the interior surface of a fabric form.

Turning to the temporal boundaries of Lane Farm Cord Impressed, one is confronted by a series of seemingly incongruous circumstances. Lane Farm Cord Impressed sherds were found between layers of red ocher in the fill of mound 43 of the Sny-Magill group (Beaubien 1953a). Mound 43 contained a Hopewell-like tomb below these sherds. This group also produced a radiocarbon date of A.D. 1053 ± 300 (M-40) from mound 55, also a Hopewell tomb (Beaubien 1953b:131). Logan (1959) has reported Lane Farm pottery from the Harper's Ferry mound group with a date of A.D. 220 ± 150 (M-743) on charcoal found stratigraphically above the Lane Farm sherds (Crane and Griffin 1961:113). He has also reported single cord-decorated rims with an interior channel from the fill of a Hopewell mound (#2) at Harvey's Island (Logan 1959:321). Lane Farm sherds from the Quandahl site have been discussed relative to their obvious Havana traits, but this site also produced such exotic items as a cut human mandible and a perforated marine shell disc.

The relatively limited geographic distribution and frequency of the Lane Farm type suggests that it has shallow time depth. There are two alternatives for resolving this temporal confusion. This type may be associated with a cultural time lag of Hopewellian mortuary customs in a small region of northeastern Iowa (cf. Logan 1959:319). Thus, while the intensifying influence of Effigy Mound culture was present in Iowa by ca. A.D. 700, several bands in the northeast corner of the state continued to preserve Hopewellian burial customs and made Havana-like vessels with fabric-impressed designs. The other alternative is that the Lane Farm type represents the *initial* appearance of fabric-impressed pottery. This was Logan's original conception of the temporal position of the Lane Farm assemblage, that is, in the Intermediate period, A.D. 300-650, in terms of this discussion. This temporal position, forerunning and overlapping with Madison Fabric Impressed, makes sense in terms of the technological attributes discussed above. The fabric designs on Lane Farm vessels were applied after the vessel was shaped just as all other types of designs were on Havana Ware, while for Madison Fabric Impressed the fabric played an integral role in the formation of vessel walls and the design was merely built into the fabric.

In looking to Wisconsin for corollary support of this discussion, one finds relatively little in the form of concrete data. Effigy Mound culture assemblages have been pursued by excavations from the initial work of W. C. McKern to the recent contributions of William Hurley and Peter Storck. Hurley (1966, 1970, 1975) has presented a detailed analysis of the fabrics, specifically from the Bigelow and Sanders sites, but both locations are at the northern margin of the Madison Ware range and are far removed from Iowa. In point of fact, his types and those from Iowa are at the opposite extremes of variation in Madison Ware for most attributes— decorative motifs, lip shape, wall thickness, and paste qualities. Nor are the Sanders and Bigelow ceramics especially similar, except in the universal corded decorations, to the Madison Ware of the southern one-half of Wisconsin. For comparisons to Iowa this discussion will concentrate on the southern portion of Wisconsin, the region south of the floristic tension zone (Curtis 1959). For the future archaeologists may want to recognize two or more regional variants of Madison Ware to account for its diversity over the wide area where it is presently recognized. If such an approach were to be considered, ceramics from the Bigelow and Sanders sites would probably be identified with the northern variant.

Hurley (1970:617) has suggested that at the sites he has studied there is a gradual shift through time from S_Z^Z corded decoration to more complex cords. This statement is not supportable with numerical proof, but when comparing examples of Madison Fabric Impressed with fabrics on a later horizon type, such as Point Sauble Collared, there appears to be some merit to his statement. However, this writer disagrees with Hurley's identification of "single cord impressed" pottery in Wisconsin. There is reason to suspect that this pottery type (that is, this design application) may not exist in any significant quantities. For this study 54 latex rim casts were taken from the largest sherds in the collections at the archaeology laboratory of the University of Wisconsin, Madison, and nearly all of the sherds in these collections were examined. Casts taken from pottery recovered at the Sanders and Bigelow, Hahn and Horicon, and Aztalan sites represent (by more than five vessels each) all of the important ceramic types—Madison Fabric Impressed, Madison Cord Impressed, Hahn Cord Impressed, Madison Plain, Madison Folded Lip, Point Sauble Collared, and Aztalan Collared. The primary corded decoration on all of these rims is a fabric, excepting the occasional presence of cord-wrapped stick notches on the lip. Fabric structures and designs on these rims vary considerably according to the ceramic type and site provenience. For instance, Madison Plain is decorated up to the lip with warp-twined fabric or is fabric rolled. Examples of Aztalan Collared are impressed with this same fabric along with varying amounts of weft-patterned, weft-twined fabric. Point Sauble

80

Collared and Hahn Cord Impressed rims are usually impressed with the most complicated fabrics, many being baroque combinations or corded triangles and rows of knots. Several large sections of vessels are clearly impressed with a single fabric sheet from rim to shoulder. Thus, the technique of forming a vessel on the interior of a fabric supporting structure seems to be present. It should also be noted that some vessel walls exhibit evidence of having been smoothed prior to the application of the fabric design.

Madison Ware of southern Wisconsin is very similar to its counterparts in northeast Iowa. This writer has no reservations about including the Late Woodland period ceramics from both regions in the same Madison Ware category. In the realm of decoration, ceramics in the southwest one-quarter of Wisconsin appear to be more similar to those in northeast Iowa than to those of any other portion of the upper Mississippi River region. These areas exactly delimit the glacially undrifted zone in both states. Impressionistically, Madison Fabric Impressed from the Driftless and Drift Border Zones is predominantly decorated with horizontal corded designs. Such fabrics have simple structures, although compound structures with corded zoned design or oblique cords over horizontal ones are also present in substantial amounts.

Other ceramic types of Madison Ware are not well represented in the Driftless zone of either state. Madison Plain is usually evidenced by a few rims in most sites, but collared ceramics have only a spotty distribution. The few specimens of Aztalan Collared found in this region (for example, Mouse Hollow rock shelter, Logan 1959; Mayland Cave, Storck 1972) appear to be trade items or deposits left by outside visitors to the area. There are very few examples of vessels which resemble Point Sauble Collared or Hahn Cord Impressed. One Hadfields specimen, Vessel 20, has a small section of paste folded over on the exterior of the uppermost rim to produce a collar. The collar is entirely covered by fabric impressions and has a single row of "knot" and punctate impressions centered on it. The total effect of this rim decoration is strikingly similar to Hahn Cord Impressed rims (Keslin 1958) from south-central Wisconsin. This type of rim design has no similar counterparts in Iowa, since virtually all of the collared and castellated material from eastern Iowa can be effectively related to the Maples Mills developments in Illinois.

The temporal position of Madison Fabric Impressed is another subject which has received intense scrutiny in Wisconsin. Before reviewing the radiocarbon dates germane to this subject, it should be acknowledged that this discussion presumes that effigy mounds and Madison Fabric Impressed ceramics exist as two different subjects for study. It is fairly obvious that the geographic distributions of these two elements in the upper Midwest are not entirely sympatric. Therefore, it seems reasonable to suggest that effigy mounds and Madison Fabric Impressed pottery may not have been entirely contemporaneous during the full time spans of their use.

Nearly all of the significant radiocarbon dates which apply to the problem of Effigy Mound culture of Wisconsin are listed by Hurley (1975:379-84). There are important errors affecting the early dates in this table, but the majority of dates fall between ca. A.D. 700 and 1200. Nearly all of these dates represent features in mounds and villages, and Madison Ware ceramics are difficult to associate with the dated context in many cases. Two instances where dates are definitely associated with Late Woodland pottery are: (1) an otter effigy, mound 18, of the Kolterman mound group that produced a cremation with two triangular projectile points, a Madison Cord Impressed vessel, and a date of A.D. 770±250 (M-398; Wittry 1956:133-34; Wittry and Bruder 1955); and (2) a date of A.D. 720±150 (I-678; Mason 1966:27-28) on carbon scraped from the walls of a Heins Creek Cord Decorated vessel. Madison Fabric Impressed pottery is also directly associated with five dates from Hurley's (1970) Bigelow (47PT26) and Sanders I (47WP26) sites in Portage and Waupaca Counties respectively. They form a surprisingly tight cluster of dates for the extensive, long-term occupations which occurred at these sites: A.D. 810±50 (Wis-200), A.D. 930±55 (Wis-203), A.D. 960±55 (Wis-219), A.D. 990±60 (Wis-226) and A.D. 1010±60 (Wis-207) (Bender et al. 1968:162-63). The remaining dates from these sites are roughly comparable but demonstrate the wide time span of occupations, for example, A.D. 620±60 (Wis-217) and A.D. 670±55 (Wis-197) (Bender et al. 1968). All of the dates outlined here seem to indicate that Madison Fabric Impressed appeared during the latter half of the seventh century. An early date (A.D. 500±150, M-871) on the Beloit College mound group (Bastian 1962) must be discounted due to its very poor context.

The temporal placement of Madison Fabric Impressed at the Hadfields site is consistent with the earliest appearance of this type in Wisconsin, as outlined above. Madison Fabric Impressed vessels at 13JN3 were deposited by A.D. 800, and undoubtedly belong within the span of time A.D. 600-800. Woodland peoples of northeast Iowa and southern Wisconsin appear to have developed this ceramic type along parallel lines at the same period in time. Design treatments in the Driftless zones of both states show the greatest degree of similarity, while there are more disparities between motifs from the drifted regions of both states.

Turning now to the regions west, south, and east of 13JN3, we must again deal with areas which are known by very scanty archaeological data. There are few radiocarbon dates available to anchor the Late Woodland assemblages of east-central Iowa in a satisfactory chronology. Temporal relationships for this area have been assumed for assemblages found in association with certain diagnostic artifacts, these diagnostic items having received their temporal identities from dated contexts in Illinois and Wisconsin.

Cord-decorated ceramics in east-central Iowa fall into two type categories: Madison Fabric Impressed and Minotts Cord Impressed. This writer has not studied all of the rims classified by Logan, but the great majority of cord decorations on both types are fabrics. It would be safe to conclude that virtually all of them are fabrics.

Minotts Cord Impressed (Logan 1959:185-88) has many of the same attributes as Madison Fabric Impressed. The Minotts type differs from the Madison type in subtle ways which could be more carefully investigated through a statistical attribute analysis at some future time. Logan's descriptions name only two characters which act to distinguish this type: (1) rims are straight or slightly flaring, can be castellated or squared, and have sharp junctures with the expanding shoulder; (2) cords of the rim decorations tend not to be paired. Other distinctive characters may include a noticeable flaring of the upper rim, lip thickening on some vessels, and generally dull paste colors of gray, black, tans, and buffs.

A few sites in the east-central region of Iowa have been excavated since the work of Logan and, generally, these have duplicated his original inferences. Caldwell's (1961) testing at the Coralville Reservoir a few miles north of Iowa City produced one site, Woodpecker Cave (13JH202), with a substantial sample of cord-decorated rims. Of 31 rims at this site, 28 were decorated with horizontal cords only, while three had opposed triangles. One rim in the latter group had raised "corners." Interesting dentate stamps occurred on the interior rims of two specimens (Caldwell 1961:115-16). At the Sandy Beach site (13JH43) in the same reservoir the assemblage of cord-decorated pottery had predominantly opposed triangle motifs (Anderson 1971a). Anderson did not establish the precise typological identity of this material as the rim sections were relatively small. Madison or Minotts Cord Impressed are undoubtedly represented by several rims, and at least two specimens have a small amount of dentate stamping on the shoulder (Anderson 1971a). Several other body sherds have rocker stamping over cord roughening. This writer's observations of 13 cord-decorated rims in this collection showed that at least eight were fabric marked. Fabric-impressed rims with horizontal cord designs have also been recovered at the Rock Run shelter (13CD10; Alex 1968) on the Cedar River east of Iowa City and at the Walters site (13JH42; Anderson 1971b) at the Coralville Reservoir. The latter site also contained a cord-decorated vessel with a squared orifice. In all four sites there seems to be a low incidence of pairing among the spaced cords composing the major rim design (cf. Logan 1959:183, 187, for this and the following observation). This is in contrast to the higher proportion of paired weft elements in the Madison Fabric Impressed at Hadfields (where pairing is found in 14 of 24 vessels) and for this type throughout the Driftless Zone in Iowa and Wisconsin.

The four sites around Iowa City probably belong to the Minotts Focus, originally conceived by Logan (1959) as being distributed in Linn and Jackson Counties. The four sites are in Johnson and Cedar Counties immediately to the south. Two more sites, the Henry Schnoor (13JK20) and Robert Battey (13JK21) rock shelters in western Jackson County, have also been recently investigated by Manfred Jaehnig (1975). All of the cord-decorated ceramics at these sites are fabric impressed. Nearly one-half of these are compound structured with oblique cords or opposed triangular motifs, and there is a low incidence (ca. 20%) of paired decorative designs composed of opposed triangles, superimposed oblique and horizontal cords, or zones of perpendicular cords. These same vessels also tend to have this same percentage of tooled or smoothed surfaces superimposed by the fabric impression. There is reason to predict that in this area of the state fabrics were used to support newly formed walls on only one-half of the vessels. These three characters—corded geometric zones of design, low incidence of paired cords, and cord-decorated surfaces with prior surface smoothing—may also be especially characteristic of the Maples Mills pottery in Illinois.

Logan placed the earliest developments of Minotts Focus at ca. A.D. 500, but he believed that Minotts Cord Impressed belonged exclusively to the Late Woodland period, or post-A.D. 700. Three sites have been radiocarbon dated in the last six years to provide some support for his interpretations. Nine dates at the Rock Run site (Bender et al. 1969, 1970a, 1970b) generally confirm the time depth involved in the sequence from Archaic cultures to Minotts Focus. Two dates from the upper levels of the Henry Schnoor rock shelter (13JK20) appear to date the Minotts component there: A.D. 970±60 (Wis-345) and A.D. 810±60 (Wis-395) (Bender et al. 1970a). Most of the pottery in this site is Late Woodland, Madison Fabric Impressed and Minotts Cord Impressed. A bundle burial at this site was also dated A.D. 820±60 (Wis-397; Bender et al. 1971), and the Middle Woodland component had two dates: A.D. 170±60 (Wis-394) and A.D. 120±55 (Wis-396) (Bender et al. 1970a and 1970b respectively). The Robert Battey shelter contained a greater variety of ceramics; among them are probably Madison Fabric Impressed and Minotts Cord Impressed, and Linn Ware types such as Spring Hollow Cord Marked and Levsen Punctate. One date, A.D. 590±50 (Wis-404; Bender et al. 1970b:641), is associated with artifacts of "early Late Woodland and Late Woodland types," according to the collector. Two other dates, A.D. 550±55 (Wis-400) and A.D. 480±55 (Wis-399; Bender et al. 1970b), are from levels stratigraphically below the first date given here, and could conceivably date the Linn Ware at the site, although the author associates Wis-400 "in the same excavation unit" with Madison Cord Impressed

84

pottery and one triangular projectile point (Jaehnig 1975:256). A fourth date, A.D. 980±60 (Wis-406; Bender et al. 1971:476), from a midden outside the shelter is supposed to date "Archaic or early Middle Woodland" material, according to the excavator. This latter date points to a common problem encountered in rock shelter midden, that of mixed deposits. For just this reason the present writer rejects Jaehnig's placement of Madison Cord Impressed at A.D. 450 (1975:393) and the assumed association of this pottery type with Levsen Stamped (1975:220, 419-20).

The Hadfields site has two ceramic ware groups which may potentially have differing dates, but again, mixing has created problems for interpreting the radiocarbon assays. Some of the descriptions of contexts published with the six dates (Bender et al. 1973:615) are slightly amended here. These changes have resulted from a careful reading and analysis of the field notes. Two dates, A.D. 295±65 (Wis-589) and A.D. 420±55 (Wis-594), were taken from carbon in the lower of two major strata in the midden. Portions of this stratum have been incorporated into the upper one. The majority of Linn Ware Variant I ceramics (one Spring Hollow Cord Marked vessel and dentate-stamped sherds) were concentrated in this stratum. Two dates, A.D. 555±55 (Wis-599) and A.D. 660±55 (Wis-588), came from features in the upper stratum. The Madison and Linn Ware vessels were deposited in this stratum, although no single vessel of either group can be specifically associated with these dates. A single date of A.D. 800±55 (Wis-597) was taken from one of the lowest levels in the midden, but it dates carbon from the bottom layer of a late period pit which intruded into the lower stratum. The sixth date, A.D. 730±60 (Wis-596), came from a pit (Feature 67) which had been superimposed along one edge by a fired area (Feature 65) which produced Wis-599. The date from Feature 67 is the least dependable assay of these six since one edge of the feature was disturbed by a rodent-run along the cave wall.

The Madison Fabric Impressed vessels at 13JN3 cannot be precisely associated with any of the radiocarbon dates. However, there are positive associations between ceramic types, stratigraphy, and the carbon dates to provide estimates of temporal positioning. The Spring Hollow Plain vessels and Madison Ware vessels were evidently deposited during different occupations of the site. Their areal concentrations in the midden differ markedly, although their stratigraphic occurrence is plainly the same. Spring Hollow Plain Vessel 13 was found primarily in Feature 69, a pit which probably opened in the lower portion of the upper stratum. Another vessel of the same type (number 11) was scattered in features in the general midden at exactly the same vertical level of the upper stratum as Madison Ware sherds.

The dates on this upper stratum, A.D. 555-800, cover enough range in time to allow for both Madison and Linn Ware types to be deposited during the periods when each was popular. Both, however, are stratigraphically very closely associated in the Hadfields midden, if not deposited contemporaneously in some cases. Logan (1959:271) has indicated that Madison Fabric Impressed and Linn Ware types may be contemporary in some eastern Iowa sites. Although it is possible to detect slight overlap in their time ranges at 13JN3, it seems more likely that one of two situations existed in east-central Iowa during the seventh century A.D.: (1) that Linn and Madison Wares were each being manufactured exclusively by one of the two groups of people for a short period of time, and that Linn Ware was fading out of use while Madison Ware was coming into popularity; or (2) that Linn Ware was abruptly dropped from usage as Madison came into vogue. The latter possibility seems less likely, since the wares are distinctly different in both technological and decorative attributes. The first alternative is more compatible with the inference that the Woodland peoples of this region had a family-band type of organization. Assuming this kind of social organization, a natural shelter like 13JN3 could have been visited in successive years (or seasons or months) by two bands bearing distinctly different cultural assemblages.

In Illinois Lake Woodland manifestations are largely undocumented. The use of cord-impressed ceramics to identify Woodland "cultures" of this period has reached almost cliché proportions in the literature. Assemblages seemingly related to material in Wisconsin and Iowa have remained unanalysed. Suffice to say, Late Woodland material seems to be chronologically later than Weaver and probably contemporary with early Mississippian culture developments (Maxwell 1947:33-34, 1951:249; Fowler 1952:138, 1955; McGregor 1957). The primary Late Woodland ceramic type in central Illinois is Maples Mills Cord design (type 5; Cole and Deuel 1937:48), first described from the Gooden Mound of the Maples Mills Focus. Traits which are apparently characteristic of this type include frequent squaring of the orifice and raised corners or nodes on the lip, lip notching, high vertical rims and expanding shoulders, and cord-impressed decorations of opposed triangles and/or unpaired horizontal rows of cords (Cole and Deuel 1937; Schoenbeck 1946:36-37; Fowler 1955:217).

This writer has had an opportunity to peruse a small sample collection of Maples Mills rims obtained from test excavations at the Winter's Knoll site (11MD20) in the LaMoine River drainage. Approximately ten vessels were represented in this group. Most of the rims were straight or slightly flaring, and the shoulders were sharply expanding. The corded rim decorations usually were divided into zones of oblique, horizontal, and/or vertical motifs, often with triangular patterns of cord-filled and plain zones lying between bands of horizontal or vertical cords. The decorative cords were not paired. One rim had a row of large punctates encircling the base of the rim below the cord design. A few of the cord-decorated rims were impressed deeply enough to evidence fabric structures, but the majority showed only decorative cord impressions over previously smoothed surfaces. A single specimen with paste and rim form like the other rims was decorated with a fabric which was identical in design and structure to many of the Madison Fabric Impressed vessels in Iowa and Wisconsin. This fabric consisted of a band of short, oblique cords applied over the lip and on both faces of the upper rim, five pairs of spaced, horizontal cords around the neck, and faintly impressed cord roughening on the body.

There are other ceramic types which have been described for the Late Woodland cultures of the northern two-thirds of Illinois. Ceramics with rim collars (for example, Starved Rock Collared; Hall n.d.) and/or corded decorations are found throughout the upper reaches of the Illinois River drainage (cf. Fenner 1961, 1963). These northern Illinois examples may have important relationships with the Wisconsin cord-impressed types. Castellated and corded-panel decorated rims similar to Maples Mills pottery were also excavated by Bennett (1945:83, Plate 8) in Jo Daviess County. In this same report Bennett describes a few assorted Lake Michigan ware sherds (possibly Madison Cord Impressed and Aztalan Collared; 1945:131-50, Plates 8, 22, 30) from the Mills mound group and village and from the John Chapman village sites.

Turning now to the central and western portions of Iowa, ceramics with probable relationships to the Minotts types have been recovered in a few very scattered locations. The Keyes collection at Iowa City contains several rim sherds from the Carr site (accession no. ML1-710), an apparent village site in Marshall County near the center of the state. Rims in this collection are predominantly squared and castellated. Tool or cord "notches" appear on the interior and exterior edges of the lips. The necks are relatively high on these vessels, and rims are recurved with everted lips and relatively sharp shoulder junctures. Corded decorations consist of oblique cord bars over horizontal, unpaired spaced cords (two cases) or geometric patterns of corded zones (three cases). Two designs in the latter group are impressed fabrics having compound structures. The remaining three designs seem to be applied as single cords or by some form of rolling technique. All five vessels have cord-roughened bodies, but only one specimen shows evidence of the body warp running into the rim fabric. Impressionistically, these ceramics are very similar in form and design to Minotts Cord Impressed.

A small number of cord-decorated vessels were found in mound 1 at the Gypsum Quarry site (13BW1), a group of mounds on the Des Moines River southeast of Fort Dodge, Iowa. The rim/shoulder juncture on these rims is very sharp and the lips are everted. Three rims have zoned decoration of unpaired, spaced cords on the rim and lip. Two specimens have rows of horizontal cords, and one of these has a band of horizontal zigzag cords as the central motif. A third example has single cord impressions over the lip and rows of dentate stamps on the rim and shoulder. This sample is too small for developing proper inferences, but the design motifs and rim profiles are tantalizingly similar to the Minotts Focus assemblage of Linn and Johnson Counties.

Another group of sherds in the Keyes collection also contains a significant number of cord-decorated rims. A total of 11 rims from the area around Glenwood, Iowa was studied by this author using rubber latex casts (accession nos. Ms199 and Ms205). All 11 rims are single cord impressed, and only three specimens are decorated with compound cords, that is, cords which have more than two elements and are double-plied. Only one example has lip decoration (cords) and the rim interior is plain in all cases. The main body of cord design is executed in horizontal rows of unpaired, spaced cords with oblique cord bars often imposed over this corded band. Nine of the 11 sherds were large enough to contain the entire rim design, and in all cases the horizontal corded element was bordered on the bottom by corded "hanging" pendants. Rims are recurved, and the shoulder/ neck juncture is round and gradual. This ceramic type has been tentatively associated with Missouri Bluff Late Woodland (Keyes 1949). There are probably long-range relationships between this type and Minotts, but similarities seem to be restricted to a few basic design motifs and the use of zoned cord decorations.

One of the most interesting assemblages of cord-decorated ceramics comes from the Loseke Creek sites (25PT9, 25PT12) in Platte County in eastern Nebraska. Kivett (1952:52-53, 98-100) has provided descriptions of the 171 rims recovered from both sites. Cord-impressed decorations are found on 63% of the rim sherds from 25PT9 and 73% of the rim sherds from 25PT12. A large portion of these rims are decorated with three to nine rows of horizontal, unpaired cords, and of these rims one-quarter and one-half respectively are also decorated with diagonal single cords or tool impressions on the outer lip. A small number (6% and 4% respectively) also have "hanging pendants" immediately below the horizontal cord band, and these pendants may be filled with horizontal cord impressions. One last vessel in this group has alternating zigzag pairs of cords superimposed over the horizontal cord band to form a diamond pattern almost identical to that on Vessel 21 at 13JN3. Most of these vessels have vertical cord roughening on the shoulders and rims up to the lip, while the bodies are cord roughened in random directions. The author notes that on the most elaborately decorated examples this cord roughening is smoothed over under the rim decoration. Kivett has named this cord-decorated type Feye Cord Impressed (1952:54-55). The undecorated, cord-roughened variety is Feye Cord Roughened. He describes the distribution of the former type as being primarily centered in northeastern Nebraska but ranging as far as the south-central part of the state and into southern South Dakota (for example, Hurt 1952).

Kivett points out that the Loseke Creek pottery is superficially similar to that from the Missouri Bluffs (Missouri Bluffs Cord Impressed; Keyes 1949:97) in the Keyes collection (1952:68-69), but he carefully recognizes that ceramics are but a small portion of a cultural assemblage. There are important similarities between the Loseke and the temporally preceding Valley Cord Roughened pottery (Kivett 1952). Thus, for this region there may be evidence for local potters superimposing a new idea of corded designs over an older pattern of cord-roughened pottery. The possibility exists that this new idea of corded designs may have diffused from the region of eastern Iowa after ca. A.D. 700. The Feye Cord Impressed material has been referred to here as single cord impressed; however, the oportunity for this writer to analyse these rims for fabrics has not been available. After scanning the fine plates of rims in Kivett's report, this writer feels the possibility that these are fabric impressed cannot be ignored.

Prehistoric Fabrics

It is self-evident that the complex fabrics found on Late Woodland vessels in the upper Mississippi River region are the products of a long-established fiber technology. That these fabrics are indelibly preserved on ceramic vessels of this time period is fortunate for the prehistorian, for the inevitable decomposition of biodegradable fibers and the paucity of the ethnographic record has left little of this technology for our scrutiny. In considering the preceding complex analyses, a few statements may be made to describe the nature of this fabric production. The ideas presented in the next paragraphs are a direct outgrowth of conversations with Dr. Kenneth Heintz, fabric technologist in the School of Home Economics, University of Wisconsin at Stout. His advice on the production of fabrics is incorporated here almost verbatim.

In general, the Madison Ware fabrics are structurally uniform. This observation does not extend to the designs incorporated in the fabrics, since those from the northern half of Wisconsin are extremely variable in design motifs. Rather, a striking homogeneity is evidenced in the few, unvarying types of twining stitches by which the warp and weft are interconnected. For the most part, fabric design elements in Madison Ware are developed by spacing, floating, or switching cords from face to fabric face. This structural simplicity seems to contrast with examples of fabrics from ethnographic sources in the upper Midwest. Fabric designs of this later time horizon were developed in color by changing the fabric stitch to bring the desired colored element forward and to obscure others.

The Madison Ware fabrics also show a striking uniformity of cord twist; a cord of any ply was usually made by alternating the twist direction of each ply. For example, two Z-spun elements would be twisted into an S-twisted cord, and two S-twisted cords would be twisted into a two-ply, Z-twisted cord. The process of alternating the direction of cord plies results in a soft cord, or for example, one in which the Z-twist of a single-ply cord tends to partially unravel the S-spinning of its component elements. (The alternative to soft cord, hard cord, gives a Z-twisted cord which tends to tighten its Z-spun component elements.) The people producing Madison Ware fabrics evidently preferred soft cord for its greater thickness.

The problem of how these fabrics were produced remains a matter of speculation. Conversation with Ken Heintz has generated several potential solutions. It is logical to suggest that these fabrics were made from the warp-twined to the weft-faced portions, or, relative to the vessel, from the shoulder to the lip. This is because in handmade fabrics it is easier to make the transition from loose-weave fabric (warp-twined) to tighter weaves (weft-faced) than to do the reverse. Additionally, the fabric was probably oriented with the weft-faced fabric down and was twined from top to bottom so that the warp elements were allowed to hang freely. In fact, this was the method most frequently employed for twining fabrics (for example, Skinner 1921). As an additional embellishment to this reconstruction, Ken Heintz has suggested that fabrics were twined on a form, for instance, an existing vessel. Such a form would preserve the uniformly cylindrical shape of the developing fabric while concurrently giving form to a constricted neck and expanded shoulder. These fabrics would have been quite rigid and nonelastic because of the nature of the fibrous raw material, and thus the form given them in production would have been permanent.

The fact that Madison Ware fabric designs are highly variable to the point of being individualistic seems to indicate that fabric production was a free-form art among Woodland peoples of this period. In point of fact, of hundreds of vessels from dozens of sites, no two vessels are impressed with the same fabric sample. Thus, it would appear that decorative fabrics were produced as much or more for aesthetic reasons than simply as supporting structures for soft clay vessels. It should be reiterated that these fabrics are decorated with corded structures twined in relief, to be impressed each to its own vessel. It is also noteworthy that the fabric was quite rigid and probably could not be pulled off of a dried vessel prior to firing (Fig. 34). Therefore, the making of each ceramic vessel would have required the production of a fabric collar for that vessel. It is significant that these fabrics were not reused, or alternatively, were not made to be reuseable, since it is possible to produce elastic, recyclable fabrics.

This system of regularized, individualistic fabric production has important implications for the archaeologist's reconstruction of past life styles and social systems. While it is not the purpose of this section to reach any conclusions on these matters, we can note a number of interesting observations. First, it is the impression of this author that Madison Ware from eastern and north-central Wisconsin has a much greater variation of design motifs than the contemporary Madison Ware from northeast Iowa. It would be interesting if this same variability was positively correlated with variability of effigy mound types, which seem to show the same degrees of stylistic variation for the two regions. Secondly, these fabrics may be a reservoir of information documenting aspects of the Woodland social system. Not only do we have design motifs as sources of stylistic variability, but one can also define structural variations—the selection of specific elements to produce a structure, the use of stitch types, the ply of cords—which may be socially or regionally specific in their use. Finally, the utilization of fabric decoration on Late Woodland period pottery across the Midwest is interesting for its technological and aesthetic variation. We may investigate the similarities and differences between the fabric-decorated pottery within the Effigy Mound sphere and areas such as central Illinois and the glacially drifted regions of Iowa. The cord-decorated ceramics of western Iowa and adjacent portions of Nebraska and South Dakota are of particular interest in that they may be related to this fabric impressing tradition of the Midwest.

Miscellaneous Ceramics

Nearly every ceramic site produces a small number of vessels exhibiting features which place them outside of the ware groups. Such vessels are often miniatures. They may have been produced by an inexperienced hand just developing the skills of pottery making. Alternatively, such vessels could have been made very rapidly to fulfill some specific function without regard for aesthetic or normal cultural styles. They may also be the products of a child's imagination copying parental domestic activities. These low-frequency attributes are often termed *aberrant* when compared to the most common attributes of a ware group.

Vessel 9 is a small jar with a wall profile like that of Vessel 17, a Madison Fabric Impressed vessel (Figs. 35-36; cf. Fig 25). Vessel 9 has a plain exterior surface and is relatively crudely formed, although its walls are extremely thin. Its paste is identical to that of Vessel 17. Vessels 9 and 17 were undoubtedly constructed at the same time from a single batch of raw material, the former possibly being produced from the left-over paste of the latter.

Vessels 6a and 6b are crudely formed miniature jars made from largely untempered pastes. Both are represented by tiny rim fragments and poorly preserved body sherds. Vessel 6b is cord roughened up to the lip on the exterior surface and has fingernail impressions decorating the upper rim. Both characters are reminiscent of Spring Hollow Cord Marked traits.

The final vessel, number 8, has several extraordinary characteristics. This is a small jar with an insloping rim, expanding shoulder, and cord-roughened exterior surface. The clay component of the paste has an exceptionally high concentration of organic debris—a high humic content and numerous partially decomposed plant parts. Much of this organic

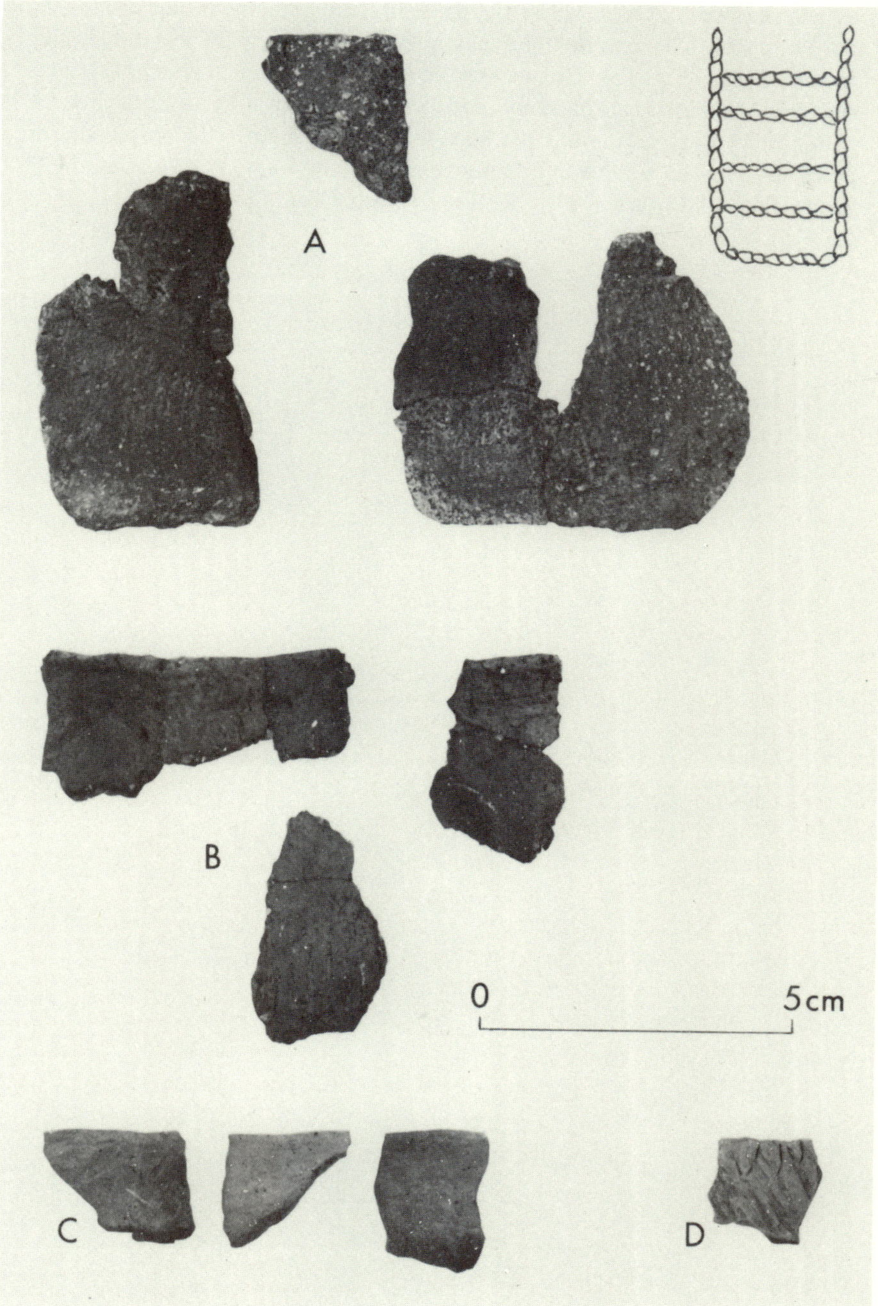

Fig. 35. Miscellaneous vessels. A, Vessel 8; B, Vessel 9; C, Vessel 6a; D, Vessel 6b.

deposit has been burned out of the paste in firing, leaving a black and gray porous paste. The exterior rim has been decorated with one ladder-like corded design (Fig. 35). This design is composed of three or four contiguous rectangular shapes, outlined by cords intertwined in a net-like fashion. A complete reconstruction has not been feasible, as the two decorated sherds presently reside in two different collections—that from the 1972 excavation, and the Keyes collection in Iowa City.

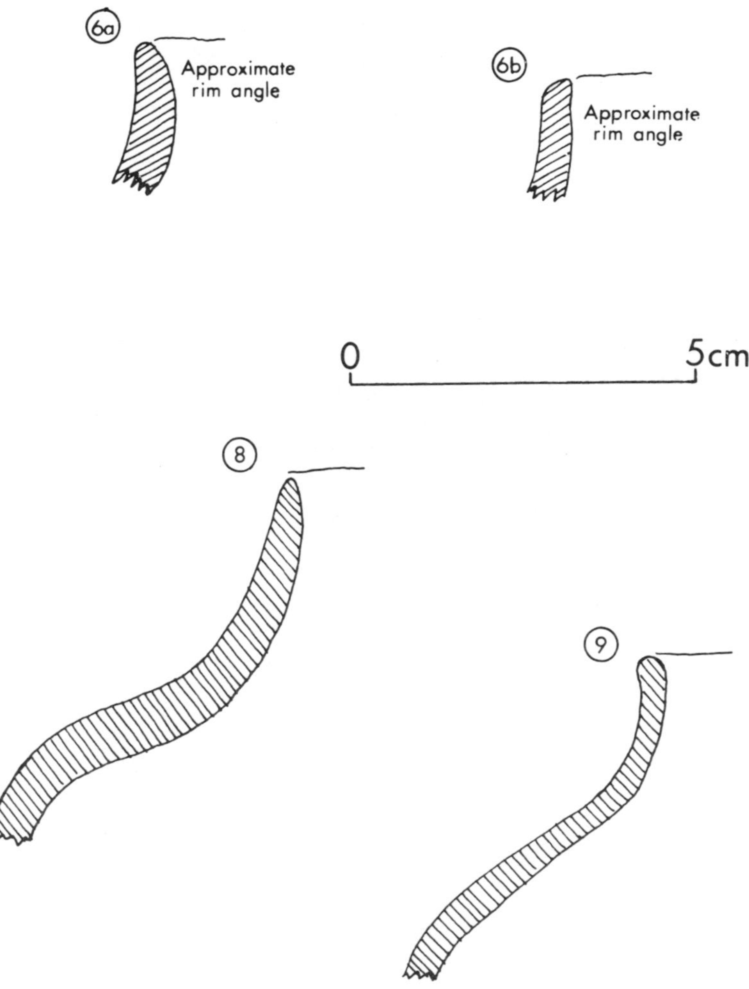

Fig. 36. Miscellaneous vessel rim profiles.

Pottery Discussion

The individualized aspects and areal distributions of pottery types and wares have been dealt with up to this point. Now it is possible to present a concise statement relating these various types through time and space, and to account for the cultural processes which may be responsible for their appearance and change. This discussion is intended to fashion a framework of fact, inference, and occasional speculation to facilitate future work in eastern Iowa.

The three ware groups have features which are peculiar to each group. Havana Ware is typified by a very coarse paste which may be either sandy and massive, or blocky due to over-tempering with crushed rock. Havana vessels have thick walls and conoidal forms with a slight constriction at the neck. In contrast, Linn Ware averages thinner walls and compact, sparse- to moderately-tempered paste. The surfaces of Linn vessels are noticeably denser, a character which reflects not only the finer paste of this ware group but also a different approach to finishing the surface. Surfaces, including those of cord-roughened varieties, usually do not have a gritty feel but instead are harder and smoother. All of the Madison Ware types have cord-roughened exterior surfaces, and nearly all of the vessels are decorated by some form of corded design. The cord roughening and corded designs characteristically occur as fabric structures. Single cord-impressed designs or cord-wrapped paddle roughening are infrequent exceptions to the use of fabrics. Madison Ware normally has very thin walls and a compact paste with variable amounts of temper inclusions.

Taking the three wares in their natural chronological order, there are two major technological innovations which characterize the inception of the latter two and thus make it possible to distinguish between the three. The first appears as the fine dense paste of Linn Ware. This innovation was closely associated with the production of Weaver Ware in Illinois. Linn Ware represents a truly sweeping technological shift, for not only does its paste differ from that of Havana, but vessel walls are thinner, shoulders and rims are more pronounced, and there are modifications in decorative styles. The transition from Havana to Linn Wares probably was relatively rapid and uniform across the east-central portions of the state. Sites on the Wapsipinicon, Cedar, Iowa, and portions of the Maquoketa Rivers generally contained large numbers of Linn Ware sherds—as many or more than other wares at each site. The vast majority of Linn Ware in these sites, ones roughly outside of the Driftless Zone, is either Spring Hollow Plain or Cord Marked, the former being in the majority. Within the Driftless Zone of Iowa the distinction between some types of Linn and Havana Wares is less intense due to the presence of heavily decorated types such as Levsen Stamped and Punctated. It is not clear whether this situation in the Driftless Zone represents a true, long-term overlap between Linn and

Havana Ware styles during the Intermediate period, or a partial breakdown in the sensitivity of the established ceramic typology.

The second major ceramic innovation to appear in eastern Iowa was the rapid development of cord decoration, the hallmark of the Late Woodland period. The seemingly abrupt appearance of cord decorations in the upper Mississippi River region apparently results from the nonexistence of this decorative form in the Illinois Havana and Weaver Wares and in their Iowa counterparts. Fabrics seem to have substantial time depth in North America, having been produced during the Middle Woodland period (Griffin et al. 1970: Plate 143a). However, they appear only sporadically as impressions on vessels beginning in the Early Woodland. Madison Ware represents a truly prolific record of the complex fabrics produced by prehistoric native Americans. This ware is but one of several cord-decorated Late Woodland wares in eastern North America.

The cord-decorated types in the Madison Ware group are remarkably uniform as they are distributed over a very large area of four states. This is due in part to the mechanical limitations of the fabric making process (twining, that is) and also in part to the inevitable influence of cultural selection, the norms of artistic design. The latter process may also be responsible for the regional variations of Madison Ware as they are described in this report. It has been stated that the east-central portion of Iowa, the same area which shows the most intense Weaver influence, is the center for Minotts Cord Impressed. The Minotts pottery has close resemblances to Maples Mills Cord Impressed from central Illinois and is undoubtedly contemporary with it. Minotts Cord Impressed is the structural/functional equivalent of Madison Fabric Impressed, and both types are found in east-central Iowa sites and are difficult to separate typologically. Minotts Cord Impressed seems to have been first manufactured 100 or more years later than Madison Fabric Impressed. However, at its inception Minotts Cord Impressed is not a regional variant of Madison Ware, but instead seems to develop independently in the broad regional shift toward cord-decorated ceramics.

It is difficult to disregard the possibility that Lane Farm Cord Impressed, which was being made by ca. A.D. 500, was the first of a wide range of cord-decorated pottery types, which were popular after ca. A.D. 650. However, this Lane Farm type should be viewed at present as a harbinger of Madison Fabric Impressed, not as the genetic precursor of all fabric-decorated ceramics. There are several ways to interpret the temporal context of Lane Farm Cord Impressed and these have been discussed previously in this report. The production of Lane Farm ceramics appears to overlap the initial development of Madison Fabric Impressed in northeast Iowa. During the short period of time when these types overlapped, they were apparently produced by different groups of people. This insight stems from the fact that Lane Farm paste and vessel form are like that of Linn Ware but substantially different from Madison Ware.

Lane Farm may realistically be identified as the combination of Linn Ware and fabric-impressed decoration—a typologically transitional pottery type.

The development of fabric decoration by the beginning of the Late Woodland period also effected a modest technological change. The employment of fabrics as the supportive structures for wet, newly formed vessels has been discussed here. The extreme thinness of many vessel walls and the continuous fabric impression on rims and shoulders of most vessels are characteristic of this peculiar technology in Madison Ware. This method of producing vessels, at least the evidence for it, appears to have a high incidence of occurrence (more than one-half) in sites within the Iowa Driftless Zone but seems to fade proportionately beyond this region in Iowa.

On a broader perspective there are at least two factors which show continuity among the three Iowa ware groups. One is the persistent use of zoned decorations. The other is the constant appearance of vessels with aberrant characteristics.

The continuity of zoned decorative motifs is strikingly evident when one looks at the ceramic sequence from Naples Stamped and Spring Hollow Incised, to Levsen Punctated and Stamped, Lane Farm Cord Impressed and Stamped, and finally Madison Fabric Impressed and Minotts Cord Impressed. Logan's (1959) Figs. 1-3, 5, 7, and 9-10 assist in making these comparisons. Naples Stamped has been given straight dentate and ovoid stamps in horizontal and vertical rows. There are usually several zones of these designs. The most common consists of a horizontal row of vertical or oblique dentate stamps immediately below the lip, and below that a horizontal row of bosses or punctates, and finally below that various types of horizontal rows or vertical columns of stamps. Spring Hollow Incised designs are less ordered than Naples designs. There is a lower frequency of bosses or punctates and a much lower frequency of upper rim and lip decoration. Spring Hollow Incised designs usually consist of incised lines in geometric patterns or fields of fingernail or tool punctates, and combinations of both. Several of these geometric patterns also appear on Lane Farm and Madison Fabric Impressed pottery: groups of parallel horizontal lines superimposed by oblique lines (Logan 1959: Fig. 1c), groups of parallel horizontal lines bordered by a row of short oblique strokes (Figs. 1b, i), and zoned oblique lines (Figs. 1a, d, e, g,). Work in the future may demonstrate that Spring Hollow Incised has close relationships with Black Sand Incised, Morton Incised, and Fettie Incised (Griffin 1952b:98-105). Pottery which is similar to these Illinois types in form and design has been found in Iowa but has not been discussed to the degree that later types have been.

Levsen decorations are stamped, punctated, or tooled in many of the same designs that appear on Spring Hollow Incised and Naples Stamped. Decorations on the Levsen types are carefully structured, as they are on

Naples Stamped. The opposed triangle motif appears (Logan 1959: Figs. 3j, 5e), and there is a heavy emphasis on the horizontal movement of designs. This emphasis on the horizontal is carried over into Lane Farm Cord Impressed as well. Lane Farm decorations are nearly always structured in horizontal cords or narrow horizontal bands of short cord impressions. Many Lane Farm vessels have designs of cord-filled geometric zones—opposed triangles or groups of oblique cords—but these motifs are either bordered or adjoined by horizontal cords. Rocker stamping on the bodies of Lane Farm vessels is not being considered here with the rim decoration, since such stamping usually covers the entire surface and seems to be a decorative analogue of cord roughening.

In Madison Fabric Impressed we find the ultimate in motif variation. Some Madison Ware designs are nearly identical to Lane Farm decorations, and the practice of placing the corded design above the shoulder is present on both types. However, Madison Ware designs are far more varied with rows of knots, punctates, cord-filled quadrilateral shapes, opposed triangles and parallelograms, and cord-described zones of cord roughening. The extensive variation of Madison Ware designs is primarily due to the wide geographic range over which it is found and the potential for individual invention within that large region.

The second general trait of Iowa Woodland pottery, the frequent appearance of typologically aberrant vessels, is a problem in nearly every site collection. Examples of this have been cited here (for example, Linn Ware Variant II), and many others, such as cord-impressed decorations on a crudely made vessel with Havana paste (for example, 13CD10, accession no. 172-619), are to be found in the state's collections. There are three potential explanations for the presence of this pottery. The first is that ceramic typologies have become outmoded and nondiscriminant as more site collections add to our knowledge. This seems unlikely, as the vast majority of sherds from the most recent excavations fit securely into the type categories. A second alternative is that there was a lag in turnover of ceramic methodologies as new ideas about decoration and technology became quickly popularized, but the older methods remained in use. This is typical of human behavior—mixing the old and the new—and has a corollary in the third explanation. This third notion is that some pockets of family-bands did not participate closely in the general social interactions which tended to stimulate regularized patterns in ceramic design. Instead, these scattered groups might have retained established modes of ceramic design long after newer kinds came into popularity with the majority population. At present we cannot absolutely reject any of the above three choices, but the second of the three makes most sense in terms of the archaeological data now in hand. There are relatively small numbers of these aberrant vessels—apparently not enough to infer the existence of a small population independent of the cultural mainstream in eastern Iowa.

Fig. 37. *The potential influence of ceramic traditions in Late Woodland Iowa.*

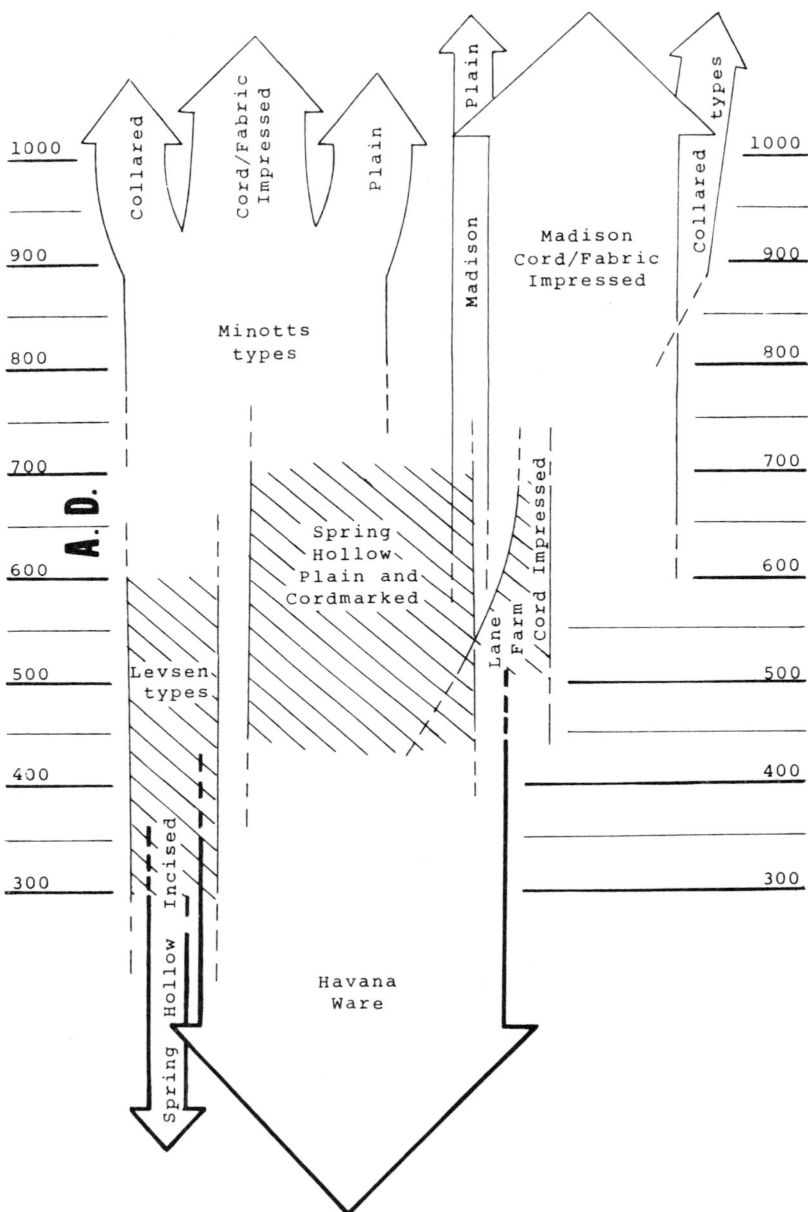

Fig. 38. Implied chronological and generic relationships in eastern Iowa ceramics.

The social forces which brought about both the standardization of Iowa Woodland ceramics and the aberrant or transitional examples discussed here are dealt with in the comprehensive summary section of this study. Much of what has been said in this section on ceramics is summarized in Figs. 37 and 38. Fig. 37 shows distributions of central Iowa variants of Madison Ware and the northeast Iowa/Wisconsin variants of Madison Ware in very preliminary terms. The most interesting aspect of this map is the attitude of the major Iowa river systems relative to the rough distributions of Madison Fabric Impressed and Minotts Cord Impressed.

The interrelationships of the ceramic types discussed here are graphically illustrated in Fig. 38. The pottery seriation, which is the foundation for Fig. 38, was accomplished by Logan and is illustrated by his Fig. 22 (1959:263). His interpretations have undergone minor temporal and typological changes for this discussion, and these modifications are incorporated in Fig. 38. In this figure a ceramic type is portrayed as first originating from other types, then being in production for a duration of time, and finally dissipating as other types come into popularity. The horizontal scale is not given absolute values (percentages), but several types have been scaled in relative terms to match their intense popularity (for example, Havana and Madison Fabric Impressed) or infrequent occurrence (for example, Madison Plain).

4

Stone, Bone, and Shell Tools

It is widely recognized that artifact types from archaeological contexts may be placed in functional categories or activity sets which indicate the composition—gender groups, age groups, special activity groups such as hunters or potters—of the human group. Summary statements concerning the stone, shell, and bone artifacts recovered from 13JN3 are included here to provide evidence for the composition of human groups at this site. Certain artifact types, such as projectile points, are diagnostic in a cultural and chronological sense. Thus, the stone, shell, and bone artifacts are also discussed as part of the entire Hadfields site assemblage.

The data base and inferences about tool functions on which this chapter depends are found in Appendices D-F. Artifacts are placed in numbered categories (types), which are differentiated largely on the basis of form. The potential functions of artifacts are suggested from references to other analyses and by considering the nature and position of the working surface(s).

Projectile Points

A total of 49 projectile points and four fragments, which are probably points, described in Appendix D, have been placed in 13 categories. Of the 53 specimens, 30 are broken in some manner. It is noteworthy that all but one of the 30 broken points are either a base or blade. Apparently, these projectile points, having been broken in use yet still attached to their shafts, were being returned to the Hadfields site to be repaired or replaced. This suggests that 13JN3 was base camp for hunters.

These point categories can be ordered such that three complexes may be recognized: categories 1-5 (Fig. 39), various stemmed points; categories 6-7 (Figs. 39-40), eared points; and categories 8-12 (Figs. 40-41), various triangular points. (Category 13, Fig. 41, includes the four fragments.) It should not be assumed that these three complexes represent only three corresponding occupations of the site, for the nature of the midden

Fig. 39. Projectile points. A-B, category 1; C-E, category 2; F-G, category 3; H-I, category 5; J, category 4; K-P, category 6.

Fig. 40. Projectile points. A-G, category 7; H-J, category 8; K-Q, category 9; R-X, category 10.

indicates that the site was visited on many occasions by small groups of people. It is more realistic to view each complex as a group of regional styles of a single time horizon, and to see each point type (category) as the output of one artisan or a group of closely related artisans.

All point categories at 13JN3 seem to be indigenous to eastern Iowa, despite the fact that at least three groups (categories 6, 7, 11) are relatively rare in other sites in the same area. Chert from local sources was utilized for at least 62.5% of these points, and it is clear from the analysis of lithic debris that some of the exotic cherts were worked into points at the site.

The relative stratigraphic position of each point category is discussed under each type heading in Appendix D. The chronological progression of point types at 13JN3 may be viewed more clearly in the seriation and cumulative graphs shown in Table 4 and Figs. 42 and 43. The typological relationships inferred from these figures would be: Linn Ware (39% of pottery vessels) and projectile point categories 1-7 (48%), and Madison Ware (61% of pottery vessels) and projectile point categories 8-12 (52%). The seriation is based on a small sample and cannot be tested for statistical significance. Despite this shortcoming, the apparent mixing of excavation level #5 is plainly seen in the cumulative graph, Fig. 43.

TABLE 4
Projectile Point Categories
by Stratigraphic Levels

	Stratigraphic Levels				
Category no.	1-2	3	4	5	6-
1-5	5	1	2	1	0
6	0	1	1	4	0
7	1	2	4	1	0
8-9	7	2	0	1	0
10	2	3	2	0	0
11	1	1	2	0	1 (feature)
12	1	1	1	0	0

Worked Bone

Bones which have been intentionally modified fall into three classes at 13JN3. One class, cut bone (Fig. 44), represents the waste products of the bone working technology. Relatively few examples were available for discussion here, these being the most striking examples and thus the most visible among the thousands of bone fragments at the site.

The second group, bone tools (Figs. 45-50), includes the largest number of worked bone elements. Tools required primarily for leather working dominate this class with as many as 36 specimens—awls, burnishers,

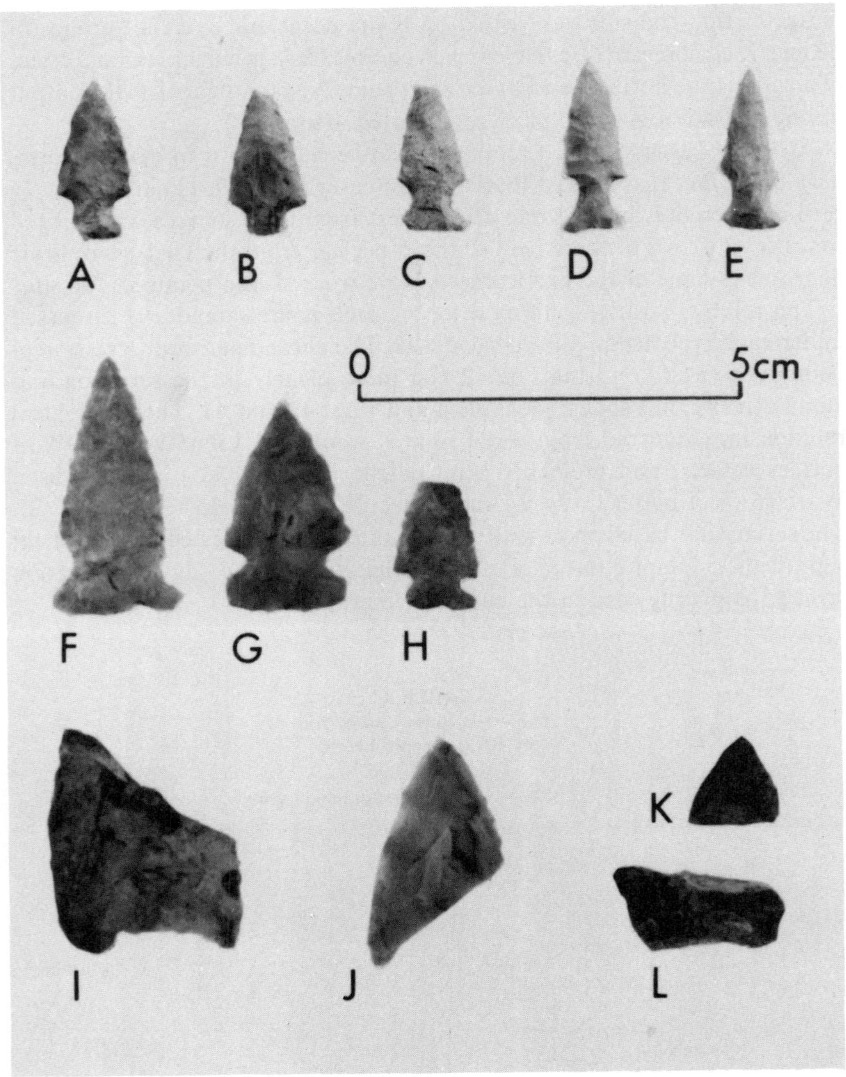

Fig. 41. Projectile points. A-E, category 11; F-H, category 12; I-L, category 13.

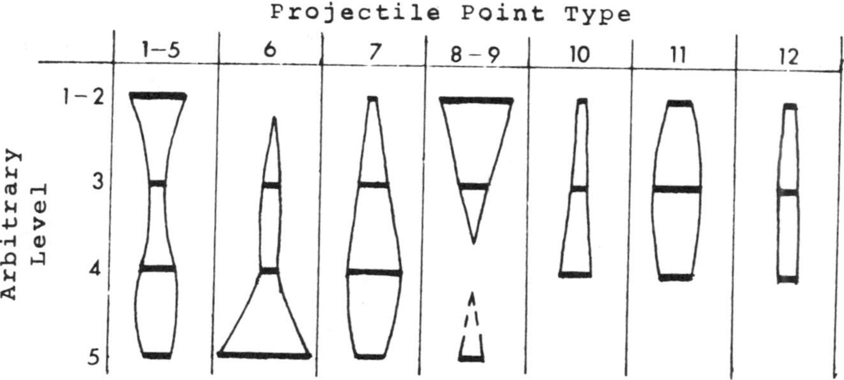

Fig. 42. Distribution of projectile point types at 13JN3.

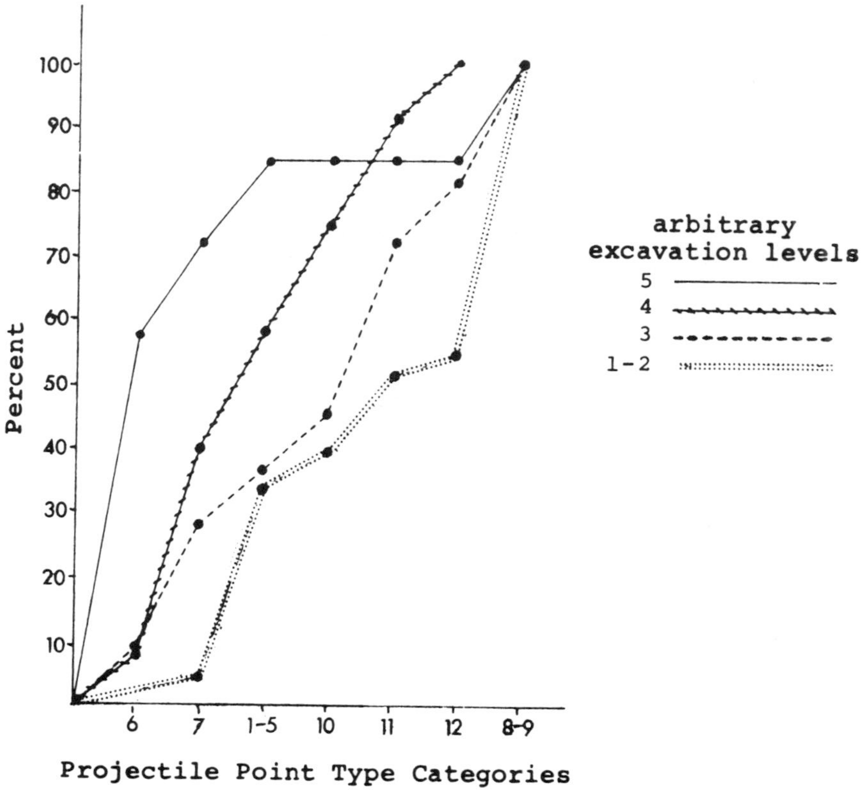

Projectile Point Type Categories

Fig. 43. Cumulative graph of the distributions shown in Fig. 42.

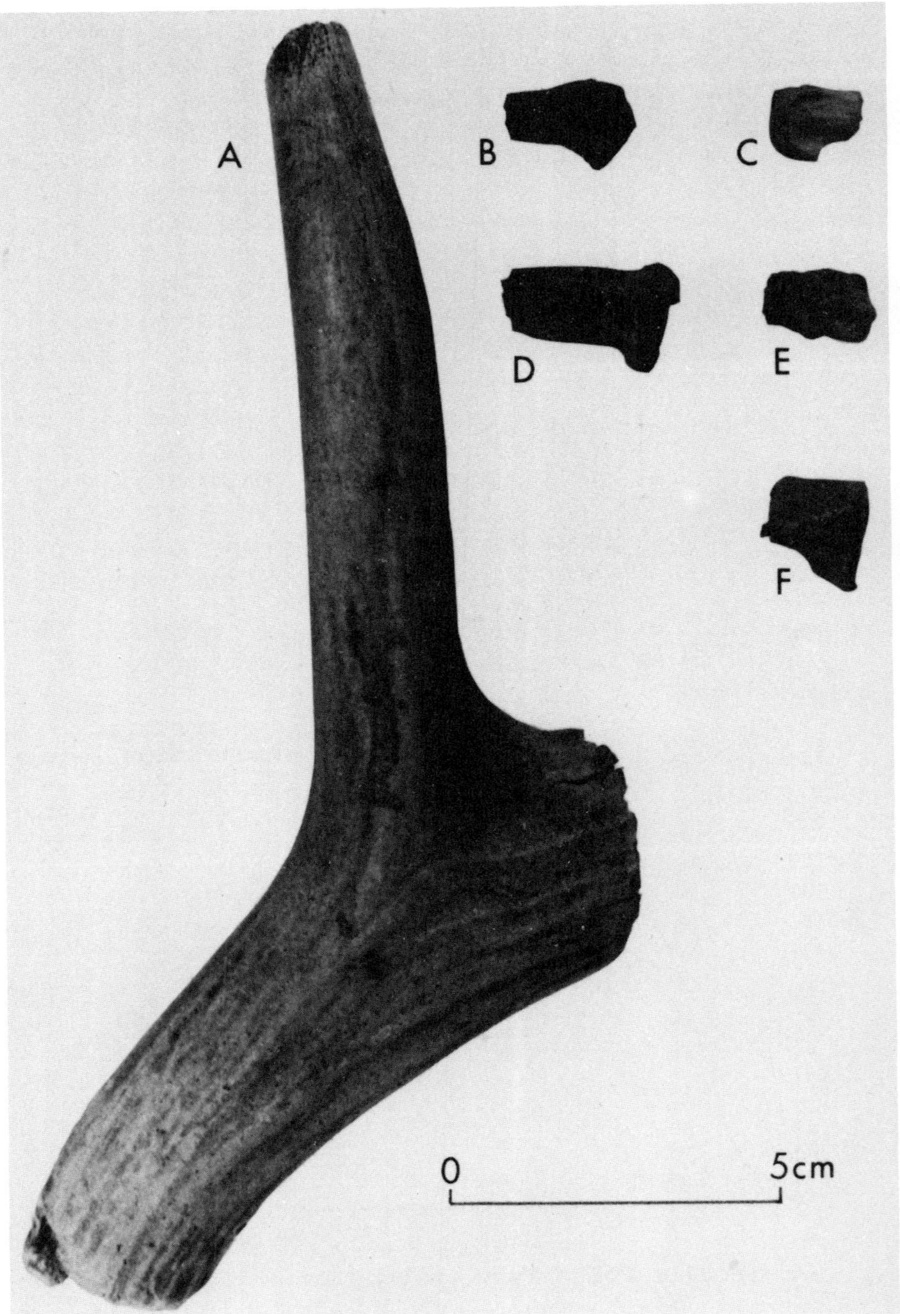

Fig. 44. Cut bones.

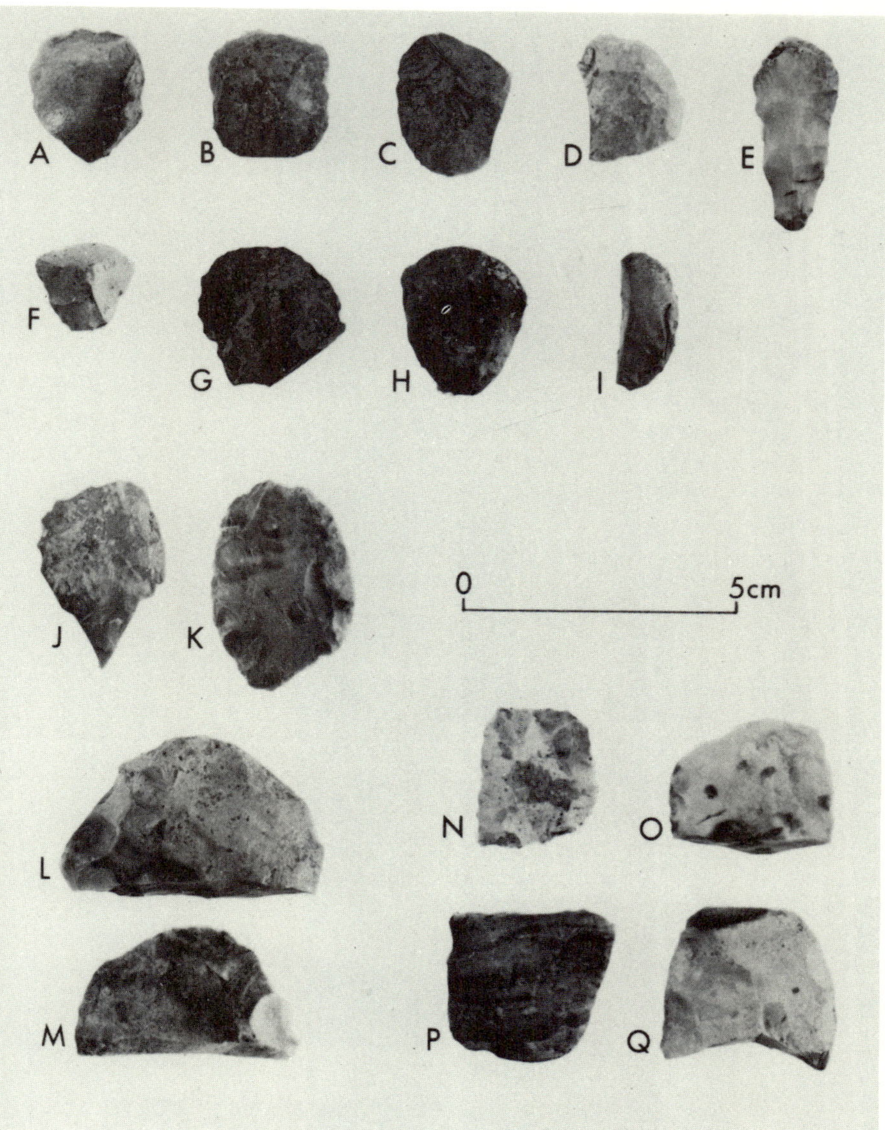

Fig. 45. Scrapers. A-I, end scrapers; J-K, oval scrapers; L-M, disc scrapers; N-Q, rectangular scrapers.

Fig. 46. Stone artifacts. A-B, knives; C-E, miscellaneous stone tools; F-J, drills; K, stone elbow pipe; L, historic pipe stem.

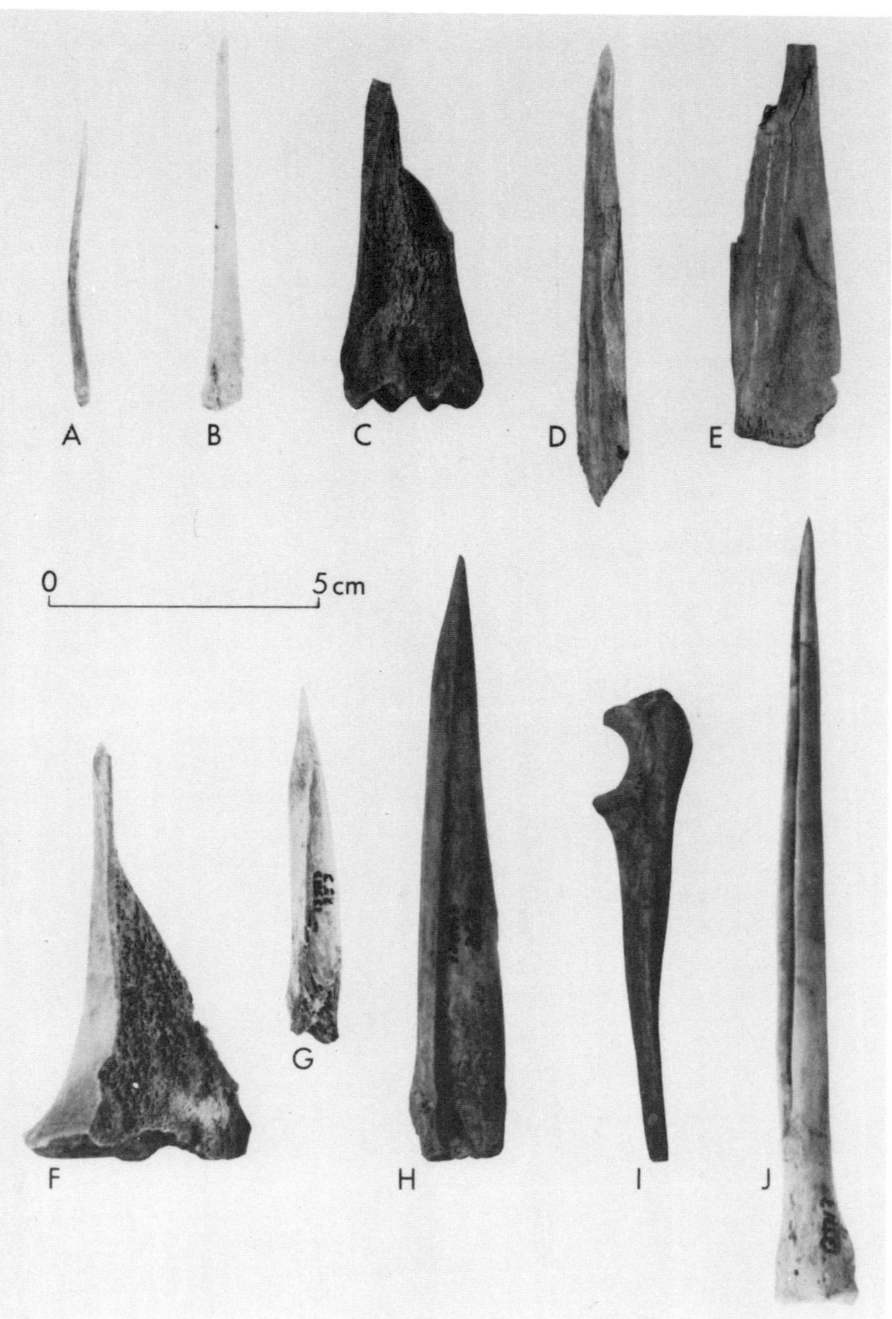

Fig. 47. Awls.

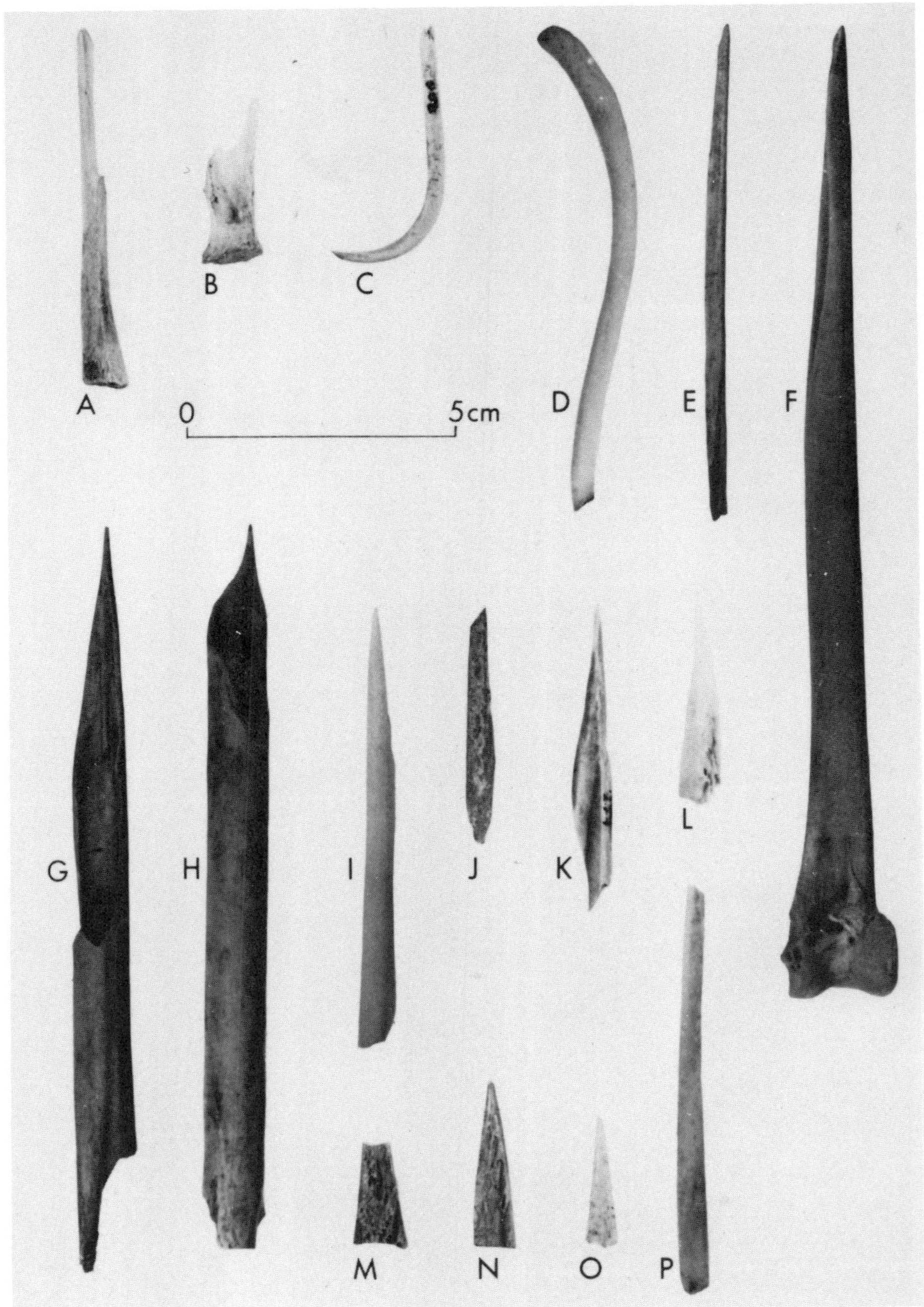

Fig. 48. Awls.

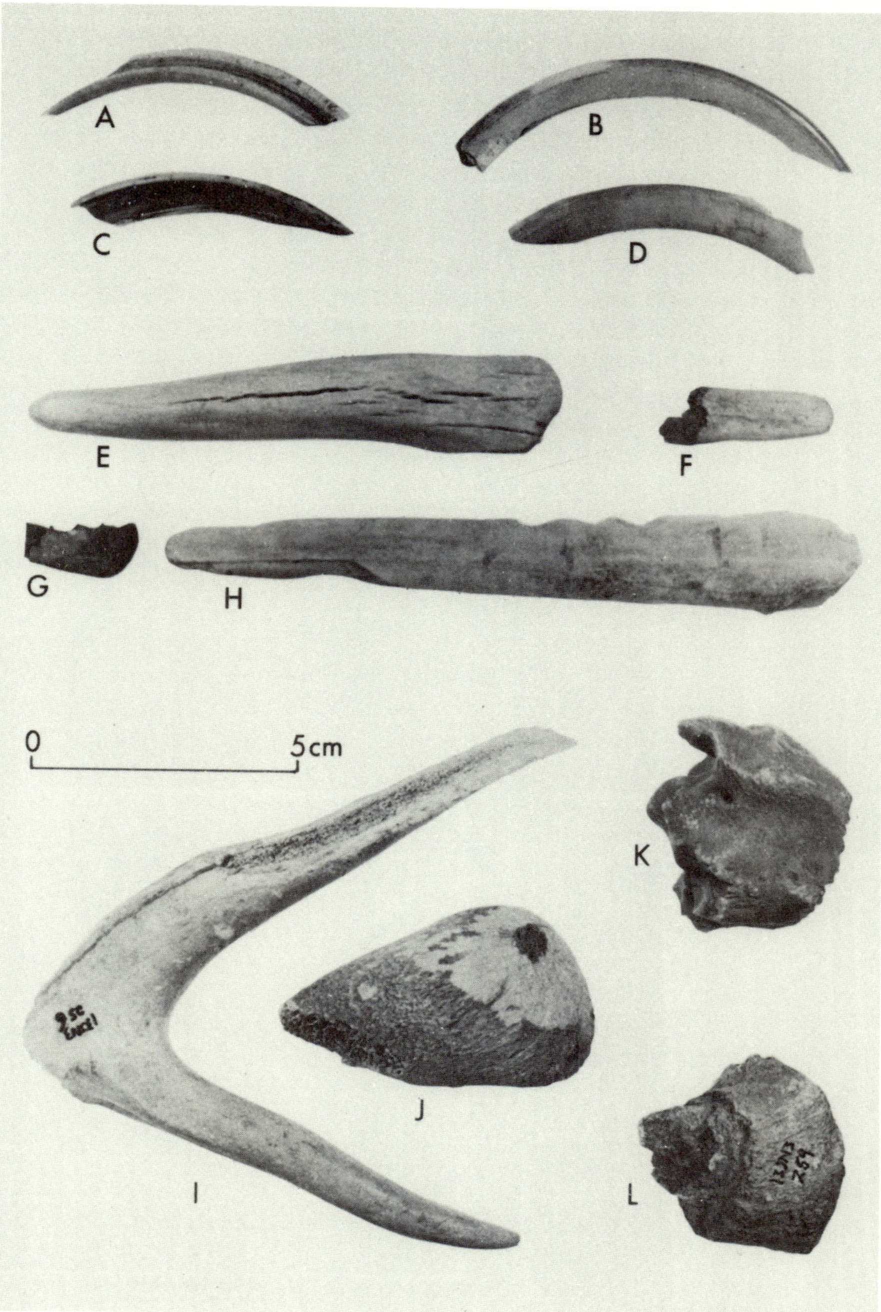

Fig. 49. Beaver incisors and burnishers. A-D, beaver incisors; E-F, burnishers; G, pendant; H, burnisher; I-L, hide grainers.

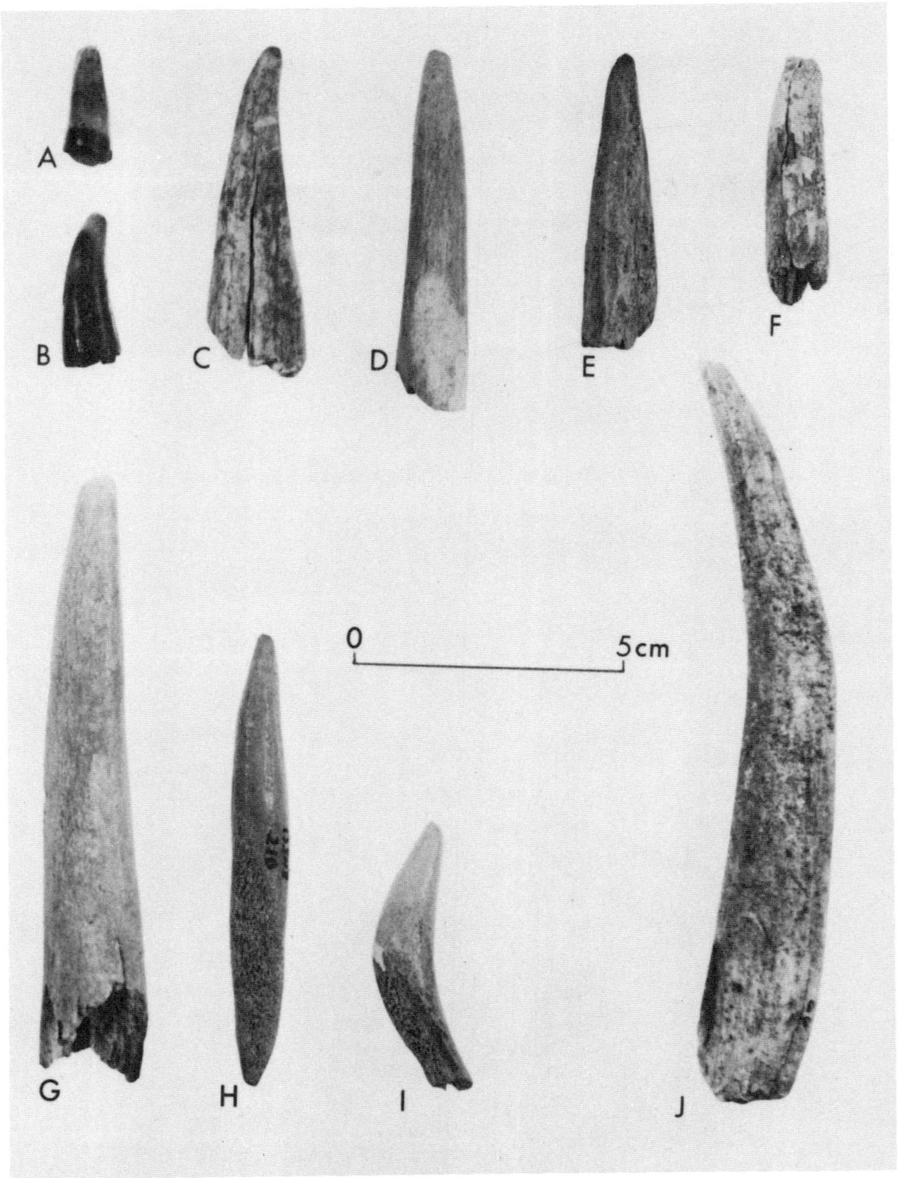

Fig. 50. Flakers. A-G, flakers; H, miscellaneous tool; I, hide grainer; J, flaker.

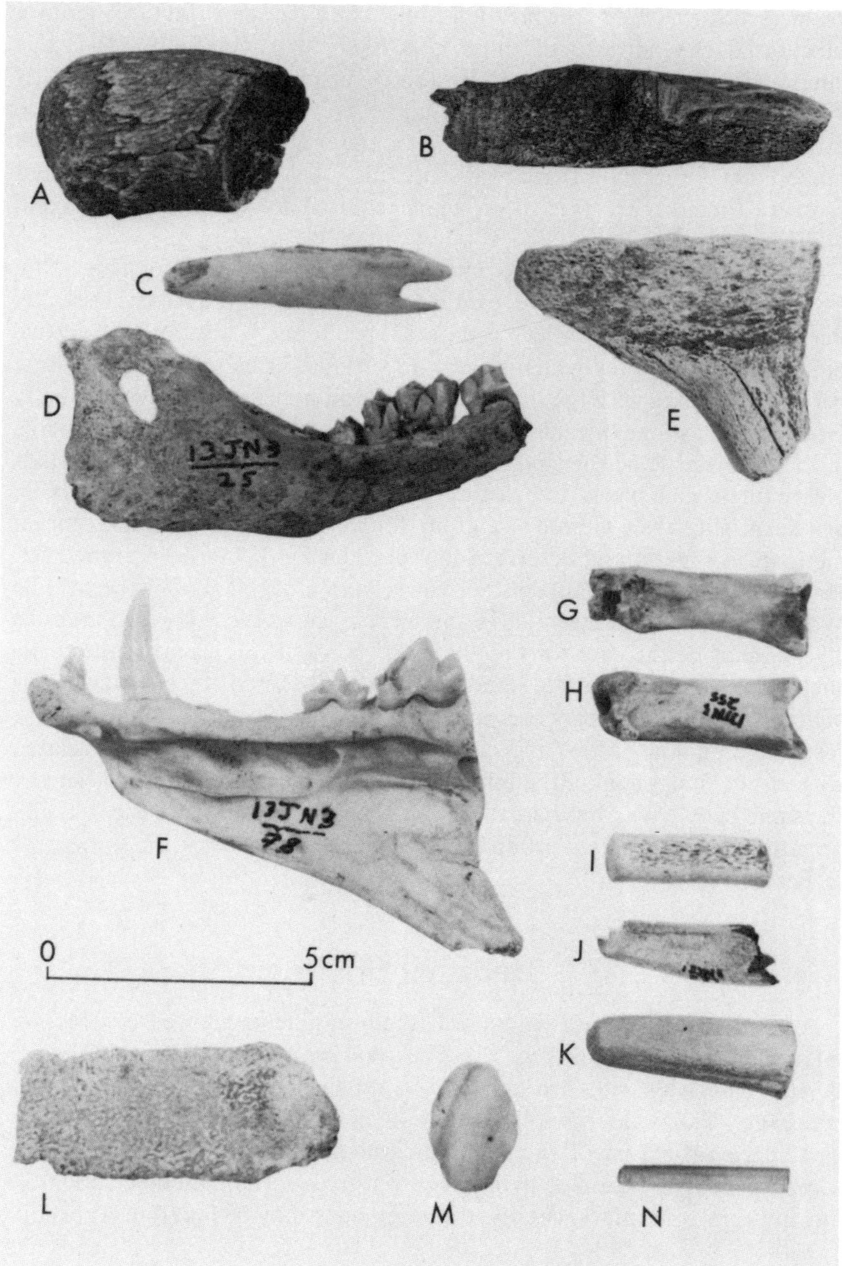

Fig. 51. Miscellaneous tools. A-E, miscellaneous tools; F, cut canid maxilla; G-H, perforated deer phalanges; I-K, antler counters; L, pendant; M, decorative bone wafer; N, bone bead.

grainers. Since hide preparation and clothing manufacture require substantial expenditures of time, it is likely that Hadfields Cave was inhabited for extended periods by family-band units. In addition, it is logical to assume that hide working activities were pursued here because deer were being hunted near the site and regularly consumed by its inhabitants. Other tools that are also present— beaver incisor "chisels" and pressure flakers—are typical of items required for daily household and hunting activities.

The third class, decorative and ceremonial bone objects (Fig. 51), includes some of the more exotic material recovered from the site. Perforated phalanges, antler "counters," pendants, beads, and decorative bits of bone are items which appear in various forms in sites of all time periods beginning with the Archaic. Woodland sites in the Midwest usually produce at least one of each of these objects, and the Hadfields assemblage of these objects is neither inordinately large or small. The additional finds of five turtle shell bowls, five rattles (Figs 52-53), and the cut canid maxilla *are* surprising when viewed as a group (cf. also the rattlesnake shell gorget pictured in Fig. 54 and described in Appendix F). It has been argued (cf. Halsey 1966:392) that turtle shell bowls were a component of the Middle Woodland household assemblage and were in use as everyday food utensils. This cannot be the case for the Hadfields bowls. It is clear that the turtle shell rattles and cut maxilla should be viewed as sacred objects, whether as charms or ceremonial paraphernalia (that is, as noise makers and as a mask respectively). The rattles and cut maxilla cannot be definitely associated with either component, although they may have been brought to the site by the same people who brought the bowls. The five rattles were undoubtedly brought to the cave as a group, for they were deposited at the same time in Feature 69.

Modified Shell

A total of 15 mollusc valves and shell fragments showed evidence of intentional modification (Fig. 55). The great majority of pelecypod species at the Hadfields site are relatively thin-shelled types, prone to easy breakage. Thus, this small number of worked shell remains may, in part, be a reflection of the high attrition rate for shell objects on the compact, heavily trampled living floor of the cave. Detailed descriptions of this material and inferences about its functions may be found in Appendix F.

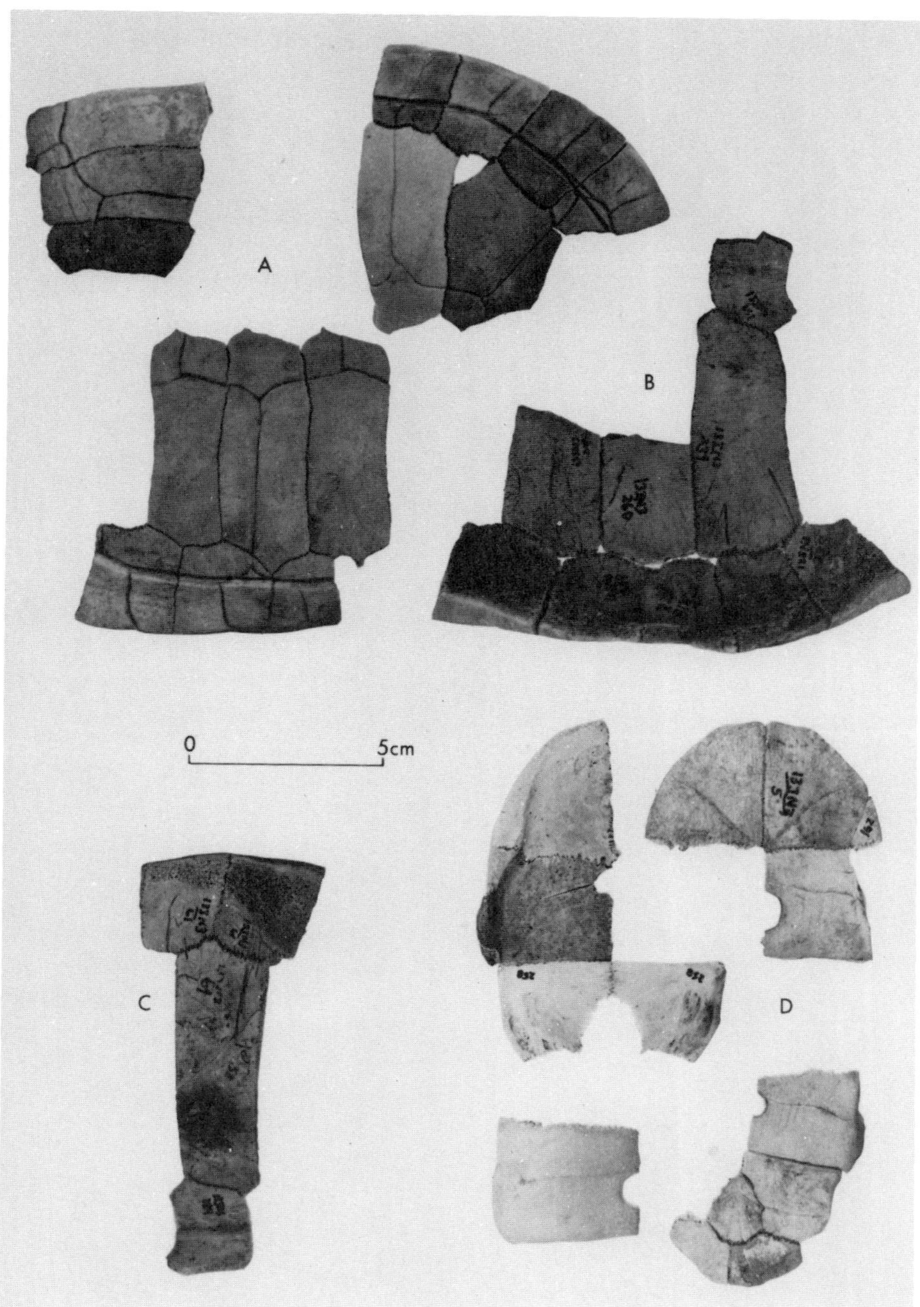

Fig. 52. Turtle shell artifacts. A-C, bowls; D, rattle.

Fig. 53. Turtle shell artifacts. A, bowl; B, rattle; C, bowl; D-F, rattles.

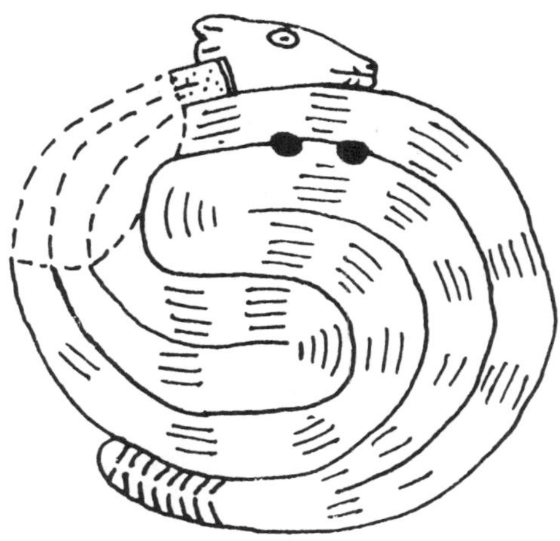

Fig. 54. Shell gorget.

Conclusions

The Hadfields tool assemblage can be characterized by two generalizations. First, the assemblage contains a wide variety of tool forms with differing functions. A rapid review of these functional classes would include various drilling and punching tools (for example, chipped stone drills, bone awls), scraping and scouring instruments (for example, end scrapers, bone hide grainers, shell scrapers), cutting tools (chipped stone knives, flake blanks with marginal wear and retouch), stone working tools (antler flakers, hammerstones), a grinding slab (Fig. 56), various decorative and ceremonial paraphernalia, and projectile points. To this assemblage we can also add ceramics, for pottery functions as containers for food preparation and storage. Within this variety of functional artifact classes, we can select specific artifact classes which are likely to have been associated with either men's or women's activities. For example, the manufacture of some lithic tools and the utilization of projectile points were probably men's activities, while women could have been responsible for the manufacture and use of pottery and the preparation of animal skins. Other items, such as the turtle shell rattles, could have been associated with group behavior, including both men and women, for it is likely that rattles were utilized for communal ceremonies and not as individuals' charms.

The second generalization is that there are several tools in each tool category. The fact that there are several examples of tools in many different functional classes suggests that 13JN3 was occupied for an

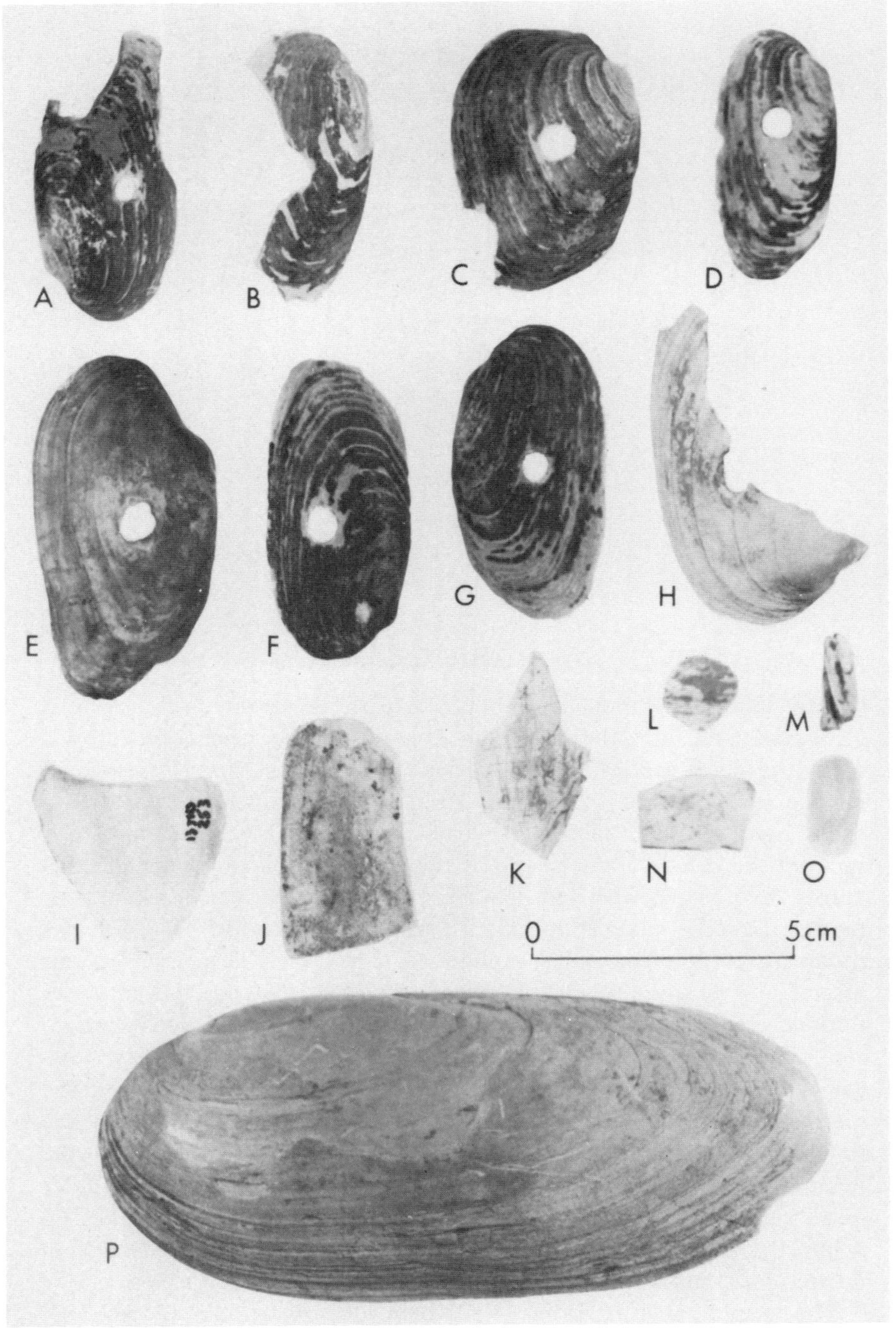

Fig. 55. Modified shell. A-G, perforated valves; H, scraper; I-L, cut shell; M, marine shell; N-O, cut shell; P, scoop or digging tool.

extensive period of time, that is, a long enough habitation to require the reproduction or reintroduction of new tools. Because the site contains two components, the site must have been occupied on at least two different occasions. But it is more reasonable to assume that *most* of the occupation debris at 13JN3 was accumulated by several extended visits to the site by human groups of both men and women. It is hypothesized that these human groups were small family-bands. Occasional short visits to 13JN3 also may have been made by hunting parties whose family camp was nearby.

Fig. 56. Miscellaneous stones. A, grinding slab; B-E, introduced cobbles and pebbles; F, abrader; G, fossil; H, fragment of hematite concretion; I, hematite "cup."

5

Studies in Paleoecology

The multifaceted approach to studying biological remains from archaeological contexts has proved to be one of the best approaches for reconstructing paleoecological relationships. The concurrent analysis of several types of remains—for example, seeds, animal bone, terrestrial gastropods, pollen—provides independent pools of evidence which may be compared with one another to produce a complete and realistic reconstruction of the environment. A number of disciplines in the biological field are usually requested to assist in the analysis of organic remains, often providing information on typical habitats, climates, soil characters, and identification of organisms. When the analyses of several types of organic remains are made available to the archaeologist, it is possible to reconstruct the environment in which those organisms lived and to recognize the interrelationships between those organisms. The study of interrelationships between organisms and their environment is, of course, the study of ecology (Odum 1971:3). In analysing the organic remains left by prehistoric man and reconstructing the relations between man and his environment, we are studying the paleoecology of man.

This chapter concerns several aspects of paleoecology as evidenced by the organic remains from the Hadfields site. The four sections here deal with plant remains, annuli in white-tailed deer teeth, seasonality, and diet reconstruction. The latter three sections are supported by an analysis of skeletal remains in Appendices G-L. These appendices contain listings of animal habitats as well as inferences concerning man's utilization of several animal species.

The final section of this chapter is devoted to reconstructing a generalized diet of the people who occupied 13JN3. Such a dietary study is not considered as part of the paleoecology of organisms evidenced at the site. Rather, the diet represents an aspect of *man's* relationship with his environment. This reconstructed diet, the theories about band size which are inferred from the reconstructed diet, and the remaining portions of this chapter are part of the groundwork for the theoretical discussion of subsistence and settlement patterns in Chapter 6.

Paleoethnobotany

Although the description of botanical remains has a long history in archaeology, sophisticated analysis and insight into the reasons for the presence of specific types of remains has been slow in developing. Many of the earliest notable reports of archaeological botanical material in the eastern United States, such as Nelson (1917), Gilmore (1931), and Jones (1936), dealt almost exclusively with cultivars and the problem of their origins in aboriginal North America. Generally these initial statements about plant remains lacked definitiveness, since their authors had few finds to interpret. Until the early 1960s the pace of paleoethnobotanical researches was slow, being stimulated primarily by the botanical section of the University of Michigan's Museum of Anthropology. But with the publication of Fowler's (1971b) discussion of plant cultivation in the central Mississippi valley, Caldwell's (1962) interpretation of aboriginal agriculture in the eastern United States, and Yarnell's (1964) general work on the Great Lakes region, paleoethnobotany entered a model building state which was to ignite new systematic researches. Moreover, the advantages of flotation for the total recovery of carbonized plant remains were quickly recognized. For some investigators, this technique has become part of standard field procedure.

Total recovery techniques and 40 years of accumulated literature now provide us sufficient data with which to attempt to link broad inferences concerning prehistoric settlement/subsistence patterns with reconstructions of material culture and chronological sequences. This approach has been taken in recent articles by Hall (1973) and Struever and Vickery (1973). Both deal with the dynamics of the development and utilization of domesticated and cultivated plants in the eastern United States. Developmental models, such as those contained in the two articles referenced above, function as testable hypotheses for analyses with limited regional scope such as the one to be presented here. Both models also provide skeletal frameworks of resource utilization to which the date of plant use at 13JN3 can be compared.

Methods

The seed remains described here were extracted from 341 liters of soil systematically sampled from features and levels of the control squares at the site. There was a total of 81 numbered features—pits, fired areas, charcoal concentrations—of which 48 (minus two lost in the field prior to processing) were considered distinct enough and sufficiently voluminous to accommodate a 6-9 liter sample. In some cases whole features were placed in plastic bags and processed. Typically, the soil samples were subsampled in laboratory washing to reduce the volume of carbonized organic remains to an analytically manageable size.

Soil samples were taken from the general 3 inch control levels in the 5x5 feet mapping squares in a systematic fashion (Steel and Torrie 1960:412; Buell and Cantlon 1951); that is, all levels were sampled from every other square in a line from end to end through the central portion of the site. Additional bags of soil were taken from squares beyond this line of regularly sampled squares. For this analysis, the population of general midden soil samples was subsampled using a table of random numbers, and the resultant 18 samples were assumed to be reasonably representative of the midden in the entire site.

Water flotation was used to separate the carbonized remains from soil and bone in all of the soil samples. During this processing every precaution was taken to fulfill the requirements for complete recovery (cf. Benn 1974:56-57; Tiffany 1974:10-13; Renfew 1973:7-15). The soil conditions at 13JN3 also necessitated either the use of chemical flotation with zinc chloride or multiple washings to separate the denser nutshell fragments from the gravel. In addition, the heavy fractions were picked by hand to remove nutshell which remained in the gravel.

The flotated debris was sorted with the aid of a binocular microscope. Nutshell, which made up the majority of the seed remains, was initially sorted with number 10 mesh (window) screen into essentially unidentifiable (smaller fraction) and identifiable (larger fraction) units. Seed and nut identifications were completed using modern comparative seed collections, with occasional reference to Martin and Barkley (1961) and the Forest Service's *Woody-Plant Seed Manual* (1948). Several one-of-a-kind seeds could not be identified, since the available comparative collections of seeds from the forest biome were incomplete.

In an effort to supplement the seed analysis, wood charcoal was also identified. The one-quarter inch field screens produced large quantities of charcoal from over 100 arbitrary levels, much of this charcoal being less than one-quarter inch in diameter. From these field samples, 15 were selected through reference to a table of random numbers, and an additional five flotation samples containing large quantities of wood charcoal were added to the analysis to provide a total of 20 samples to represent the entire site. The identification procedure followed mainly after Conrad and Koeppen (1972:52) in that wood fragments large enough to be snapped by hand became the identifiable sample. This for the most part precluded using fragments smaller than one-quarter inch in the greatest dimension. Identifications were made with the *Textbook of Wood Technology* (Panshin et al. 1964) and with modern wood specimens, and were checked by Mr. Lawrence Conrad (at that time a graduate student, Department of Anthropology, University of Wisconsin-Madison).

A summary table (Table 5) of wood charcoal has been constructed using counts of identified fragments per species rather than weights. As Conrad and Koeppen (1972:52) point out, interpretive units have yet to be developed for charcoal analysis. This writer noticed that disparities

124

TABLE 5
Charcoal Remains

Catalogue no.	Square no.	Level	Juniperus virginiana	Populus/ Salix	Juglans nigra cinerea	Carya ovata glabra	Ostraya virginiana	White Oaks	Red Oaks	Ulmus americana	Cf. Ulmus rubra	Cf. Celtis sp.	Prunus serotina	Acer saccharum	Tilia sp.	Fraximus Cf. americana	Knots/Bark	Sample Total
33	113	15	—	—	—	—	—	2	5	—	—	1	—	—	—	—	2	10
39	129	3	—	—	—	—	1	—	7	—	—	—	—	—	—	—	—	8
41	143	4	2	—	—	—	—	1	3	—	1	—	—	—	—	—	—	7
77	94	4	2	—	—	—	—	—	24	—	—	—	—	1	4	—	5	36
93	124	3	4	—	—	2	2	7	47	—	2	2	—	—	—	5	6	77
117	113	5	—	—	—	—	—	3	36	1	13	—	—	—	—	—	7	60
196	124	6	—	—	—	—	3	3	40	2	—	—	—	1	—	—	2	51
197	124	5	2	—	—	11	2	9	87	1	—	2	—	—	—	10	18	142
204	126	3	—	—	—	3	4	12	4	—	—	1	—	—	—	2	—	26
228	135	3	9	—	—	4	2	2	44	—	2	—	—	—	—	—	2	65
233	127	3	3	—	—	—	—	2	27	1	7	—	—	—	—	1	5	46
245	96	5	—	—	—	—	—	6	25	6	—	—	—	—	—	—	6	43
265	141	3	—	—	—	—	—	4	16	—	—	—	—	—	—	—	1	21
300	128	4	20	—	3	2	2	2	1	—	—	—	—	1	—	—	3	34
334	125	6	—	—	1	1	—	4	24	1	—	—	—	—	—	—	2	33
	Fea.	lev.																
36	30	3	2	—	8	14	7	7	112	—	1	—	1	5	—	2	8	167
64	10	4	—	—	4	1	6	—	55	—	3	3	—	—	—	—	4	76
100	64	—	2	1	6	5	3	2	63	—	33	1	—	—	—	1	7	123
106	56b	—	6	—	1	7	1	3	36	—	—	—	—	—	—	—	2	56
146	5	4	—	—	—	—	1	2	35	—	1	1	—	—	—	—	4	44
Species Totals			52	1	23	50	34	71	691	12	63	11	1	8	4	21	84	

TOTAL 1,042

between species density and friability would have resulted in unequal weighting of certain species if weights had been employed as the unit of analysis. Specifically, the oaks are particularly dense and appear to be less prone to breakage. The use of fragment counts for this analysis should not imply that this is the preferred method for any future analyses, but only that in this instance counting specimens was easier than weighing after first snapping (and often shattering) for the identification.

Results

Tabulation of the seeds recovered at 13JN3 has been provided in Tables 6, 7, 8, and 9. In scanning Tables 6 and 7, the most striking aspect is the uniformity of sample yields. This probably reflects the relatively short time span of occupation (ca. 500 years) during which virtually all of the midden was deposited. It may also reflect the possibility that these Woodland peoples had a stabilized, secure subsistence base which remained static for this time period.

Of all seeds recovered, the nuts—hickory, walnut, butternut—contribute by far the greatest weight and numbers. These resources clearly played a substantial role in the fall and winter diet. Another type of seed resource, the chenopods, dominates the remainder of the sample in numbers. The presence of chenopods may be significant in terms of their link to corn agriculture, also evidenced at 13JN3. A wide range of species is present in the remaining seeds in this sample, but the numbers of individuals of each type are very small. Seeds in very small numbers could indicate that such species were not utilized in ways which left large numbers of them carbonized. But alternatively, in the historic period many of these poorly represented types of seeds may have been utilized when seasonally available, or occasionally when required for technological, medicinal, or ceremonial purposes. Thus, sporadic and specialized uses of these seeds or their parent plants would have drastically reduced the chances for carbonization and survival in the excavator's screens.

One especially important factor to consider for the presence of several seed species is that they were clearly introduced into the site by rodents. It is clear, when comparing the uncarbonized species (Table 8) with the carbonized species of seeds, that *Rhus* sp., *Physalis heterophyla*, *Scirpus* sp., *Juniperus virginiana*, *Ostrya virginiana*, and acorns occur in both groups. However, as there was an absence of teeth marks on any of these seeds, it cannot be positively stated that the carbonized specimens were rodent introduced as were the modern ones. But the possibility that any or all of these are rodent deposited casts doubt on any interpretations of their potential use by man. Many of the *Celtis* sp. pits, including burned examples, had a single punched hole which is typical of rodent feeding.

TABLE 6
Carbonized Seed Remains
from Features

	36	37	44	49**	50	56	58	64
Catalogue no.	36	37	44	49**	50	56	58	64
Feature no.	30	75	50	65	54	21	40	10
Stratigraphic Level	3	—	6	3	5	—	5-6	4
Sample volume	4¼	7½	7½	4	9	6	4	2½
Charcoal	42.6	16.4	14.8	36.7	63.5	30.6	16.0	24.4
Juniperus virginiana	—	—	—	—	3fr	—	—	—
Graminae	—	—	—	—	—	—	—	—
Stipa sp.	—	—	—	—	—	—	—	—
Zizania aquatica	—	—	—	1	—	—	—	—
Zea mays	—	—	—	—	—	1fr	—	—
Scirpus sp.	—	—	1	—	—	—	—	—
Juglans cinerea	0.2	0.25	0.1	0.1	0.4	1.0	0.2	0.7
Juglans nigra	0.1	0.1	0.1	0.1	0.4	1.2	0.1	0.3
Carya ovata	4.2	2.4	1.8	0.4	18.5	41.1	2.2	0.7
Corylus americana	0.2	T	T	—	T	T	—	T
Quercus spp.	T	T	—	T	T	T	T	T
Celtis occidentalis	—	+1	+2	—	1	—	+1	—
Polygon pennsylvanicum	—	—	—	—	—	—	—	—
Chenopodium hybridum	9	3	—	20	44	79	3	2
Chenopodium album	—	—	—	1	4	9	1	—
Chenopodium spp.	24	4	2	23	75	68	7	5
Amaranthus spp.	—	—	—	—	—	—	—	—
Ranunculus sp.	—	—	1	—	—	—	—	—
Aquilegia columbia	—	—	—	—	—	—	—	—
Brassica spp.	—	—	—	—	—	—	—	—
Pyrus sp.	—	—	—	—	—	—	—	—
Lespedeza sp.	—	—	—	—	—	—	—	—
Strophostyles sp.	—	—	—	—	—	—	—	—
Rhus sp.	—	2	—	5	—	2	—	—
Hypericum sp.	—	—	—	—	—	—	—	—
Viola sp.	—	—	—	—	—	—	—	—
Apocynum sp.	—	—	—	—	—	—	—	—
Cuscuta spp.	—	—	—	—	—	—	—	—
Monarda fistulosa	—	—	—	—	*1*	—	—	—
Physalis heterophyla	—	—	—	—	—	—	—	—
Ambrosia sp.	—	—	—	—	—	—	—	—
Helianthus annuus	—	—	—	—	—	—	—	—
Nut spp. (shell)	1.1	0.5	0.5	8.0	1.9	10.0	0.6	0.1
Nut spp. (meat)	0.1	0.1	T	T	0.1	0.2	0.1	—
Unidentifiable gm.	0.1	—	—	0.1	0.1	0.1	—	—
seeds	—	—	—	—	+8	—	3	1
Unidentified seeds	1	—	1	5				

Stratigraphic Level	3	2	3	2	—	4	—	—
Sample volume	2	6	4	4	6¾	4	4	8
Charcoal	6.4	29.7	31.1	22.0	74.9	30.8	12.6	75.1
Juniperus virginiana	—	—	1fr	—	—	—	—	—
Graminae	—	—	—	—	—	—	—	—
Stipa sp.	—	—	—	—	—	—	—	—
Zizania aquatica	—	—	—	—	—	—	—	—
Zea mays	—	—	1fr	—	1	—	—	—
Scirpus sp.	—	—	—	—	—	—	—	—
Juglans cinerea	—	0.7	0.2	0.1	0.7	0.35	0.1	1.4
Juglans nigra	0.1	0.2	3.1	0.5	0.9	0.2	0.1	2.7
Carya ovata	—	7.1	19.4	3.4	3.8	1.2	0.4	3.8
Corylus americana	0.1	0.3	T	0.1	0.2	T	—	0.1
Quercus spp.	—	—	T	0.1	0.3*	0.1	—	0.2@
Celtis occidentalis	T	—	T	1	+10	T	+1	+10
Polygon pennsylvanicum	—	—	—	—	—	—	—	—
Chenopodium hybridum	—	20	45	1	27	7	1	9
Chenopodium album	—	5	3	—	4	3	—	3
Chenopodium spp.	1	9	62	3	+46	16	12	27
Amaranthus spp.	—	—	—	—	1	—	—	1
Ranunculus sp.	—	—	—	—	—	—	—	—
Aquilegia columbia	—	—	—	—	—	—	—	—
Brassica spp.	—	—	—	—	—	—	—	—
Pyrus sp.	—	—	—	—	—	—	—	—
Lespedesa sp.	—	—	—	—	—	—	—	—
Strophostyles sp.	—	1	—	—	—	—	—	—
Rhus sp.	—	8	—	1	5	3	—	—
Hypericum sp.	—	—	1&1fr	—	—	—	—	—
Viola sp.	—	—	—	—	—	—	—	—
Apocynum sp.	—	—	—	—	—	—	—	—
Cuscuta spp.	—	—	—	—	—	—	—	—
Monarda fistulosa	—	—	—	—	—	—	—	—
Physalis heterophyla	—	—	—	—	—	—	—	—
Ambrosia sp.	—	—	—	—	—	—	—	—
Helianthus annuus	—	—	—	—	—	—	—	—
Nut spp. (shell)	0.2	1.7	2.5	0.8	1.8	0.8	0.1	5.4
Nut spp. (meat)	—	—	0.1	0.1	0.1	—	—	0.1
Unidentifiable gm.	—	T	0.1	—	0.1	0.1	T	0.3***
seeds	—	—	—	—	0.1	0.1	—	8
Unidentified seeds	—	1	—	—	2	—	—	6
TOTALS gm.	6.8	39.7	56.5	25.1	82.8	33.55	13.3	89.2
seeds	1	44	113	6	+96	29	+14	+64

	101	102	103	104	106	110	111	117
Catalogue no.	101	102	103	104	106	110	111	117
Feature no.	53&33	57	27	72	56b	45	70	78
Stratigraphic Level	3	—	3	4	—	3	3	5
Sample Volume	4	4	8½	4	4	4	4¾	4
Charcoal	45.2	20.8	38.0	0.9	18.7	1.5	17.6	45.8
Juniperus virginiana	1fr	—	—	—	—	—	—	—
Graminae	—	—	—	—	—	—	—	—
Stipa sp.	—	—	—	—	—	—	—	—
Zizania aquatica	—	—	—	—	—	—	—	+1
Zea mays	4fr	—	—	—	—	—	—	—
Scirpus sp.	—	—	—	—	0.1	—	0.1	1.6
Juglans cinerea	1.3	—	—	—	0.1	—	0.1	0.6
Juglans nigra	1.0	0.4	0.1	—	1.1	—	0.4	2.4
Carya ovata	24.9	6.4	8.1	0.5	T	0.1	—	T
Corylus americana	—	0.15	T	0.1	T	—	—	T
Quercus spp.	1.5@*	T	T	—	+3	1	+2	—
Celtis occidentalis	T	2	+3	2	—	—	—	—
Polygon pennsylvanicum	—	—	—	—	12	—	1	6
Chenopodium hybridum	188	4	38	—	—	—	—	—
Chenopodium album	14	1	3	—	16	—	1	6
Chenopodium spp.	53	10	28	—	—	—	—	—
Amaranthus spp.	1	1	—	—	—	—	—	—
Ranunculus sp.	—	—	—	—	—	—	—	—
Aquilegia columbia	—	—	—	—	1	—	—	(1)
Brassica spp.	—	—	—	—	—	—	—	—
Pyrus sp.	—	—	1	—	—	—	—	—
Lespedeza sp.	—	—	—	—	—	—	—	—
Strophostyles sp.	—	—	—	—	—	—	—	—
Rhus sp.	2	2	2	—	1	—	—	—
Hypericum sp.	—	—	—	—	—	—	—	—
Viola sp.	—	—	—	—	—	—	—	—
Apocynum sp.	1	—	—	—	1	—	—	(1)
Cuscuta spp.	—	1	—	—	—	—	—	—
Monarda fistulosa	—	—	—	—	—	—	—	—
Physalis heterophyla	—	—	—	—	—	—	—	—
Ambrosia sp.	—	—	—	—	—	—	—	1fr
Helianthus annuus	—	1	—	—	—	—	—	0.2
Nut spp. (shell)	8.8	0.9	2.5	0.1	0.2	0.1	0.1	0.1
Nut spp. (meat)	0.5	0.1	0.1	T	0.1	—	T	0.1
Unidentifiable gm.	0.1	0.2	0.1	—	—	—	—	—
seeds	—	2	—	—	1	—	—	—
Unidentified seeds	2	5	—	—	1	[illegible]	[illegible]	1

129

Stratigraphic Level	3	3	3	—	3	3	—	3
Sample volume	4	4	4	4	4	4	4	4
Charcoal	26.1	17.5	31.5	23.0	21.6	2.8	2.8	4.1
Juniperus virginiana	—	—	1	—	—	—	—	—
Graminae	—	—	—	—	—	—	—	—
Stipa sp.	—	—	—	—	—	—	—	—
Zizania aquatica	—	—	—	—	—	—	—	—
Zea mays	—	—	—	—	+1	1	—	—
Scirpus sp.	—	—	—	—	1	—	—	—
Juglans cinerea	0.9	0.3	0.6	0.1	0.2	0.2	—	0.1
Juglans nigra	0.1	0.1	0.3	—	1.0	0.1	—	0.1
Carya ovata	1.8	3.3	1.8	0.6	2.4	0.3	—	0.2
Corylus americana	T	T	T	T	T	0.1	0.3	0.1
Quercus spp.	T	T	T	T	T	—	0.1@@	—
Celtis occidentalis	—	+5	1	1	—	T	—	+2
Polygon pennsylvanicum	—	—	—	—	—	—	—	—
Chenopodium hybridum	7	20	10	—	5	—	5	5
Chenopodium album	—	—	2	—	2	—	—	1
Chenopodium spp.	20	24	11	2	15	—	—	3
Amaranthus spp.	—	—	—	—	—	—	—	—
Ranunculus sp.	—	—	—	—	—	—	—	—
Aquilegia columbia	—	—	—	—	—	—	—	—
Brassica spp.	—	—	—	—	—	—	—	—
Pyrus sp.	—	—	—	—	—	—	—	—
Lespedeza sp.	—	1	—	—	—	—	—	—
Strophostyles sp.	—	—	—	—	—	—	—	—
Rhus sp.	3	5	2	—	2	—	—	—
Hypericum sp.	—	—	—	—	—	—	—	—
Viola sp.	—	—	—	—	—	—	—	—
Apocynum sp.	—	—	—	—	—	—	—	—
Cuscuta spp.	—	—	—	—	1	—	—	—
Monarda fistulosa	—	—	—	—	—	—	—	—
Physalis heterophyla	—	—	—	—	—	—	—	—
Ambrosia sp.	—	—	—	—	1	—	—	—
Helianthus annuus	—	—	—	—	—	—	—	—
Nut spp. (shell)	0.6	0.3	0.2	0.1	0.6	0.1	0.1	0.1
Nut spp. (meat)	—	—	0.1	—	0.1	—	—	—
Unidentifiable gm.	0.1***	0.1	0.1	—	0.1	—	T	—
seeds	3	—	—	1	1	—	—	—
Unidentified seeds	3	—	2	—	—	—	1	—
TOTALS gm.	29.6	21.6	34.6	23.8	26.0	3.6	3.3	4.7
seeds	36	+55	29	4	+29	1	6	+11

130

	130	131	132	133	134	143	144	145
Catalogue no.	130	131	132	133	134	143	144	145
Feature no.	13	32	61	55	33b	80	48	27b
Stratigraphic Level	3	33	3	4	—	—	—	—
Sample volume	4	4	4	4	2¼	6	5	4¼
Charcoal	21.1	12.5	26.6	6.0	12.8	36.8	82.1	19.2
Juniperus virginiana	—	—	—	—	1fr	—	1fr	—
Graminae	—	—	—	—	—	—	1	—
Stipa sp.	—	—	—	—	—	1	—	—
Zizania aquatica	—	—	—	—	—	1	2	—
Zea mays	1	—	—	—	—	—	—	—
Scirpus sp.	—	—	—	—	—	—	—	—
Juglans cinerea	0.1	0.1	0.3	—	0.3	0.9	0.6	0.1
Juglans nigra	—	—	0.4	0.1	0.5	0.6	1.0	0.2
Carya ovata	1.5	0.7	3.9	0.2	3.7	27.9	3.4	4.1
Corylus americana	—	—	0.1	—	—	T	T	0.1
Quercus spp.	—	—	T	—	T	T	T	0.2@
Celtis occidentalis	1	—	1	T	—	—	1	T
Polygon pennsylvanicum	—	—	—	—	—	—	—	—
Chenopodium hybridum	2	20	30	—	7	34	6	10
Chenopodium album	—	—	10	1	1	2	—	2
Chenopodium spp.	—	15	102	4	22	27	10	10
Amaranthus spp.	—	1	—	—	—	1	—	—
Ranunculus sp.	—	—	—	—	—	—	—	—
Aquilegia columbia	—	—	—	—	—	—	—	—
Brassica spp.	1	—	—	—	—	—	—	—
Pyrus sp.	—	—	—	—	—	—	—	—
Lespedeza sp.	—	—	—	—	—	—	—	—
Strophostyles sp.	—	—	—	—	—	—	—	—
Rhus sp.	1	—	23	2	—	—	2	—
Hypericum sp.	—	—	—	—	—	—	—	—
Viola sp.	—	—	—	1	—	—	—	—
Apocynum sp.	—	—	—	—	—	—	—	—
Cuscuta spp.	—	—	—	—	—	—	—	—
Monarda fistulosa	—	—	—	—	—	—	—	—
Physalis heterophyla	—	—	—	—	—	—	—	—
Ambrosia sp.	—	—	—	—	—	—	—	—
Helianthus annuus	—	—	+3	—	1	—	1	—
Nut spp. (shell)	1.5	0.2	1.7	0.3	0.4	3.8	0.6	0.7
Nut spp. (meat)	T	—	T	—	0.1	0.2	0.1	0.1
Unidentifiable gm.	T	—	0.1	T	0.1	0.2	T	T
seeds	—	3	—	—	—	—	—	—
Unidentified seeds	—	—	2	—	—	—	2	1
TOTALS gm.	24.2	13.5	33.1	6.6	17.9	70.4	87.8	24.7
seeds	6	38	+171	8	31	66	25	23

131

Stratigraphic Level	8	33	16	20	9	1	4	Provenience
	4	5	4	3	4	2	2	ience
Sample volume	5	4	3¾	8	½	¼	¼	
Charcoal	28.2	10.8	38.2	20.5	11.7	7.6	0.5	
Juniperus virginiana	—	—	—	—	—	—	—	
Graminae	—	—	—	—	—	—	—	
Stipa sp.	—	—	6fr	—	—	—	—	2
Zizania aquatica	—	—	—	1	—	—	—	
Zea mays	—	—	—	1fr	—	—	—	
Scirpus sp.	—	—	—	—	—	—	—	
Juglans cinerea	0.5	—	0.8	0.2	—	—	0.1	
Juglans nigra	0.7	0.1	0.8	0.8	0.1	—	—	
Carya ovata	2.8	1.1	35.6	11.3	0.4	—	0.2	
Corylus americana	—	T	0.1	0.2	—	—	0.1	
Quercus spp.	—	T	0.2	0.1@@	—	—	—	
Celtis occidentalis	—	—	—	T	—	—	—	
Polygon pennsylvanicum	—	—	—	1	—	—	—	
Chenopodium hybridum	5	—	137	22	—	—	—	
Chenopodium album	—	—	9	1	—	—	—	
Chenopodium spp.	1	3	+204	10	1	—	—	
Amaranthus spp.	—	—	17	2	—	—	—	
Ranunculus sp.	—	—	—	—	—	—	—	
Aquilegia columiba	—	—	—	—	—	—	—	
Brassica spp.	—	—	1	—	—	—	—	1
Pyrus sp.	—	—	3	—	—	—	—	
Lespedeza sp.	—	—	1	1	—	—	—	
Strophostyles sp.	—	—	—	—	—	—	—	
Rhus sp.	—	—	1	4	—	—	—	
Hypericum sp.	—	—	—	—	—	—	—	
Viola sp.	—	—	—	—	—	—	—	
Apocynum sp.	—	—	25	—	—	—	—	
Cuscuta spp.	—	—	2	—	—	—	—	
Monarda fistulosa	—	—	1	1	—	—	—	
Physalis heterophyla	—	—	1	—	—	—	—	
Ambrosia sp.	—	—	—	—	—	—	—	
Helianthus annuuss	—	—	1fr	—	—	—	—	
Nut spp. (shell)	0.3	0.2	10.7	4.4	3.0	0.1	0.3	
Nut spp. (meat)	0.1	—	0.2	—	—	—	—	
Unidentifiable gm.	—	0.1	0.3	T	—	—	—	
seeds	1	—	—	—	1	1	—	
Unidentified seeds	—	—	4	1	—	—	1	
TOTALS gm.	32.6	12.3	86.9	37.5	15.2	7.7	1.2	2
seeds	7	3	+413	45	2	1	1	5

*cf. *Q. alba*; **unidentified nutshell utilized for C¹⁴ date; ***cf. bulb; fr=fragments;
f=fired area; b=bone pit; T=trace < 0.1; @cf. *Q. macrocarpa*; @@cf. red oak group

TABLE 7
Carbonized Seed Remains from General Squares

	73	76	83	84	95	96	163	198	216
Catalogue no.									
Square no.	102	86	104	115	116	104	86	105	102
Stratigraphic Level	3	4	5	3	3	4	3	4	4
Sample Volume	8	4	8	5	8	6	4	4	4
Charcoal	19.1	22.3	11.1	23.7	19.3	30.2	16.7	27.9	8.6
Juniperus virginiana	—	1	—	—	—	—	—	—	—
Stipa sp.	1&1fr	—	—	2fr	—	—	—	—	1fr
Zizania aquatica	—	—	—	—	—	1	—	1	—
Zea mays	1	—	—	—	—	—	—	—	1fr
Juglans cinerea	0.4	0.4	—	0.2	0.1	0.1	0.4	0.1	1.5
Juglans nigra	0.5	0.5	—	0.1	—	0.1	0.3	0.5	1.9
Carya ovata	5.0	2.0	0.2	3.5	0.5	1.0	2.1	1.0	4.8
Corylus americana	0.5	—	0.1	0.7	T	T	0.2	T	0.1
Ostrya virginiana	—	—	—	—	—	—	2	—	—
Quercus spp.	0.1	T	—	—	T	T	0.2*	0.3	0.1
Celtis occidentalis	—	17	—	—	—	—	5	—	—
Chenopodium hybridum	23	13	5	13	12	13	31	12	6
Chenopodium album	1	2	—	3	8	5	—	2	1
Chenopodium spp.	52	21	12	42	87	22	46	40	24
Amaranthus spp.	—	—	—	—	—	—	—	—	—
Aquilegia cf. *columbine*	—	—	—	—	—	—	—	—	—
Brassica spp.	—	—	—	—	—	—	—	—	—
Rhus sp.	5	1	—	5	—	—	2	—	2
Cuscuta spp.	—	—	—	—	—	—	—	—	—
Helianthus annuus	—	—	—	—	—	—	—	1	—
Nut spp. (shell)	2.9	1.0	0.1	2.2	0.4	0.4	0.7	0.6	2.7
Nut spp. (meat)	0.1	0.1	—	T	T	0.1	0.1	0.1	0.1
Unidentifiable gm.	0.1	0.1	T	0.2	0.1	T	T	T	0.1
seeds	2	—	—	1	—	—	—	—	—
Unidentified seeds	1	1	—	—	—	—	3	—	3
TOTALS gm.	28.7	26.4	11.5	30.6	20.4	31.9	20.7	30.5	19.9
seeds	87	56	17	66	107	41	82	56	38

	373	414	415	416	420	426	429	436	437
Catalogue no.									
Square no.	104	118	45	121	116	102	117	44	102
Stratigraphic Level	1-2	1-2	3	3	1-2	2	6-7	1-2	5
Sample Volume	3½	4	4	4	8	2	4	4	2
Charcoal	3.1	20.8	3.5	13.7	36.3	8.1	0.9	11.8	1.3
Juniperus virginiana	—	—	—	—	—	—	—	—	—
Stipa sp.	—	—	—	—	—	—	—	—	—
Zizania aquatica	—	—	—	—	—	—	—	—	—
Zea mays	—	—	—	—	1	2	—	—	—
Juglans cinerea	0.1	0.1	—	0.1	0.3	0.2	—	—	0.1
Juglans nigra	0.2	0.1	0.1	0.1	0.2	0.2	0.1	0.3	—
Carya ovata	0.7	1.9	0.1	0.7	1.8	1.6	0.1	0.4	1.1
Corylus americana	0.2	0.1	0.1	—	T	0.3	0.1	0.1	—
Ostrya virginiana	—	—	—	—	—	—	—	—	—
Quercus spp.	—	0.1	—	T	T	T	—	—	0.1**
Celtis occidentalis	—	—	—	—	—	—	1	—	—
Chenopodium hybridum	—	—	1	—	—	—	—	—	—
Chenopodium album	—	—	—	—	—	1	—	—	—
Chenopodium spp.	—	2	1	8	20	6	—	1	—
Amaranthus spp.	—	1	—	—	—	—	—	—	—
Aquilegia cf. *columbine*	1	—	—	—	—	—	—	—	—
Brassica spp.	—	1	—	—	—	—	—	—	—
Rhus sp.	1	—	—	—	2	—	—	—	—
Cuscuta spp.	—	—	—	—	—	—	—	—	—
Helianthus annuus	—	—	—	—	1	—	—	—	—
Nut spp. (shell)	0.1	0.8	0.2	0.6	0.6	0.3	0.1	0.2	1.0
Nut spp. (meat)	—	0.1	—	T	—	0.1	—	—	—
Unidentifiable gm.	—	0.1	T	T	—	T	—	T	—
seeds	+3	—	—	—	+10	—	—	—	1
Unidentified seeds	—	1	—	—	2	—	—	—	—
TOTALS gm.	4.4	24.1	4.0	15.2	39.2	10.8	1.3	12.8	2.6
seeds	+5	5	2	8	+46	9	1	1	1

fr=fragment; T=trace < 0.1; *cf. *Q. alba;* **cf. *Q. macrocarpa*

134

TABLE 8
Uncarbonized Seeds

Catalogue no.	Juniperus Fragments	Graminae	Phalaris sp.	Panicum capillare	Eleocharis spp.	Scirpus spp.	Ostrya virginiana	Polygonum sp.	Polygonum pennsylvanicum	Polygonum convolvulus	Chenopodium sp.	Chenopodium album	Chenopodium hybridum	Portulaca oleracea	Geum sp.	Rubus sp.	Euphorbia maculata	Rhus sp.	Lappula redowskii	Verbena hastata	Physalis heterophylla	Bidens cernua
36	—	—	—	—	—	—	—	—	—	—	—	—	—	—	—	—	—	—	—	—	1	—
44	1	—	—	—	—	—	—	—	—	—	—	—	—	—	—	—	—	—	—	—	—	—
56	3	—	—	—	—	—	—	—	—	—	—	—	—	—	—	—	—	—	—	—	—	—
57	—	—	—	—	—	2	—	—	—	—	—	—	—	—	—	1	—	1	—	—	—	—
58	—	—	—	—	—	—	—	—	—	—	—	—	—	—	—	1	—	—	—	—	—	—
64	—	—	—	—	—	—	—	—	—	—	—	—	—	—	—	—	—	—	—	—	1	—
73	—	1	—	—	—	4	—	—	—	—	—	—	—	—	—	—	—	1	—	1	—	—
74	—	—	—	—	—	—	—	—	—	—	—	—	—	—	—	—	—	3	—	—	—	—
76	—	—	—	—	—	—	—	—	—	—	—	1	—	—	—	—	—	—	—	—	1	—
81	1	—	—	—	—	—	—	—	—	—	—	—	—	—	—	—	—	—	—	—	—	—
83	—	—	—	—	—	—	—	—	—	—	—	—	—	—	1	—	—	—	—	—	—	—
84	16	—	1	—	2	—	—	—	—	—	—	—	—	—	—	—	—	1	—	—	—	—
92	2	—	—	—	—	—	—	—	—	—	—	—	—	—	—	—	—	1	—	—	1	—
95	1	—	—	—	2	1	—	—	—	—	1	—	—	1	—	—	—	—	—	—	2	1
96	1	1	—	—	—	—	—	—	1	1	—	—	—	—	—	—	—	—	—	—	—	2
100	2	—	—	1	—	—	—	—	—	—	—	—	—	—	—	3	—	—	—	—	—	—
101	—	—	—	—	—	—	—	—	—	—	—	—	—	—	—	—	—	3	—	—	—	—
117	—	—	—	—	—	—	—	—	—	—	1	—	—	—	—	—	—	—	—	—	—	—
118	1	—	—	—	—	—	—	—	—	—	—	—	—	—	—	—	—	—	—	—	1	—
122	1	—	—	—	—	—	—	—	—	—	—	—	—	—	—	—	—	1	—	—	—	—
130	—	—	—	—	—	—	—	—	—	—	—	—	—	—	—	—	—	—	—	—	1	—
132	—	—	—	—	—	—	—	—	—	—	—	—	—	—	—	—	—	3	—	—	—	—
133	1	—	—	—	—	—	—	—	—	—	—	—	—	—	—	—	—	—	—	—	—	—
143	—	—	—	—	—	—	—	—	—	—	—	—	—	—	—	1	—	—	—	—	—	—
144	—	—	—	—	—	—	—	—	—	—	—	—	—	—	—	—	—	1	—	—	—	—
153	2	—	—	—	—	—	—	—	—	—	—	—	—	—	—	1	—	—	—	—	1	—
163	3	—	—	—	—	—	2	—	—	—	—	3	—	—	—	1	—	3	1	—	5	—
373	2	—	—	1	—	—	—	—	—	—	—	—	1	1	—	—	—	2	—	—	1	—
414	6	—	—	—	2	—	—	—	—	—	—	—	1	2	—	1	1	—	—	—	1	—
419	1	—	1	—	—	—	—	1	—	—	—	—	—	—	—	—	—	5	—	1	1	—
420	—	—	—	—	—	—	—	—	—	—	—	—	—	—	—	—	—	1	—	—	—	1
426	—	—	—	1	—	—	—	—	—	—	—	—	—	—	—	1	—	2	—	—	1	—
436	—	—	—	—	—	2	—	—	—	—	—	3	—	—	—	1	—	1	—	1	1	—
437	2	—	—	—	—	—	—	—	—	—	—	—	—	—	—	—	—	—	—	—	—	—

Many of the uncarbonized chenopods also had a single "bite" removed from the margin of the seed, but unlike the hackberry pits, no carbonized chenopods showed such evidence of rodent feeding. Members of the genera *Peromyscus* (white-footed mice) and *Microtus* (meadow mice) are known to consume and cache quantities of seeds of many types (Jackson 1961:209-45). *Peromyscus* sp. is currently an occupant of Hadfields Cave.

Wood charcoal (Table 5) is weighted so heavily in favor of the red oak group that it is clear the occupants of 13JN3 were selecting this type for fires. The predominance of a few species of wood can be cited as a lesson on how man selectively exploits his environment and renders the task of paleoenvironmental and paleoecological reconstruction difficult. The extensive use of the red oaks (primarily *Quercus rubra* and *velutina*) for firewood is predicated on a relatively high availability of heat (BTUs) per unit of wood, slow burning, and the glowing coals produced in the combustion of this wood (Pond 1974:41-42). White oak and shagbark hickory rate slightly higher than the red oaks in the above three categories, but the nuts of these two species are potential food sources for man and are less likely to have been exploited extensively for wood. The 15 species evidenced in the carbon samples probably were collected largely as fallen limbs to supplement the red oak wood supply.

Environment

The reconstruction of paleoenvironments by utilizing macrobotanical remains from archaeological contexts is typically a hazardous and frustrating task. This is because the intense selectivity practiced by prehistoric peoples tends to preclude any use of relative species frequencies, the numbers which are usually employed to identify specific types of plant communities. For this study the typical habitats for all plants evidenced in the Hadfields flotation samples must be compared so that inferences can be drawn about the number and composition of plant communities surrounding the site.

If the seed lists are tabulated according to typical habitat, the breakdown is as follows: 12 woodland species, 3 species from openings and forest borders, a single species from low, wet areas, 3 species from prairies, and 8 species of wastes (that is, weeds). The wood charcoal can be grouped according to the forest community in which it achieves optimum importance (Curtis 1959:520-69): southern mesic forest—*Acer saccharum, Ulmus rubra, Tilia americana, Ostrya virginiana, Juglans cinerea*; southern xeric (dry) forest—*Quercus alba, Prunus serotina*; southern xeric (dry-mesic) forest—*Quercus rubra, Fraximus americana, Juglans nigra*; southern lowland (wet) forest—*Salix nigra, Populus deltoides*; southern

TABLE 9
Plant Descriptions

Species	Common Name	13JN3 Remains	Optimal Habitat	Season Available (fruit)
Juniperus virginiana	red cedar	wood and seed parts	limestone bluffs and dry woods	Sept.-Oct.
Stipa sp.	needle grass	seed awn	dry prairies and sands	mid-late summer
Zizania aquatica	wild rice	seeds	quiet waters	Sept.
Scirpus sp.	great bulrush	seeds	marshes and shallow water	rootstock: fall-spring seed: July-winter
Salix sp. or *Populus* sp.	willow poplar	wood	Southern hardwood (wet) forests	—
Juglans cinerea	butternut	seeds and wood	Southern hardwood (mesic) forests	Sept.-Oct.
Juglans nigra	black walnut	seeds and wood	Southern hardwood (dry-mesic) forest	Sept.-Oct.
Carya ovata	shagbark hickory	seeds and wood	oak openings and dry forests	Sept.-Oct.
Corylus americana	hazelnut	seeds	Southern hardwood (dry) forests	late summer-early fall
Ostrya virginiana	ironwood	seeds and wood	Southern hardwood (mesic) forests	summer
Quercus macrocarpa	burr oak	seeds	oak barrens and openings	late summer-fall
Quercus alba	white oak	wood and seeds	Southern hardwood (dry) forests	late summer-fall
Quercus spp.	"red oaks"	wood	Southern hardwood (dry-mesic) forests	—
Ulmus americana	white elm	wood	Southern hardwood (wet-mesic) forest	—
Ulmus rubra	slippery or red elm	wood	Southern hardwood (mesic) forest	—
Celtis occidentalis	hackberry	seeds and wood	Southern hardwood (wet-mesic) forest	autumn
Polygonum pennsylvanicum	heart seed	seeds	moist ground along streams, wastes, cultivated areas	autumn-spring

Chenopodium spp.	lamb's-quarters pigweed goose foot	seeds	wastes and disturbed areas	fall-winter
Amaranthus spp.	pigweed wild beet	seeds	wastes and disturbed areas	fall-winter
Ranunculus sp.	crowfoot	seeds	thickets, rich woods, clearings	rootstock: spring seeds: fall
Aquilegia columbia	wild columbine	seeds	rich woods	late summer
Brassica sp.	mustard	seeds	disturbed areas	fall
Pyrus sp.	crabapple	seeds	wooded slopes, thickets, bottoms	Oct. (first frost)
Prunus serotina	black cherry	wood	Southern hardwood (dry) forests	—
Lespedeza sp.	—	seeds	dry, open soil	fall
Strophostyles sp.	wild bean	seeds	river banks and sandy soils	late fall
Rhus spp.	sumac	seeds	dry, open soil	mid-summer-early winter sap: March
Acer saccharum	sugar maple	wood	Southern hardwood (mesic-wet) forest	
Tilia americana	basswood	wood	Southern hardwood (mesic) forest	—
Hypericum sp.	St. John's wort	seeds	thickets and woods borders	fall
Viola sp.	violet	seeds	open woods or prairies	—
Fraximus cf. *americana*	white ash	wood	Southern hardwood (dry-mesic) forest	—
Apocynum sp.	dogbane	seeds	thickets and woods borders	fall
Cuscuta sp.	doddler	seeds	dry-wet prairies and thickets	late fall
Monarda fistulosa	wild bergamot	seeds	open areas, prairies, sandy places	fall
Physalis heterophylla	ground cherry	seeds	dry open woods and clearings	fall
Ambrosia sp.	ragweed	seeds	prairies, openings, wastes	fall

Sources: Cooperrider 1962; Hartley 1966; Fernald 1950; Curtis 1959; Fernald and Kinsey 1958

lowland (wet-mesic) forest—*Ulmus americana, Celtis occidentalis*; oak openings—*Quercus macrocarpa, Carya ovata*; oak barrens—*Quercus velutina*.

A paleoenvironmental reconstruction can be aided by considering the physical nature of the North Maquoketa valley. The valley proper and its feeder gullies are V-shaped, narrow, and sharply distinguished from the rolling prairies above. Moisture collects in the valley and its intermittently running tributaries, so that the entire valley system, including its bluffs and feeder gullies, remains moist and protected from the drying winds and hot rays of the summer months. Conditions in plant habitats can range from soggy lowlands near the river, to the mesic conditions of the gallery forest slopes, and finally to the xeric bluff tops adjoining the prairie. Modern botanical distributions in the valley are reflective of these microenvironmental conditions; mature stands of maple, basswood, and red oak occur in the low areas and grade into mature stands of white oak, black walnut, and shagbark hickory on the bluff tops. Limited lumbering was undertaken about 50 years ago in the valley, but it was selective, and relatively natural forest climax conditions appear to have remained intact.

In many ways the modern distributions of forest communities in the valley are generally analogous to what the forest conditions must have been while the site was occupied, ca. A.D. 300 to 800. Returning to the seeds and charcoal, the presence of large quantities of hickory and black walnuts, as well as a few burr and white oak acorns, argues for a xeric forest, or Conrad's (1952:19-22) burr oak association, near the site. Other members of this forest community would have included the white ash, black cherry, and a member of the red oaks, *Q. velutina*. All are evidenced in the charcoal. This xeric oak forest community probably bordered on the prairie which covered much of prehistoric Iowa, and the three forest edge species of seeds from the site could have been found along the transition zone. As for the mesic regime, the sugar maple, slippery elm, basswood, ironwood, and butternut are typical members of the southern mesic forest community, or Conrad's red oak association (1952:18-19). The red oak is believed to have dominated the forest stands in the gully where Hadfields Cave is located. This portion of the valley is well watered and protected from the dry summer climate, yet it is sufficiently well drained to prevent saturation. The forests which currently border the river bottom proper are standing in wet to wet-mesic soils. This was undoubtedly the condition in the past, and charcoal from the site identified as hackberry, American elm, cottonwood and/or black willow represents a portion of this wet forest community, or Conrad's willow and elm associations (1952:15-18).

Because of the work of John T. Curtis and others in Wisconsin, it is not difficult to realize that in the above reconstruction we are dealing with a forest continuum (Curtis and McIntosh 1951; Curtis 1959:94-102). The forest continuum is presently and was in the past probably composed of the following: wet-mesic forests of the valley bottom at one extreme, the mesic forests of the talus slopes near the center of the continuum, and the xeric oak forests of the bluffs at the opposite end. The abrupt contours of the Maquoketa valley act as a foreshortening agent on this continuum, so that in many of the narrowest sections a complete transition from prairie through the forest continuum and back to prairie on the opposite side occurs within less than 1 mile. Of course, the finger-like feeder gullies greatly extend the forest and forest edge. In a reconstruction of Iowa's virgin forests from the first land survey documents (Fig. 57) great expanses of forests covered the river valleys and uplands in the ca. 40-mile-wide Driftless Zone in northeast Iowa (Conrad 1952:12). Much of the upland forest was composed primarily of xeric species—the burr, white, and black oaks, shagbark hickory, and black walnut. From the charcoal and seed remains at 13JN3 it is apparent that the cave's occupants relied heavily on wood from the dry-mesic and mesic forest communities and on plant food resources from the xeric oak forest and forest edge communities. Wood could have been gathered in the immediate vicinity of the cave. The nut resources, which account for nearly all of the evidence of the plant foods taken from this area, probably were gathered just above the site on the bluffs or within a few thousand feet of the site in the oak savannah adjoining the prairie. In the xeric oak forests and openings hickory and walnut trees would have been plentiful. Gathering a large quantity of these nuts probably would have required only a short day's labor for a family.

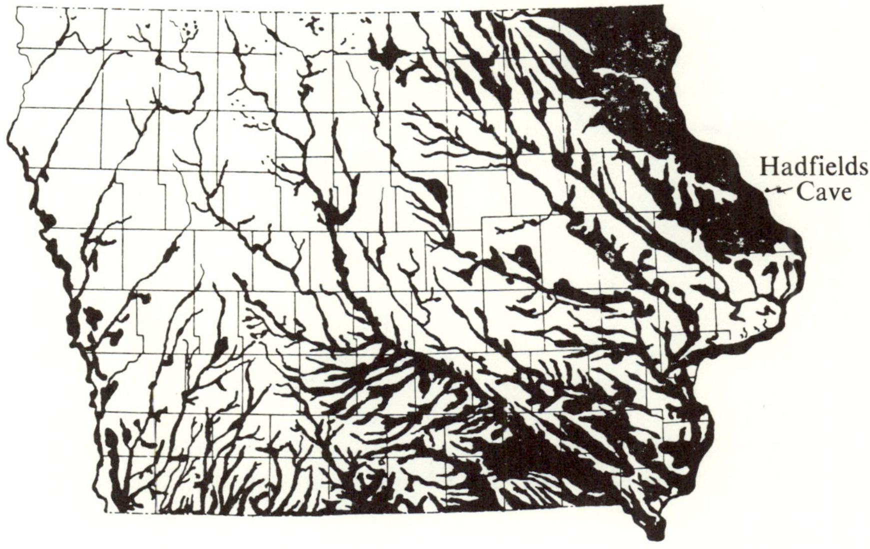

Fig. 57. Forests in Iowa prior to European settlement.

Agriculture

Domesticated crops, corn (*Zea mays*) and sunflowers (*Helianthus annus macrocarpus*), were evidenced in approximately one-third of the flotation samples. Only individual corn kernels and fragments were recovered, some of these being merely the endosperm of the seed. All of the kernels were too distorted by carbonization to provide useful measurements, but the robust shape of the most complete specimens suggests that they may have had traits found in Eastern Complex maize (cf. Ford 1973:190). Several fragments of sunflower seeds were also recovered, and three complete specimens (with achenes) measured 6 mm., 6 mm., and 9 mm. in length. All of the sunflower seed fragments appeared to have been as long and robust as the measureable ones. The apparent significance of seed size as it relates to sunflower domestication in aboriginal America has been discussed elsewhere (Benn 1974a). At the present time the sunflower is assumed to have been an aboriginal domesticate (cf. Struever and Vickery 1973:1205).

A total of 20 flotation samples contained corn or sunflower seeds, and three of these evidenced both. The associations and contexts for these 20 samples are summarized in Table 10.

From the preceding discussion it is clear that remains of corn and sunflower seeds are liberally sprinkled throughout midden attributable to the upper stratum, that is, the latter portion of the occupation. Corn and sunflower seeds from the lower stratum and stratigraphic contexts of apparently intermediate date raise the possibility that these cultigens were also present in small quantities during the early period of occupation. If we consider the fact that only a portion of the plant foods brought to the site were eventually carbonized and recovered in our screens, then the specimens described here would seem to suggest that domesticates, corn and sunflowers, were brought to this site frequently after A.D. 300.

It is difficult to judge the significance of these domesticates in the context of the Intermediate period between Middle and Late Woodland. Cutler and Blake (1973:6; cf. Struever and Vickery 1973:1213, 1215) have stated that corn has yet to be found in a dated context of this time period, but as Hall (1973:37) has indicated, the absence of such remains is probably a consequence of the general lack of carefully excavated, immediately post-Hopewellian sites in the Midwest. Despite this void of evidence for the A.D. 300-700 span, corn has been found in Middle Woodlands contexts in Illinois. These finds are summarized in Struever and Vickery (1973:1200): the Jasper Newman site (Moultrie County) with nine cobs having a mean row number of ten (Cutler and Blake 1969:133); the Peisker site (Calhoun County) with 12- and 14-rowed ears (Cutler and Blake 1969); the Macoupin site (Jersey County) with a 12-rowed ear, probably a flint or flour corn and not Northern Flint corn (Cutler and

Blake 1969). One of three reports of corn in Wisconsin comes from the Late Woodland Dietz site (Baerreis and Nero 1956; Cutler 1956), where the type of corn was found to be more similar to the older "Hopewell" corn than to Eastern Complex maize. Corn was also found in 13 of 17 samples from the "generalized" Woodland levels at the Brogley rock shelter near Platteville, Wisconsin (Tiffany 1974), and has been found in the Woodland component at the Boy Scout rock shelter near LaFarge, Wisconsin (Barbara Mead 1974: personal communication). The Brogley site also contained sunflower seeds of a relatively large size. No corn has been reported for Iowa prior to ca. A.D. 800, when it appears in quantity in the Great Oasis and Mill Creek Culture sites in the western two-thirds of the state.

TABLE 10
Flotation Samples from 13JN3

Catalogue No.	Square	Level	Feature	Corn Kernels	Sun-flower Seeds	Context Associations
198	105	4	—	—	1	lower stratum
216	102	4	—	1 fr.	—	lower stratum A.D. 295±65 (Wis-589)
117	—	5	78	+1	1 fr.	lower stratum
73	102	3	—	1	—	upper stratum
420	116	1-2	—	1	1	upper stratum
426	102	2	—	2	—	upper stratum
56	—	—	21	1 fr.	—	upper stratum
81	—	3	33F	1 fr.	—	upper stratum
92	—	—	66	1	—	upper stratum
101	—	3	53, 33	4 fr.	—	upper stratum
102	—	—	5F	—	1	unclear
126	—	3	35	+1	—	upper stratum
127	—	3	15	1	—	upper stratum
130	—	3	13	1	—	upper stratum
132	—	3	61	—	+3	upper stratum
134	—	—	33b	—	1	upper stratum
143	—	—	80	1	—	early-upper stratum
144	—	—	48	2	1	late-upper stratum
154	—	(4)	16	—	1 fr.	upper stratum A.D. 800±55 (Wis-597)
419	—	3	20	1 fr.	—	upper stratum

Other finds of corn are considerably more far-ranging, for instance, corn from Renner (23PL1; Wedel 1938:101) and the Lawson site (25PT12) in Nebraska (Kivett 1952:47), but they do not afford us a clear sequence of maize development in eastern North America. Hall (1973:36-38) and Struever and Vickery (1973) make it abundantly clear that an understanding of the development of Eastern Complex flint and flour

142

corns, the varieties best adapted to the northern United States, must ultimately come from the remains of corn grown prior to the Late Woodland period. The immediate barrier to our understanding of this development is an insufficient sample of corn from Middle Woodland contexts and the absence of corn from ca. A.D. 350-700. The Hadfields corn may be the first to fall in the latter period of time. However, the kernels from this site are wholly deficient as a data sample upon which a sequence of development can be built. The 13JN3 corn included only a single whole grain, the remainder being fragments. This grain is 5.8 mm. long and 6.6 mm. wide and appears in shape to be related to the Eastern Complex of flint and flour corn, but it was not possible to determine the row number.

The fact that the Hadfields site, as well as two rock shelters in Wisconsin (Brogley and Boy Scout), evidence corn fits well with the developmental steps proposed by Hall (1973:34-37) for Eastern Complex maize. Hall suggests three factors which may have contributed to the selective modification which produced corn adapted to the northern latitudes of the United States. First, Yarnell (1964:135-40, 150) has commented that many of the sites in the northeastern states which have produced cultigens are also located where the mean annual frost-free period is above the latitudinal average. The Mississippi trench, extending well above La Crosse, Wisconsin, is precisely such an area where the climate is ameliorated to such an extent that the growing season at La Crosse averages 34 days longer than in interior Wisconsin (USDA 1941:746; Yarnell 1964:127; Hartley 1966:11). As Hall indicates (1973:35), these protected extensions into the northern latitudes would have allowed prehistoric peoples to cultivate southern-adapted tropical flints far north of their optimal habitat. Extending these tropical flints northward could theoretically have brought about changes in the plants' photoperiodicity; that is, a plant would become adapted to the shorter nights and longer days of the northern latitudes as well as the shorter growing season (Hall 1973:29).

A second factor noted by Hall is that cooler, moister conditions of the Scandic climatic episode (Baerreis and Bryson 1965; Griffin 1960) may have selected for Eastern Complex corn characteristics in the tropical flints already being cultivated in the Midwest. One especially important characteristic of the Eastern Complex flints is their ability to germinate in the cool, moist soils of the spring season.

A third factor may be related to the apparent fragmentation of settlement patterns and social units in the post-Hopewellian Woodland period. Hall envisions a fractionalized settlement pattern at this time period that would have isolated a multitude of small corn plots from the generalized crossbreeding of wind pollination. The resultant inbreeding within corn plots on the northern limits of agriculture would have selected for the traits of the Eastern Complex flint corn, such as the need for early germination and rapid maturation (Hall 1973:37).

The tremendous numbers and general distribution of chenopods in the 13JN3 soil samples suggest that this plant was more to Woodland peoples than simply a seasonally exploited wild plant resource. A reconstructed estimate of the total carbonized chenopods in the site is about 300,000 (Tables 11 and 12), and this number is probably only a fraction of the total actually brought to the site for food. The number of seeds reconstructed here could have been gathered from about ten well-developed plants with very efficient threshing techniques (cf. Herron 1953). It is more likely, though, that we are seeing only the tip of the iceberg as it were, because at 13JN3 we seem to have evidence for a systematized use of *Chenopodium* seeds as a food source. In speculating on a source for the seeds we can probably discount the North Maquoketa valley. It is narrow and wooded today and does not supply extensive expanses of disturbed or waste area which is the habitat preferred by the chenopods (Cooperrider 1962; cf. Zawacki and Hausfater 1969). Rather, this writer believes that the chenopods are associated with the maize and sunflowers, and that all three were brought to the Hadfields site to be stored as winter food supplies. The chenopods probably were brought from summer villages where these Woodland people were cultivating small amounts of maize and sunflowers. Whether *Chenopodium* was actually being cultivated along with corn or simply was gathered from weedy plants around the village is virtually impossible to determine at present.

The argument for *Chenopodium* as a cultigen in the Midwest has been vigorously endorsed by Struever and Vickery (1973:1209; Struever 1968a:67-72) on rather flimsy archaeological evidence. Their case involves a few widely scattered finds of exceptionally large chenopod seeds (*C. hybridum gigantospermum*) found in Early Woodland contexts beyond their natural range, and the relatively frequent occurrence of this seed in several other Woodland sites in Illinois. But it is not clear in their argument whether it is the probability of cultivation or of domestication that is being advocated, although the latter is definitely implied. Yarnell (1965:79-80) has clearly documented the status of both terms. In domesticates we find morphological changes brought about by man; such changes render the plant and its products more advantageous than its wild ancestors. In addition, a domesticate is technically not able to survive beyond a few generations without the hand of man. Cultigens do not have to display any morphological changes from the wild form, but are simply plants which man protects from competition with other plants and may propagate within or beyond their natural range. In point of fact, as Yarnell notes, the only real difference between weeds and cultigens is their cultural context, and in the Eastern Woodlands many apparent cultigens are in fact also common weeds (for example, *Chenopodium* spp., *Helianthus* spp.).

TABLE 11
Estimated Feature Total of Carbonized Remains
(based on flotated remains from features)

Catalogue no.	Feature no.	Sample Size	Estimated Feature Volume	Volume Correction	Charcoal	All Nuts	Carbonized Seeds	C. ovata	J. nigra	J. cinerea	Nut spp.	Unidentifiable	Unidentifiable seeds	Unidentified	Chenopodium spp.
Fired Areas			1.		gm.	gm.		gm.	gm.	gm.	gm.	gm.			
49	65	41	7.32	1.83	36.7	9.1	50	0.4	0.1	0.1	8.0	0.1	0	5	44
64	10	2.5	1.6	1	24.4	1.9	7	0.7	0.3	0.7	0.1	0	1	0	7
65	53	2	2	1	6.4	0.4	1	0	0.1	0	0.2	0	0	0	1
74	60	6	6	1	29.7	10.0	43	7.1	0.2	0.7	1.7	T	0	1	34
81	33f	4	56.3	14.1	31.1	25.3	112	19.4	3.1	0.2	2.5	0.1	0	0	110
82	24	4	61	15.2	22.0	5.0	5	3.4	0.9	0.1	0.8	0	0	0	4
98	44	4	8.35	2.1	30.8	2.7	29	1.2	0.2	0.4	0.8	0.1	0	0	26
99	56f	4	30.1	7.5	12.6	0.7	13	0.4	0.1	0.1	0.1	T	0	0	13
101	51	4	72.4	18.1	45.2	37.5	264	24.9	1.0	1.3	8.8	0.1	0	2	255
102	57	4	30.8	7.7	20.8	7.9	20	6.4	0.4	0	0.9	0.2	2	5	15
103	27	8.5	12.8	1.5	38.0	10.9	72	8.1	0.1	0	2.5	0.1	0	0	69
104	72	4	10.5	2.6	0.9	0.7	0	0.5	0	0	0.1	0	0	0	0
110	45	4	5.77	1.44	1.5	0.2	0	0	0	0.1	0.1	0	0	0	0
111	70	4.75	4.75	1	17.6	0.7	2	0.4	0.1	0.1	0.1	0	0	0	2
118	34	4	18.1	4.5	26.1	3.5	31	1.8	0.1	0.9	0.6	0.1	3	3	27
120	25	4	11.7	2.9	17.5	4.1	50	3.3	0.1	0.3	0.3	0.1	0	0	44
121	38	4	4.92	1.2	31.5	3.0	26	1.8	0.3	0.6	0.2	0.1	0	2	23
126	35	4	5.9	1.5	21.6	4.3	28	2.4	1.0	0.2	0.6	0.1	1	0	22
127	15	4	40.16	10.1	2.8	0.9	1	0.3	0.1	0.2	0.1	0	0	0	0
130	13	4	30.1	7.5	21.1	3.1	5	1.5	0	0.1	1.5	T	0	0	2
131	32	4	5.58	1.4	12.5	1.0	36	0.7	0	0.1	0.2	0	3	0	35

132	61	4	4	1	26.6	6.4	168	3.9	0.4	0.3	1.7	0.1	0	2	142
133	55	4	6.58	1.65	6.0	0.6	8	0.2	0.1	0	0.3	T	0	0	5
146	5	5	7.4	1.48	28.2	4.3	6	2.8	0.7	0.5	0.3	0	1	0	6
153	39	4	18.6	4.6	10.8	1.5	3	1.1	0.1	0	0.2	0.1	0	0	3
154	16	3.75	14.7	3.9	38.2	48.2	409	35.6	0.8	0.8	10.7	0.3	0	4	+250
419	20	8	32.6	4.1	20.5	17.0	45	11.3	0.8	0.2	4.4	T	0	1	33
446	9	0.5	10	20	11.7	3.5	1	0.4	0.1	0	3.0	0	1	0	1
447	1	0.25	12	48	7.6	0.1	0	0	0	0	0.1	0	1	0	0
448	4	0.25	13.1	52.4	0.5	0.7	0	0.2	0	0.1	0.3	0	0	1	0
Pits															
37	75	7.5	15	2	16.4	3.3	9	2.4	0.1	0.25	0.5	0	0	0	7
44	50	7.5	7.5	1	14.8	2.5	4	1.8	0.1	0.1	0.5	0	0	1	2
50	54	9	9	1	63.5	21.3	125	18.5	0.4	0.4	1.9	0.1	8	0	123
58	40	4	40.4	10.1	16.0	3.1	11	2.2	0.1	0.2	0.6	0	3	0	11
92	66	27	27	1	74.9	7.7	84	3.8	0.9	0.7	1.8	0.1	0	2	+ 77
100	64	8	8	1	75.1	13.6	40	3.8	2.7	1.4	5.4	0.3	9	6	39
105	43	12	12	not considered due to laboratory accident											
106	56b	4	30.1	7.5	18.7	1.6	30	1.1	0.1	0.1	0.2	0	1	1	28
117	78	4	157.5	39.4	45.8	4.9	15	2.4	0.6	1.6	0.2	0.1	0	1	12
122	52	4	8	2	23.0	0.9	2	0.6	0	0.1	0.1	0	1	0	2
128	81	4	68.5	17.1	2.8	0.5	5	0	0	0	0.1	T	0	1	5
134	33b	2.5	2.5	1	12.8	4.9	31	3.7	0.5	0.3	0.4	0.1	0	0	30
143	80	6	12	2	36.8	33.3	66	27.9	0.6	0.9	3.8	0.2	0	0	63
144	48	5	5	1	82.1	5.7	22	3.4	1.0	0.6	0.6	T	0	2	16
145	27b	4.25	4.25	1	19.2	5.4	22	4.1	0.2	0.1	0.7	T	0	1	22
Miscellaneous															
36	30**	17	25.6	1.22	42.6	5.8		4.2	0.1	0.2	1.1	0.1	0	1	33
56	21	6	10.03	1.67	30.6	53.4		41.1	1.2	1.0	10.0	0.1	0	0	156
129	30@@	4	—	—	4.1	0.6		0.2	0.1	0.1	—	—	0	0	9

f=fired area; b=bone pit; T-trace; **Square 142; @@Square 134

TABLE 12
Estimated Site Total of Carbonized Remains
(based on general square flotated remains)

Catalogue no.	Square no.	Stratigraphic Level	Sample Size	Charcoal	All Nuts	Carbonized Seeds	C. ovata	J. nigra	J. cinerea	Nut spp.	Unidentifiable	Unidentifiable seeds	Unidentified seeds	Chenopodium spp.
			1.	gm.	gm.		gm.	gm.	gm.	gm.	gm.			
73	102	3	8	19.1	9.4	83	5.0	0.5	0.4	2.9	0.1	2	1	76
76	86	4	4	22.3	3.9	38	2.0	0.5	0.4	1.0	0.1	0	1	36
83	104	5	8	11.1	0.4	17	0.2	0	0	0	T	0	0	17
84	115	3	5	23.7	6.65	63	3.5	0.1	0.2	2.2	0.2	1	0	58
95	116	3	8	19.3	1.1	107	0.5	0	0.1	0.4	0.1	0	0	107
96	104	4	6	30.2	1.7	41	1.0	0.1	0.1	0.4	T	0	0	40
163	86	3	4	16.7	3.9	81	2.1	0.3	0.4	0.7	T	0	3	77
198	105	4	4	27.9	2.5	56	1.0	0.5	0.1	0.6	T	0	0	54
216	102	4	4	8.6	11.1	34	4.8	1.9	1.5	2.7	0.1	0	3	31
373	104	1-2	3.5	3.1	1.3	2	0.7	0.2	0.1	0.1	0	3	0	0
414	118	1-2	4	20.8	3.8	4	1.9	0.1	0.1	0.8	0.1	0	1	2
415	45*	3	4	3.5	0.5	2	0.1	0.1	0	0.2	T	0		8
416	121	3	4	13.7	1.5	8	0.7	0.1	0.1	0.6	T	0	0	7
420	116	1-2	8	36.3	3.0	24	1.8	0.2	0.3	0.6	0	10	2	0
426	102	2	2	8.1	2.6	9	1.6	0.2	0.2	0.3	T	0	0	1
429	117	6-7	4	0.9	0.4	0	0.1	0.1	0	0.1	0	0	0	0
436	44*	1-2	4	11.8	1.0	1	0.4	0.3	0	0.2	T	0	0	20
437	102	5	2	1.3	1.3	0	1.1	0	0.1	1.0	0	1.0	0	2

T=trace

	Sample Volume	Estimated Site Volume	Total Remains (gm.)				
			C. ovata	J. nigra	J. cinerea	Nut spp.	Chenopodium Cheno spp.
Back Squares	78.5 1.	39,900 1.	28.0	4.8	4.1	14.5	508 seeds
Front Squares*	8.0 1.	9,590 1.	0.5	0.4	0.1	0.4	28
	Correction Factor		Estimated Site Total Remains (gm.)				
Back Squares	X509		14,252	2,443.2	2,086.9	7,380.5	258,572
Front Squares	X1196		598	478.4	119.6	478.4	33,488
	Est. Totals (gm.)		14,850	2,921.6	2,206.5	7,858.9	292,060
	Est. # Nuts		23,386	1,119	604	12,376	seeds
	Est. gm. Meat		31,922	2,575	768	16,894	175.24
	Est. Calories		228,240	17,301	5,213	120,789	

For each feature the grams of nuts multiplied by the correction factor gives:	Total Remains (gm.)				
	C. ovata	J. nigra	J. cinerea	Nut spp.	Chenopodium spp.
Est. Site Totals (gm.)	1,411.05	129.59	123.96	445.14	8,651 seeds
Est. # Nuts	2,222	49.7	34	701	
Est. gm. Meat	3,033	114.2	43.2	956	5.19 gm.
Est. Calories	21,687	767	293	6,842	

148

Returning to the Hadfields site, it is this writer's belief that chenopods are associated with the maize and sunflowers. In light of the frequent occurrence and time depth for *Chenopodium* in the Woodland period it seems reasonable that, by the time Hadfields Cave was occupied in the Late Woodland period, this plant would have been cultivated along with domesticates. Here *cultivation* implies protection from competition by undesirable plants and possible propagation by spreading seed in a suitable location. This system of raising both domesticated plants and "weeds" is analogous to Struever and Vickery's (1973:1211) "simple mud-flat horticulture," which they hypothesize was an "important feature" of Hopewellian development in the Illinois River valley (Struever 1964, 1968a). The *Chenopodium* plant is peculiarly adapted to this type of relatively casual cultivation, since the plant produces copious terminal inflorescences and retains seeds long after the first hard frost. The plant's seeds could have been easily gathered and would have been available for a long period beginning in September when the corn was ripe (Fernald and Kinsey 1958:177).

Ethnobotany

Ethnographic accounts are virtually the only source of information about the uses of certain plant resources by the American Indian. This is especially true for the hundreds of herbal concoctions employed by the Indian to cure an assortment of physical ailments as well as various deviate conditions of the mind. The most useful accounts are the compilations of plant usages made by ethnobotanists working with Indian groups in the final stages of the dissipation of their aboriginal culture in the late nineteenth and early twentieth centuries. The value of these reports for archaeologists is that they provide data on the various possible uses of a particular plant. Hopefully such a data pool will show specific instances of a plant's use which can be located in an analogous archaeological context.

The ethnobotanical accounts of plant usages are summarized in Table 13 for each plant evidenced at 13JN3. This listing is not intended to be comprehensive of all the available literature as many references are highly repetitious. In addition, it is not necessarily implied that these are the uses to which the plants from the Hadfields site were put. As has been indicated, many species found in small amounts at the site may have been introduced by rodents.

Of specific interest is the seed evidence for hemp, *Apocynum*. The stems of this plant were one important source of fiber for making cordage, a material utilized to decorate and produce the Hadfields pottery. Yarnell (1964:92) states that largely whole plants were collected when mature, thus creating the possibility of transporting the plants' seeds to a site where the processing for cordage took place. The importance and popularity of this and other sources of cordage for aboriginal peoples in the Midwest probably should not be underestimated, although they are not frequently evidenced in the flotation samples. Early historic period accounts of the Huron and Petun culture (Hunt 1967:43, 56) indicate that they were cultivating *Apocynum* for the production of thread to make fishnets. The Huron also collected nettles (*Urtica* spp.) and during the winter "wove collars . . . made sacks, and from the hemp raised for them by the Petuns they made fishnets" (Hunt 1967:59).

Ethnographers' observations of Indian groups in Wisconsin and Iowa are more explicit about the use of plant fibers for technological purposes. The Menomini employed basswood (*Tilia americana*) and slippery elm (*Ulmus rubra*) bark fiber, cedar bark (*Juniperus virginiana*), or rotting nettle fiber (*Urtica* sp.) to weave storage and corn hulling bags (Skinner 1921:232; Hoffman 1896:260). They also used yarn made from buffalo wool (Hoffman 1896). The Ioway (Skinner 1926: 286) made bags of basswood or nettle fiber in addition to utilizing buffalo wool for the same purpose. The Sauk used nettle, basswood, and cedar bark to make bags. A single tiny fragment of carbonized thread was recovered in a flotation sample from 13JN3. This fragment is a Z-twisted thread composed of between 8 and 12 fibers. It is approximately 1 millimeter in diameter and appears to be made of some type of mammal hair.

The remaining plant species and their uses, as described in Table 13, are self-explanatory. To conclude this section on paleoethnobotany, it should be emphasized that the preceding data and discussions view cultural behavior from only one aspect, the utilization of selected plant species. A better understanding of plant uses may be achieved by studying several aspects of the subsistence cycle. This broader purpose is undertaken in the following three sections.

Analysis of Dental Cementum in White-tailed Deer

Archaeologists are continually in search of new techniques which will provide a more complete understanding of prehistoric conditions. In this case we are borrowing the technique of counting cementum annuli in white-tailed deer teeth from the wildlife ecologists (cf. Benn 1974b). A wide range of population and age distribution studies of the white-tailed deer (*Odocoileus virginianus*) is available in the literature of this discipline, providing a solid understanding of modern deer which can be applied to archaeological remains of this species.

TABLE 13
Hadfields Site Ethnobotany

Species	Common Name	13JN3 Remains	Uses	Sources
Juniperus virginiana	red cedar	wood and seed parts	fruits for medicine leaf smoke inhaled bark for weaving	Gilmore 1919 Yarnell 1964:186
Stipa sp.	needle grass	seed awn	stem and leaves for brushes	Gilmore 1919
Zizania aquatica	wild rice	seed	grain provides food	Jenks 1900; Smith 1923, 1928, 1932, 1933
Scirpus sp.	great bulrush	seed	tubers eaten stems woven into mats	Densmore 1928:293 Smith 1923:74; 1933:112
Salix sp. or *Populus* sp.	willow or poplar	wood	fiber made into cordage	Yarnell 1964:187-88
Juglans cinerea	butternut	seeds and wood	seed for food and dye	Smith 1923:68, 1928:259, 1932:405, 1933:103
Juglans nigra	black walnut	seeds and wood	seed for food black dye from root	Smith 1928:259 Gilmore 1919
Carya ovata	shagbark hickory	seeds and wood	seeds for food wood for tools	Smith 1928:259, 1932:419
Corylus americana	hazelnut	seeds	food and medicine dye	Smith 1932:397, 1923:63 Densmore 1928:289
Ostrya virginiana	ironwood	seeds and wood	seeds eaten when starving medicine for kidney	Fernald and Kinsey 1958:152 Densmore 1928:291
Quercus spp.	burr, white and red oaks	seeds and wood	seeds for food after leaching tannin medicine	Densmore 1928:320 Yarnell 1964:69-70

Species	Common name	Part	Use	Reference
Ulmus americana	white elm	wood	medicine	Smith 1933:86
Ulmus rubra	slippery or red elm	wood	wood cambium used for medicine laxative and cordage	Smith 1932:392, 1933:86 Gilmore 1919
Celtis occidentalis	hackberry	seeds and wood	berries for food	Smith 1928:265
Polygonum pennsylvanicum	heart seed	seeds	seeds for medical beverage	Smith 1923:47; Densmore 1928:291
Chenopodium spp.	lamb's-quarters, pigweed, goosefoot	seeds	seeds for food medicine leaves as greens	Harrington 1967:57, 69, 234; Johnson 1962; Fernald and Kinsey 1958:177; Smith 1933:47, 98, 1928:209; 1923:28
Amaranthus spp.	pigweed, wild beet	seeds	leaves for potherb seeds for food	Fernald and Kinsey 1958: 184-85
Ranunculus sp.	crowfoot	seeds	medicine, dye	Smith 1933:75, 123, 1932:426
Aquilegia columbia	wild columbine	seeds	medicine from root perfume from crushed seeds	Smith 1932:383 Gilmore 1919
Brassica sp.	mustard	seeds	leaves as potherb, seeds for seasoning	Fernald and Kinsey 1958: 216
Pyrus sp.	crab apple	seeds	fruits for food	Smith 1928:263
Prunus serotina	black cherry	wood	medicine for food from berry	Smith 1923:71, 1932:385, 1933:77
Lespedeza sp.	—	seeds	tea and medicine	Gilmore 1919
Strophostyles sp.	wild bean	seeds	seeds may have been eaten	Fernald and Kinsey 1958: 256

Rhus spp.	sumac	seeds	beverage and medicine leaves smoked dye	Fernald and Kinsey 1958:256 Yarnell 1964:180 Smith 1932:424
Acer saccharum	sugar maple	wood	sugar from sap	Smith 1923:61, 1932:394, 1933:93
Tilia americana	basswood	wood	bark fiber for cordage	Smith 1923:76, 1933:114; Densmore 1928:293
Hypericum sp.	St. John's wort	seed	medicine	Smith 1923:37, 1933:60
Viola sp.	violet	seeds	medicine	Smith 1932:392, 1933:87
Fraximus (americana)	white ash	wood	technology	Yarnell 1964:190
Apocynum sp.	dogbane	seeds	medicine fiber for cordage	Smith 1932:354, 1933:38 Yarnell 1964:191
Cuscuta sp.	doddler	seeds	orange dye	Gilmore 1919
Monarda fistulosa	wild bergamot	seeds	medicinal beverage	Smith 1923:39
Physalis heterophylla	ground cherry	seeds	berries eaten	Smith 1928:264
Ambrosia sp.	ragweed	seeds	leaves as medicine	Gilmore 1919

The nature of cementum annuli has been admirably summarized by Klevefal and Kleinenberg (1969). They state that cementum consists of yearly deposits of calcium and organic substances on the roots of many animal teeth. In white-tailed deer these deposits are characterized by two annular rings: (a) a wide, nontransparent band composed of several organic compounds and relatively little calcium (hypocalcified); (b) a narrow, transparent band with a high calcium content (hypercalcified) and lower in organic compounds (Klevefal and Kleinenberg 1969:13-33). The narrow, "winter" band is deposited during the cold season for ungulates in the Midwest (Low and Cowan 1963; Ransom 1966; Gilbert 1966).

Klevefal and Kleinenberg (1969) also describe a variety of annular layers found in teeth and bones representing nearly every taxonomic family of vertebrates presently living in North America. Although this study will deal only with deer, many genera recovered from archaeological sites exhibit annular growth rings. With the proper foresight during excavations it should be possible to recover a variety of animal types which would pinpoint seasonal harvesting of animals. Among the animals which could be considered are the beaver (*Castor*), vole (*Microtus*), muskrat (*Ondatra*), woodchuck (*Marmota*), bear (*Ursus*), mink (*Mustela vison*), and others.

For nearly a decade cross-sectioning and counting of these rings has been utilized by game biologists to determine age at death of modern deer populations. Age determination by cementum rings has been found to be consistently more reliable for deer in all types of environments than the traditional age estimates by degree of tooth wear developed initially by Severinghaus (1949). While rates of tooth eruption and wear may vary considerably according to individual animals and their diets, the deposition of cementum is relatively regular and consistent throughout the life of deer. In addition, wear aging has been viewed as somewhat unreliable in animals older than five years (Gilbert 1973:46).

The potential usefulness of annuli in teeth has been emphasized for archaeologists by Saxon and Higham (1969) and more recently by Gilbert (1973). The advantages of this technique for analysis of midwestern fauna are clear. First, the jaws and teeth of white-tailed deer are commonly among the most numerous and best-preserved bones to be found, and thus we are assured of adequate samples from many sites. Secondly, cementum ring counts are more reliable than wear aging of jaw fragments for establishing age composition of prehistoric deer harvests. Most importantly, cementum annuli provide an estimate of the season of death for each animal analysed, thereby permitting an estimate of the seasonal occupation of a site.

Materials and Methods

Sources cited here described two teeth in the jaw of white-tailed deer which provide the best cementum annuli: the first incisor, $I_{\overline{1}}$, and first molar, $M_{\overline{1}}$. The first incisor has been used most frequently (Low and Cowan 1963; Gilbert 1966; Erickson and Seliger 1969), but this tooth passes though one-quarter inch screen and is less frequently recovered. Also, incisors are rarely found in place in the jaw, while the first molar usually is. The cementum of first molars in modern deer has been studied by Ransom (1966), apparently with the same results as those achieved by others on incisors. Ransom (1966) and Gilbert (1966) found that annular cementum ring counts in captive deer of known ages were nearly identical to their real ages. The problem confronted in this experiment is whether first molars from archaeological deer will also produce identifiable annular rings that compare favorably with wear ages previously determined from the same teeth.

The sample of teeth from the Hadfields site utilized for this study consists of 22 lower left first molars, all of which were removed from jaw fragments for processing. All but four had been wear aged using the Severinghaus method (1949) before removal from the jaw (Table 14; see also Fig. 61). Wear aging was entirely unreliable on four molars because these jaw fragments contained only one or two teeth, including the first molar.

The method used to process the first molars for cementum rings follows the procedure outlined by Erickson and Seliger (1969) with some modifications. Molars were carefully removed from the socket with pliers and a dissecting needle, exercising care not to chip or crack any part of the root. Each tooth was then marked with its site catalogue number to introduce as much anonymity into the processing as possible. Counting cementum rings can be difficult and occasionally somewhat subjective, and it was felt that for this experiment the cementum should be studied without knowing the exact wear age of each tooth. The molars were then embedded in bio-plastic, a casting resin, to support the tooth structure as it was being sectioned. Embedding involved forming a small mold of aluminum foil, pouring a thin film of catalyzed resin into the mold, allowing this to set slightly, positioning one or more teeth in the mold, and then filling the mold with a catalyzed resin until the teeth were completely covered. An advantage of the resin is that it is clear, and therefore sectioning of the teeth can be carefully planned after the teeth are mounted.

When the resin had thoroughly hardened, the molds were cut into blocks, each containing a molar. Blocks were cut in such a way as to produce two parallel faces: one sectioning the tooth from which cementum lines were to be read, and the other for resting on the microscope table. Cutting was done on a small table saw with a diamond blade of thickness .040 inches. After considerable experimenting, it was found that a longitudinal section, medially (anterior to posterior) through the molars, removing about one-third of the tooth, produced the largest exposure of cementum. This exposed face was then ground and polished on a series of carborundum grits of decreasing sizes (320, 14, 3 microns). The working face was reground as many times as necessary to produce readable cementum rings. Before viewing, the molar face was wetted with ethylene glycol (commercial antifreeze), which sharpened the image of the rings under magnification (X100 to X160). A stain, Alizarin Red S, was applied to several teeth to sharpen seasonal ring contrasts, but this was entirely unsuccessful.

TABLE 14
Tooth Aging on M_1 of *O. virginianus*

Catalogue no.	Wear Age	Ring Age	w-r=d	Season of Death	Production Time	Comments
					(min.)	
163 (3)	—	5.0	—	end of winter	45	—
194	—	(4.0)	—	(winter)	35	obscure lines
195	—	3.0	—	end of winter	55	—
230	—	3.0	—	end of winter	35	—
10 (1)	2.5	2.0	+0.5	end of winter	50	—
10 (2)	6.5	7.0	-0.5	winter	60	obscure lines
36	1.0	0.5	+0.5	early winter	35	—
66	6.5	7.0	-0.5	winter	—	—
134	2.5	1.5	+1.0	fall	45	M_1
162	5.5	5.0	+0.5	winter	—	—
163 (1)	3.0	3.5	-0.5	fall	55	—
163 (2)	3.5	5.0	-1.5	end of winter	60	—
197	2.0	2.0	0	end of winter	80	obscure lines
200	4.5	5.0	-0.5	end of winter	30	—
206	7.5	9.0	-1.5	winter	25	—
211	2.5	2.0	+0.5	winter	—	—
232	6.0	5.5	+0.5	fall	35	—
243	3.0	4.0	-1.0	winter	—	—
245	6.5	8.0	1.5	winter	70	obscure lines
256	5.5	3.5	+2.0	fall	45	—
259	1.0	1.0	0	end of winter	45	—
265	6.5	9.0	2.5	winter	60	—

$$\bar{x} = 48 \text{ min.}$$
$$\bar{d} = -0.25 \text{ years}$$
$$SS = 21.25$$
$$var. = 1.18$$
$$st.dev. = 1.08$$
$$S_d = 0.256$$
$$t_d = -0.9765$$
$$C1_1 = -0.79$$
$$C1_2 = 0.29$$

Results and Discussion

Annual growth rings were found in some portion of the cementum in all 22 molars sectioned for this study. However, not all of the teeth produced rings which were clear and continuous. The molars of older animals tended to have more obscure rings, and many of these sections had be be reground a number of times. There are several explanations for vague rings, the most important being that tooth cementum is normally very thin and becomes increasingly irregular as the animal grows older. Also, it has been suggested that changes in metabolism during the rutting season or when the animal is sick may result in additional "false" lines appearing among the seasonal rings (Low and Cowan 1963:469).

The microphotograph (Fig. 58, cf. Fig. 59) accompanying this discussion shows a series of cementum rings which are typical of many of the teeth sectioned for this experiment. In this specimen the dentine/cementum interface is not visible, since the photograph was taken with transmitted light. Winter rings appear light and summer rings dark like the dentine under transmitted light. The illustration indicates that this animal was just completing its seventh year of growth and was killed during the winter. The seventh winter ring is thin and very light in the photograph.

A statistical summary of the molars sectioned is presented in Table 14. If we assume that the ring ages shown in the table are reliable indicators of an animal's real age, then the relatively close agreement of ring and wear ages is encouraging for those utilizing the Severinghaus method only. It should be noted that almost all of the molars sectioned were taken from jaw fragments containing two to four molars and pre-molars, not the usual complement of seven in the lower jaw. Thus we should expect to find wear ages differing in some cases from the ring ages, since wear aging depends on a comparison of the degree of wear among several teeth in a jaw. The differences between wear and ring ages of 18 molars were subjected to an analysis of variance, presented at the bottom of Table 14. The differences between wear and ring ages were found to be non-significant at the .05 level ($t_d = .9765$). Therefore, it seems clear that any inferences about aboriginal deer harvests at this site would be the same using either aging method. However, the mean of the differences ($\bar{d} = -0.25$) and the slightly skewed confidence limits ($1_1 = -0.79$ and $1_2 = 0.29$, for the .05 level) suggest that there is a tendency to underestimate the real age of a deer using the Severinghaus wear aging method. This is especially true of animals older than five years.

Probably the most striking results appear in the column headed Season of Death. By carefully determining the nature of the outermost (youngest) ring in the cementum it is possible to estimate in which part of the year the animal died. In the Hadfields sample of left first molars all animals had been killed at some point during the formation of a winter ring, unmistakably identifying this site as a fall/winter/early spring, seasonal occupation.

Fig. 58. Microphotograph of deer tooth cementum.

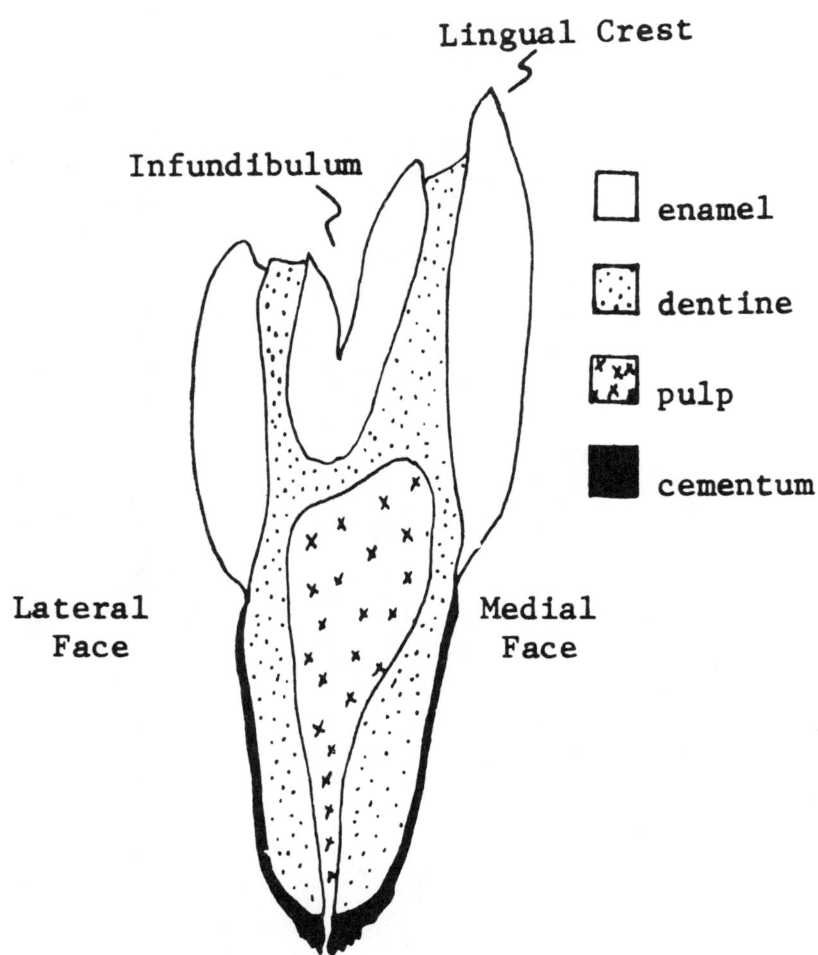

Fig. 59. Cross-sectional view of a deer tooth.

An age composition curve for the Hadfields deer has been constructed (Fig. 60) for comparison with a small number of such curves already published. The Hadfields sample is small and probably should only be considered for the general trends it shows. The ages of these 22 deer have a wide disparity, but there is a moderate concentration of individuals between the ages of two and five years. Of greater interest, however, is that 27% of this sample lies between the ages of five and a half and nine years. This contrasts with present-day age compositions of deer harvests for the one week deer hunting season in the Midwest. Modern hunters usually kill large numbers of young deer—over 25% of the kill population is typically only one-half year old—and very few animals survive to their fifth year today (Elder 1965).

Elder (1965:369) has postulated that pre-contact Indians may have practiced a certain amount of conservation with young white-tailed deer, allowing them to mature and develop better hides and more meat. As evidence for population conservation he cites age compositions from Eschelman (Guilday et al. 1962) and three Missouri sites (Elder 1965), all of which show large numbers of deer in the two-to-six-year age range. Early historic Indian middens, however, seem to show a trend toward the killing of larger numbers of younger animals, possibly as a result of the introduction of firearms and the opening of new meat markets to Europeans (Elder 1965). But the age distribution found by Pillaert (1969: 100) at the Millville site, a Middle Woodland village in Grant County, Wisconsin, is identical to those described by Elder for the early historic Indian middens in Missouri. Therefore, additional judgments concerning aboriginal conservation tactics probably should be withheld pending the development of more age compositions for deer harvests for prehistoric middens.

Another alternative to the Elder hypothesis has been presented by Bruce Smith (1974a). He suggests that, because the age composition of deer harvests made by wolves is precisely opposite that for prehistoric Indians (that is, large numbers of fawns and old adults), as predators, humans and wolves ". . .apparently concentrated on almost mutually exclusive segments of the deer population" (1974a:37). He suggests, in other words, that because the wolves were killing many fawns, this youngest age class was not available to man in large numbers. Smith does not discuss what impact selective hunting for substantial meat sources and high quality skins (both of which are best found in deer two to five years of age) may have had on the age composition of the harvest. Until we can establish whether prehistoric hunters actually were selective of particular traits in animals, we cannot know what impact other competing predators such as wolves had on man's hunting behavior.

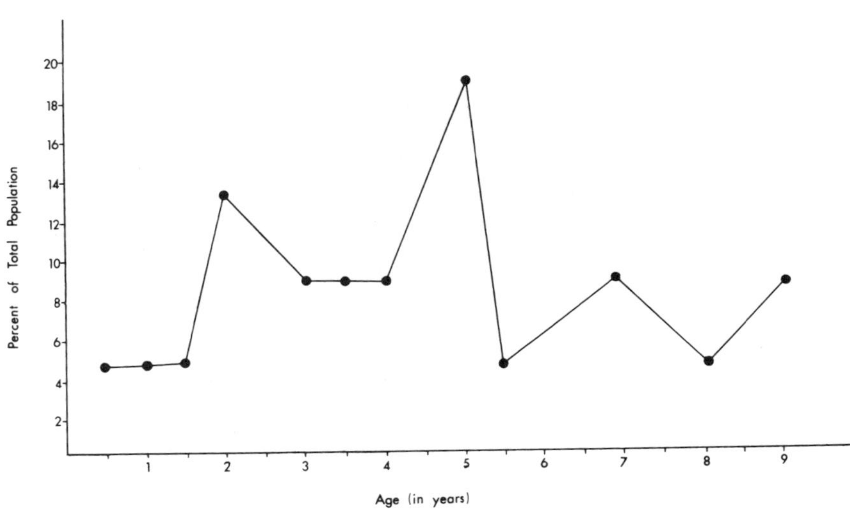

Fig. 60. *Age composition of white-tailed deer found at 13JN3.*

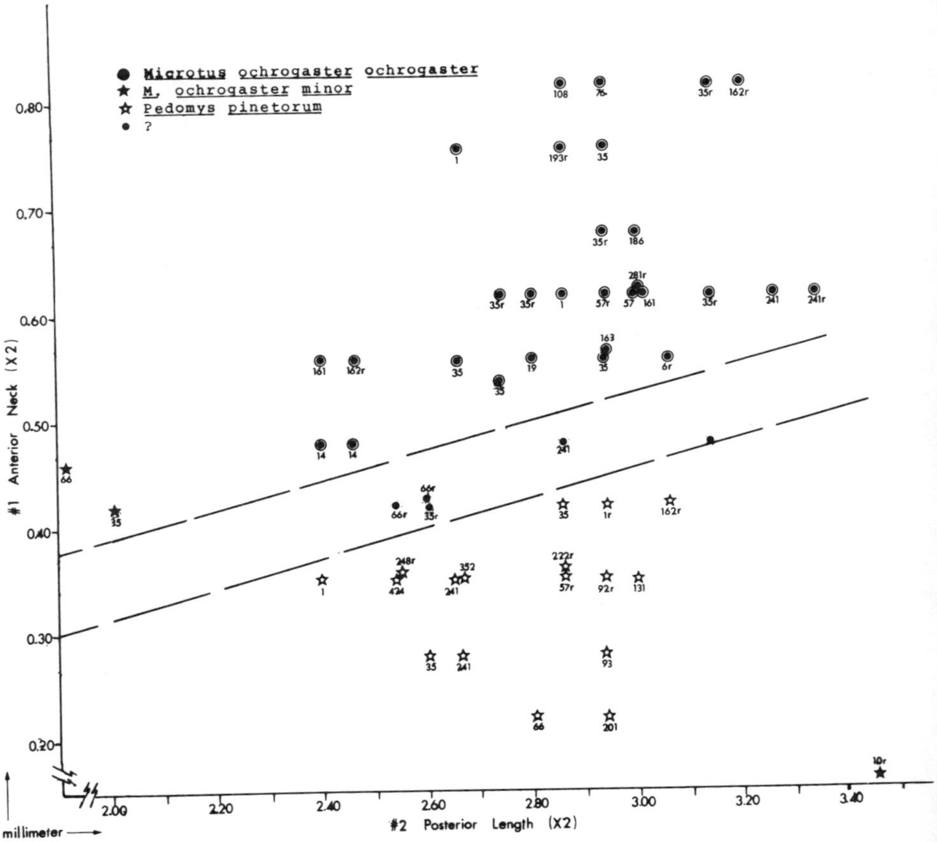

Fig. 61. *Microtine identification based on M_1 measurements.*

Seasonality

The Hadfields site was probably inhabited by small bands of transitory peoples; therefore, it is imperative that the seasons in which the site was occupied be identified. Determinations of seasonal occupation are nearly always dependent on deposits of floral or faunal material in good contexts. Even in sites where such material is recovered, only a few organisms with the qualities of seasonal sensitivity may be present. The greatest problem encountered in pinpointing seasonality, and for that matter in all paleoenvironmental studies, is that of man as a cultural filter for all material recovered by archaeologists. The people who created a particular site also tended to mix the natural stratigraphy they deposited. They also brought in organisms foreign to that environment, carried others away, and disposed of quantities of plant and animal remains in their middens in ratios not necessarily representative of the natural ecological conditions around the site. Thus, in developing seasonal or environmental inferences it is wise to avoid using negative evidence and to collect a broad range of variables which are independent of each other.

The technique of reading cementum annuli in the teeth of prehistoric white-tailed deer as an absolute test for seasonality is presented here for the first time in the Midwest. The term *absolute* is employed because, with further refinements in the techniques used by the writer and with the testing of other types of animal teeth and bones, the annual growth cycles of several animals could be cross-correlated for many sites with very little subjectivity. The results of sectioning all 22 left lower molars identified from 13JN3 have been discussed (Table 14). By identifying the outermost annual ring on each tooth it was determined that all of the deer were killed in the period between the fall and spring of the year. To be more specific, the winter ring in all of those specimens was in one of three stages of growth: a) fall—a winter ring had not yet been started but a fully developed summer band had been laid down; b) early winter or winter—some portion of the winter band was present; or c) late winter to spring—a full winter band was present but no sign of the new summer band had yet developed. The nature of the winter band is not fully understood, but Low and Cowan (1963) have indicated that it is deposited as a result of the harsh climate and sparse food conditions of this season. In east-central Iowa such conditions would correspond to a period beginning during October and ending in April.

All other potential sources of seasonal information for 13JN3 have been studied, but as time is always the limiting factor in these types of analyses, the remaining evidence follows more familiar lines of research. Alone, these traditional approaches to spotting seasonal habitations are frequently subjective; that is, they depend on negative evidence, or they are not comprehensive enough to describe an entire component. However, when they complement similar inferences based on deer teeth annuli—and

162

hopefully in future studies fish bone and mussel shell growth rings—the ultimate conclusions about seasonality are all the more powerful.

Birds are important seasonal indicators in almost any site. Many have migratory habits which are highly regularized by locations and movements in annual cycles. In many species the female bird deposits excess calcium, or medullary bone, in bone cavities immediately prior to developing and laying her eggs. The latter character, however, is difficult to spot in prehistoric bone collections due to variations in preservation and the thoroughness of laboratory washing procedures. A chart (Table 15) has been prepared to illustrate the seasonal availability of several species of birds found at 13JN3. The Passeriformes have been excluded from Table 15 because of the questionable nature of identifications and their problematical utilization by man. Of the birds listed, roughly one-half are migrants, and the remainder are permanent residents in the area around the site. Nearly all of the migrants, except the passenger pigeon and occasionally the mallard, are not present in the Hadfields area during the summer, but they winter in this area or pass over the site on their spring and fall migrations. Virtually all of the birds represented here could have been taken in the fall, winter, or spring, and many of the migratory birds would not have been available in the summer. However, these seasonal availabilities are not sharply definable. Hadfields Cave lies at a peculiar latitude where the modern summer and winter ranges of several migratory species of birds overlap. In addition, there were considerably larger numbers of every type of bird prior to the arrival of Europeans in the New World, and their ranges were probably much wider than we know them to be today.

Seasonal information is occasionally available when death interrupts the natural growth of mammals. Antlers on the male deer are grown and shed annually and are potential indicators of seasonality. Antlers begin development in April or May and are thoroughly hardened by November. They are usually shed between mid-December and late January (Jackson 1961:414-15). Of five bucks evidenced by crania at 13JN3, three were killed in the fall, as their antlers were developed and had not been dropped, and two died during the winter or very early spring, since their antlers had only recently dropped (Table 16).

Several other animals were found to be immature and had been killed at stages of growth which under normal circumstances would identify them as winter or spring kills. The absence of extremely young animals, however, should not be construed to mean that the site was not occupied during the summer, since very young animals were ordinarily not taken by Indians. The following animals in the Hadfields collection were noted at the juvenile stage of growth: turkey—two, great horned owl—one, beaver—two, bison—one. Young turkeys are hatched in the late spring while great horned owls are hatched in late winter. The three juvenile birds were taken during the first winter of their lives. Beavers are born in late May or June,

TABLE 15
Seasonal Availability of Birds

Common Name Species	FALL	WINTER	SPRING	SUMMER
Loon *Gavia immer*	transient	resident	transient	rare
Swan *Olor* sp.	transient	resident	transient	
Canada goose *Branta canadensis*	transient	resident	transient	
Mallard *Anas platyrhynchos*	transient	resident	transient—rare	rare
Green-winged teal *Anas carolinensis*	transient		transient	
Common golden eye *Bucephala clangula*		resident		
Merganser *Mergus merganser*		resident		
Redtailed hawk *Buteo jamaicensis*	resident	resident	resident	resident
Prairie chicken *Typanuchus cupido*	resident	resident	resident	resident
Ruffed grouse *Bonasa umbellus*	resident	resident	resident	resident
Bobwhite quail *Colinus virginianus*	resident	resident	resident	resident
Turkey *Meleagris gallopavo*	resident	resident	resident	resident
Passenger pigeon *Ectopistes migratorius*	resident—transient	rare	transient—resident	resident
Great horned owl *Bubo virginianus*	resident	resident	resident	resident
Saw-whet owl *Aegolius acadica*	resident	resident	resident	resident
Long-eared owl *Asio otus*	rare	resident	rare	rare

*after: Dent 1923, 1925, 1932, 1937, 1938, 1946; Gromme 1963;
     Scott 1972; Sprunt 1955.
Key: transient | | | | | | | | | | | | | |
         resident ::::::::::::::::::::::::
         rare — — — — — — — —

TABLE 16
O. virginianus **Remains—**
Identification of Sex

Site Catalogue no.			
57	Lt. frontal and cut antler bases	M	fall
66	Lt. frontal	F	—
92	Frontals and parietal	F	—
196	Lt. frontal and antler of immature individual	M	late fall
200	Frontals and parietal fragments	?	—
227	Frontals, parietal, posterior nasal, and cut antler bases	M	winter
244	Lt. frontal and cut antler bases	M	winter
247	Rt. frontal and antler base	M	winter
259	Rt. cut antler base	M	late fall
261	Frontal fragments	F	—

Minimum counts   Males=5
Females=3

and the two represented here are small enough to have been killed in the winter or spring following their births. Bison are born in April, May, or June, and the specimen at 13JN3 was taken in the spring at the end of its first year of growth.

Botanical remains are notoriously poor seasonal indicators and in most cases should only be relied on as supplemental devices. One problem of botanical data is that it is difficult to identify the origin, whether human or rodent activity, of all remains, carbonized or not. Another major problem is that practically every plant resource—seed, tuber, or fruit—can be preserved by some means of processing and stored for many months. Thus, a plant part may have been consumed or carbonized several months after it was gathered. Despite these problems the seed data from 13JN3 are relatively uniform in reflecting a fall occupation. A review of the season of availability (Table 9) demonstrates this most effectively. Large quantities of nuts were collected in September and October by the cave's residents and were undoubtedly stored for winter food reserves. Practically all of the remaining seed species are also available during the fall although many are hard, dry seeds which can survive several seasons of weathering before decomposing or germinating. Only one species of fleshy fruit was evidenced, *Pyrus* sp. (crab apple). Some ethnographic accounts state that it is possible to dry and store fleshy fruits, but many were simply collected and eaten when they were in season.

The presence of five species of turtles raises a number of questions concerning potential occupation of the site in those months not predominantly cold. All of the turtle species represented here hibernate most of the winter and would normally not have been available to man in these cold months. All of them could have been taken in September, October, late April, and May as well as in the summer. Three of the turtles—*Terrapene ornata, Chrysemys picta,* and *Emys blandingii*—had been modified into utilitarian items and may have been brought to the site in this condition.

To summarize, it is clear that Hadfields Cave was occupied during the fall, winter, and spring months. No single example of evidence contradicts this conclusion, although there is evidence of several organisms which are also available in the summer months. The fall season is represented by independent evidence from several different types of organisms: birds, seeds, and deer. This is the only season for which there is justification for estimating the time of initial annual occupation. The site probably was regularly inhabited sometime in the month of September, for this is when nut resources are usually most abundant. Evidence for occupation during the winter and spring months stems from deer teeth, other seasonal indicators of the time of death, and bird remains. The specific limits for inhabiting the cave during these two seasons are unknown.

These conclusions are utilized to construct a hypothetical seasonal procurement cycle in Chapter 6.

Dietary Reconstruction

This section represents a foray into an undeveloped region of archaeological reconstruction; however, it is only one of several such researches which are presently under way. Most notably, Lathel Duffield (1974) has discussed the advantages and some proposed methods for comparing the contributions to the aboriginal diet of various animal resources using calories rather than pounds of meat as the basic unit of measure. He points out that the protein and caloric contents of various animals differ considerably, and that the use of meat weights does not provide an accurate account of every animal's contribution to the diet.

For the Hadfields material the caloric method of analysis has been chosen so that the contribution of plant foods to the diet could also be included. The obvious advantage of this approach is that we can now make quantitative comparisons between some of the plant and animal food remains recovered. Such comparisons, however, are made using minimum counts of faunal and floral remains. We have no way of determining how much of the faunal and floral food remains was not preserved or was not recovered in our excavations. At Hadfields Cave shortcomings inherent in prehistoric biological remains were partially redeemed by the protection from weathering which the cave affords to the site, the near-perfect preservation of bone, and the extensive use of microrecovery techniques which ensured a sufficient sample.

The sample to be considered in the diet reconstruction consists of all identified mammal, bird, fish, and turtle bones, the freshwater mussels, and three kinds of nuts. The remaining seed remains were so sparsely represented that their caloric contributions are insignificant. It was clear, however, that even before minimum counts were calculated the sample was biased in favor of hard remains like bone. Due to the somewhat destructive nature of the method by which the carbon was recovered, flotation, that is, seeds are probably underrepresented. In addition, the manner by which foods were processed for consumption left some for permanent deposition, others with only a representative sample of what was eaten, and still others with no permanent record. For instance, bones with marrow were usually broken, but careful recovery and identification of as many different elements and fragments as possible probably provides a reasonable representation of what was consumed. But the same does not hold for the nuts utilized as food. Although all nutshell would have been discarded as inedible, nutshell requires carbonization to survive in prehistoric contexts. Certainly, not all of the discarded nutshell was carbonized, and we have no way at present of estimating what percentage of the nuts actually consumed were finally recovered in a carbonized condition. Finally, cultigens are probably grossly underrepresented at 13JN3 where they were being consumed but not processed. To be more precise, the maize, sunflowers, and chenopod seeds were probably brought to this site from a summer agriculture village. Cultigens probably arrived already processed (hulled, winnowed, and parched) and would have required only cooking or grinding and baking to be consumed. Thus, the opportunity for carbonization and preservation may have been infrequent.

It is necessary to determine the minimum numbers of each vertebrate and freshwater mussel species before estimates of available meat can be derived. Minimum counts for this study were found using White's (1953) criteria, the most widely utilized method at the present time. This involves using the largest count of any single element from one side of the animal as the minimum number of individuals present. White's method was further modified here to account for glaring age differences. Age differences are indicated when both a left and right of the same element come from different individuals. Therefore, in a few cases the minimum count of a species is higher than the count of any one element for one side. The minimum counts for mammals, birds, and turtles were then converted to total pounds of usable meat using figures for live weights and percent of usable meat (Tables 17, 18, and 19). The average live weight and usable meat percentage for each specie are somewhat less than are standard in the literature. Therefore, the estimates used in the present calculations were taken from a wide range of faunal studies (White 1953; Pillaert 1969; Duffield 1970; Lippold 1971). The estimates of fish weights were calculated for each specimen by utilizing a growth curve (cf. Figure 62) and the element occurring most frequently and in the best condition (Tables 20-25, cf. Figs. 63-65). The freshwater mussels were likewise measured for volume using growth curves constructed with the size and corresponding weight ranges given in Parmalee and Klippel (1974).

Tables 11 and 12 document the calculations used to arrive at an estimate of the weight of nut meat for the entire site, although the soil samples contained only a small portion of the site's volume. In these calculations the weight of nutshell found in each feature was multiplied by the proportion of soil not sampled from that feature. In this way an estimate of how much nutshell was in the entire feature was obtained (Table 11). The same procedure was followed for the general control level soil samples (Table 12), although the totals of the nutshell taken from the front and rear sections of the site were multiplied by the proportion of unsampled soil for each section. For the general level calculations, the site was divided into two sections—the front one having less midden accumulation than the rear—so that a more accurate extrapolated estimate could be obtained. After the weight of carbonized nutshell for the entire site had been calculated, the conversion to total available nut meat was accomplished using the following conversion factors developed for this study:

Hickory (*C. ovata*)	charred nutshell	.635 gm/nut
	dried meat	1.365 gm/nut
Butternut (*J. cinerea*)	charred nutshell	3.65 gm/nut
	dried meat	1.27 gm/nut
Walnut (*J. nigra*)	charred nutshell	2.61 gm/nut
	dried meat	2.30 gm/nut

The category Nut spp. in Table 12 was converted to grams of nut meat and calories using the conversion factors for hickory, since nearly all of the fragments assigned to this group appeared to belong to *C. ovata* but were too small to be realistically identified. Finally, the chenopods were changed to a total weight for the entire site using the conversion for *C. album* in Earle and Jones (1962).

The conversion from the weights of foods to their caloric equivalents (Table 26) is not intended to duplicate the aboriginal diet. There are several reasons for this, one being that this site is being treated as one unit and not as a series of seasonal occupations scattered over a 500-year span.

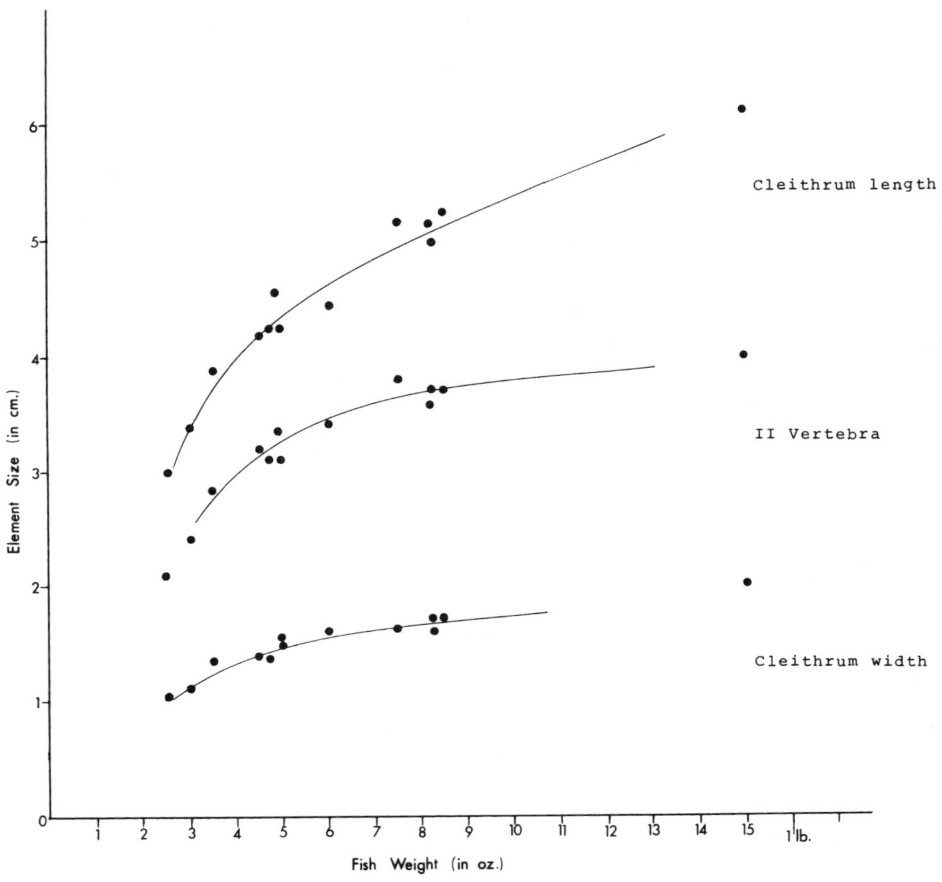

Fig. 62. Growth curve for black bullheads (Ictalurus melas).

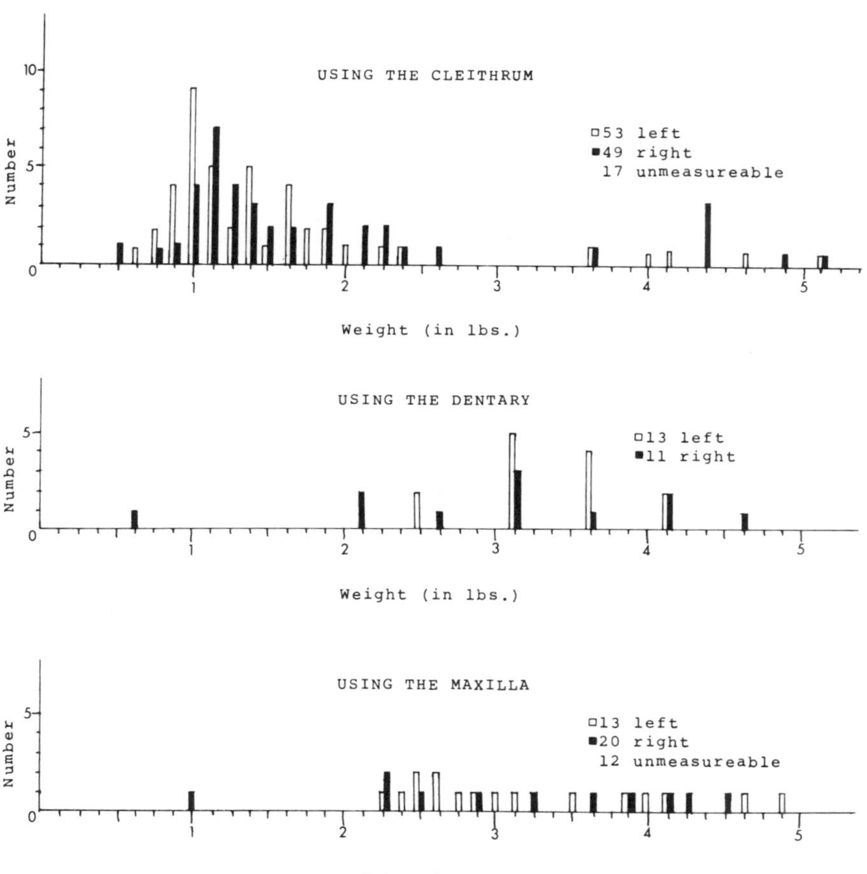

Fig. 63. Moxostoma *sp. size estimates.*

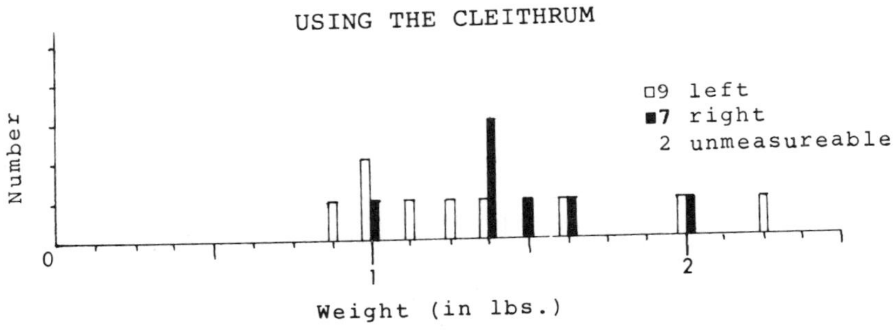

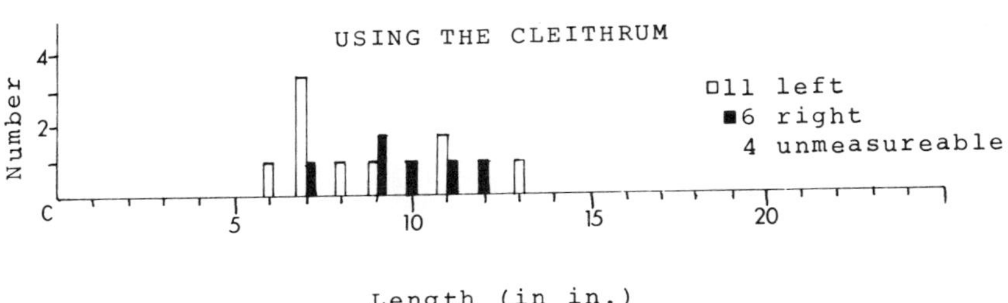

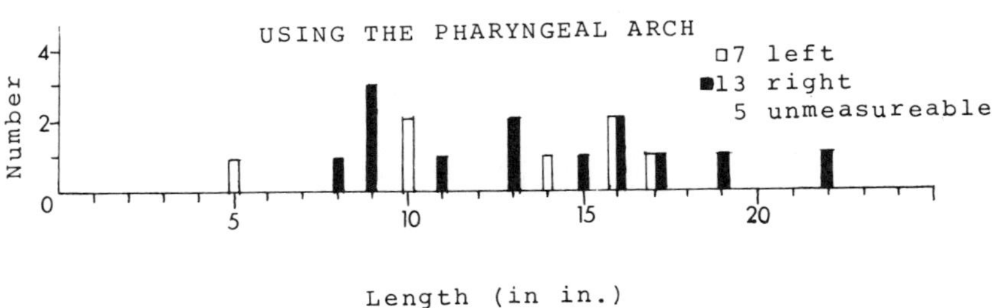

Fig. 64. Hypentelium *sp. size estimates.*

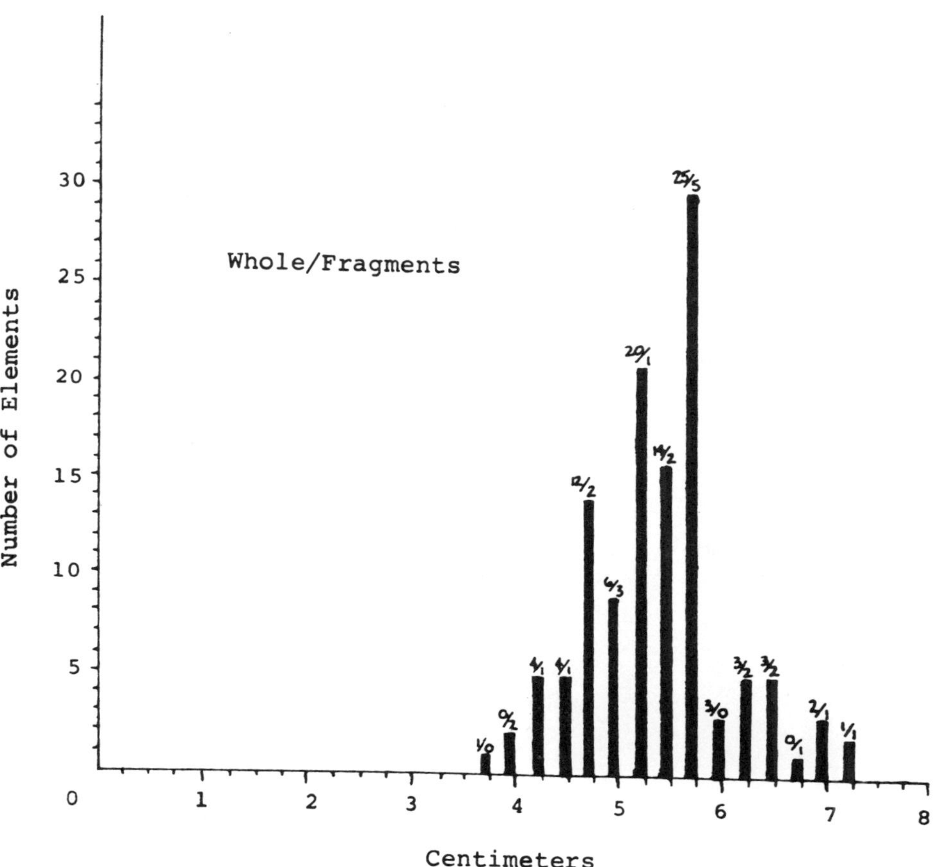

Fig. 65. Cyprinidea *sp. size estimates.*

TABLE 17
Available Meat from Mammals

Species	Total Elements	Minimum no.	Average Live Wt.	Usable Percent	Meat (lbs.)
Didelphis marsupialis	17	1	12	70	8.5
Sylvilagus floridanus	122	8	3.5	50	14
Marmota monax	45	6	8	70	33.6
Sciurus carolinensis	236	21	1	50	11.5
Sciurus niger	74	8	3	50	12
Tamiasciurus hudsonicus	6	2	(1)	50	1
Glaucomys volans	2	1	.5	70	.35
Geomys bursarius	111	11	1	70	7.7
Castor canadensis	96	5	55	70	192.5
Ondatra zibethicus	32	3	3	70	3.3
Erethizon dorsatum	4	1	15	70	10
Canis lupus	5	1	60	50	30
Canis latrans/familiaris	117	4	25	50	50
Vulpes fulva	5	1	8	50	4
Ursus americanus	80	2	300	70	420
Procyon lotor	93	8	25	70	140
Mustela vison	6	2	1.5	70	2.0
Taxidae taxus	6	1	18	70	12.5
Mephitis mephitis	25	4	7	70	19.6
Lutra canadensis	4	1	18	70	12.5
Lynx rufus	11	1	30	50	15
Cervus canadensis	18	1	700	50	350
Odocoileus virginianus	2516	26	200	50	2600
Bison bison	4	1	400*	50	200
TOTALS	3635	120			4118.05

*one-year-old individual

TABLE 18
Available Meat from Birds

Species	Total Elements	Minimum no.	Average Live Weight (lbs.)	Usable Percent	Meat (lbs.)
Gavia immer	4	1	7.0	70	4.9
Olor sp.*	2	1	—	—	—
Branta canadensis	7	1	8	70	5.6
Anas platyrhynchos	1	1	2.5	70	1.75
Anas carolinensis	1	1	13 oz.	70	9 oz.
Bucephala clangula	8	2	1.3	70	1.8
Mergus merganser	7	1	3.0	70	2.1
Buteo jamaicensis	8	1	2.75	70	1.9
Tympanuchus cupido	180	12	2.1	70	18
Bonasa umbellus	19	3	1.5	70	3
Colinus virginianus	5	1	6 oz.	70	4 oz.
Meleagris gallopavo	138	8	12	70	68
Ectopistes migratorius	161	26	1.5	70	26
Bubo virginianus	25	2	2.8	70	4
*Strix varia**	2	1	—	—	—
*Asio otus**	2	1	—	—	—
*Aegolius acadica**	2	1	—	—	—
Passeriformes not considered					
TOTALS	572	64			137.9

*bones are made into tools
**probably not utilized for food but instead taken for body parts

TABLE 19
Available Meat from Turtles

Species	Total Elements	Minimum no.	Usable Meat Per individual (lbs.)	13JN3 (lbs.)
Chelydra serpentina	21	1	5	5
Terrapene ornata	138	7	1	7
Chrysemys picta	46	4	1	4
Emys blandingii	52	3	*	*
Trionyx sp.	6	1	2	2
TOTALS	263	16		18

*represented by turtle shell bowls only

TABLE 20
***Ambloplites rupestris* Size Estimates**
(based on cleithrum measurements*)

Length in.	Length cm.	Elements left	Elements right
3-		—	—
	-8	—	—
½	-9	—	—
—		1	1
4-	-10	—	1
—	-11	—	—
—		1	—
—	-12	—	—
5-	-13	—	1
—	-14	1	1
—		—	2
—	-15	—	—
6-	-16	—	1
—		—	—
—	-17	—	—
—	-18	1	—
7-		—	—
—	-19	—	—
—		—	1
—	-20	—	—
8-		—	—
indeterminant		1	—
TOTALS		5	8

*length measured as average of three cleithrum
measurements: spine width (1st-3rd), cleithrum
width, posterior length.

TABLE 21
Micropterus dolomieui Size Estimates
(based on cleithrum width measurements)

Length		Elements	
in.	cm.	left	right
5-		—	—
	-13	—	1
½	-14	—	—
	-15	—	—
6-	-16	—	—
	-17	—	—
	-18	—	—
7-	-19	—	—
	-20	—	—
		—	—
8-	-21	—	—
	-22	—	—
	-23	—	—
		—	—
9-	-24	—	—
	-25	—	—
	-26	—	—
		—	—
10-	-27	—	—
	-28	1	—
	-29	—	—
		—	—
11-		—	—
indeterminant		1	—
TOTALS		2	1

TABLE 22
Ictalurus cf. *melas* Size Estimates
(based on cleithrum measurements)

Left			Right		
Cat. no.	Fragments	Weight (oz.)	Cat. no.	Fragments	Weight (oz.)
11	X	1.25	261		1.25
			12	X	1.5
95	X	1.75	163		1.75
219	X	2.5	187	X	2.5
239	X	2.5	188	X	2.5
257	X	4.75			
5		12.75 TOTALS	5		9.5

TABLE 23
Ictaluridae Size Estimates
(based on cleithrum and II vertebra measurements)

Cleithrum			II Vertebra		
Cat. no.	Fragments	Weight (oz.)	Cat. no.	Fragments	Weight (oz.)
248	X	1.25			
434	X	1.25			
1	X	1.5			
93	X	1.5			
117	X	1.5			
14	X	1.75			
35	X	1.75			
100	X	1.75			
135	X	1.75			
241	X	1.75			
241	X	1.75			
331	X	1.75	205	X	1.75
14	X	2.0			
66	X	2.0			
100		2.0			
246		2.0			
263		2.0			
323	X	2.0			
253		2.25	66	X	2.25
2		2.5	566	X	2.5
6		2.5			
220		2.5			
			12	X	2.75
			36	X	2.75
			77	X	2.75
			241	X	3.0
22		41.0 TOTALS	7		17.75

TABLE 24
***Catostomus* sp. Size Estimates**
(based on cleithrum measurements)

Size (lbs.)	Numbers left	right		Size (in./cm.)		Numbers left	right
-0				-1	-1		
—				—	-5		
—				—			
—				—	-10		
—				-5			
—				—	-15	1	
—	1	2		—		1	4
—		1		—	-20	3	2
-1	3	2		—			1
—	1			—	-25	1	1
—	1	3		-10			3
—		1		—	-30	1	
—		1		—			
—		2		—			2
—	1			—	-35		
—		1		—			
-2				-15			1
—		1		—	-40		
—				—			
—				—	-45		1
—				—			
—				—	-50	1	(probably)
—				-20		underestimated)	
—				—	-55		
—				—			
-3				—			
—	1	1		Broken		1	2
—	(probably under-estimated			TOTALS		9	17
—							
—							
—							
Broken	1	2					
TOTALS	9	17					

TABLE 25
Available Meat from Fish

Family/Species	Site Minimum Count	Minimum no. Measurable	Weights
Lepisosteidae	1	0	
Catostomidae	28	0	
Catostomus sp.	19	16	25 lbs. 6 oz.
Moxostoma sp.	57	40	75 lbs. 8 oz.
Hypentelium sp.	14	9	13 lbs. 10 oz.
Cyprinidae	128	125	31 lbs. 4 oz.
Ictaluridae	27	22	2 lbs. 4 oz.
Ictalurus sp.	5	5	12 oz.
Centrarchidae	3	0	—
Micropterus dolomieu	3	negligible	
Ambloplites rupestris	8	negligible	
TOTALS	293	217	148 lbs. 8 oz.

Therefore, we are not dealing with a single complete diet in this reconstruction but rather with a generalized model which accounts for the relative differences in the utilization of the major food sources for as many as three seasons (fall, winter, spring). A second reason is that the various bones and seeds have reached this analysis through differing and nonequivalent processes of preservation. This has been discussed in previous paragraphs. Thirdly, standard calorie conversion factors (in calories/100 grams) are available for only a limited number of plant and animal species. Among those which are available, very few have both the raw and cooked caloric values. The calorie conversions used for this study were taken from Bradley (1942), McCance and Widdowson (1947), Canadian Department of National Health and Welfare (1951), Watt and Merrill (1963), and Parmalee and Klippel (1974).

Table 26 is a summary of the diet reconstruction for 13JN3. This chart has been calculated for raw foods only because of the lack of caloric conversion factors for the cooked flesh of fish, many birds, and the mussels. Certainly much of the flesh eaten by aboriginal peoples was cooked, and the heat of cooking usually breaks down living tissues and releases a large number of calories for human consumption. However, the several means of cooking (boiling, roasting, steaming, etc.) also produce differing numbers of calories for the same species. Since we do not have enough information on how all of the kinds of foods were processed in the past, and as we do not possess sufficient calorie conversion factors, it seemed prudent to leave this study with the raw food values.

Considering the number of qualifications outlined thus far, there would appear to be grounds for criticizing the potential usefulness of Table 26. But the table has been developed as a vehicle for comparing the dietary contributions of major groups within the environment—land animals, birds, seeds, and so on—and was not intended to be used for comparisons between specific species. The caloric counts appearing in this reconstruction must be viewed as the *lowest* estimates which can be made from the material recovered. It would not be unreasonable to suggest that the calorie count for animal foods could be one-quarter again as large if we had recovered the remains of every animal utilized at this site. As for the seed remains, there is really no way of determining how much of this material was never carbonized. It would not be surprising if the estimate for this study was five or ten times too low.

The flesh of the white-tailed deer (*Odocoileus virginianus*) dominates all other foods in the reconstructed diet with a representation of 48.2%. The remaining mammals provide 32.1%, making a total of 80.3% for all mammals. If we also account for the other products made from these animals—skins, tools from bone and sinew, oil from the fat—the contribution of deer and other mammals to the survival of these Woodland peoples cannot be overestimated. The birds total only 3.6% of the overall calorie count, most of this coming from the turkey (*Meleagris gallopavo*), passenger pigeon (*Ectopistes migratorius*), and prairie chicken (*Tympanuchus cupido*). From birds came other items as well, such as feathers for decoration and utensils, bone for tools and beads, and various body parts for amulets and charms. Several bird species, specifically the three smallest owls, the swan, and the Passeriformes, have not been included in the dietary analysis for this very reason; they seem to be represented in the faunal sample only because they were being utilized for purposes other than food.

Fish, turtles, and freshwater mussels contribute only 2.5%, .3%, and .1% respectively to the diet. It is possible that most were taken during one season, the spring. At this time of year the urge to spawn carries many kinds of fish, particularly the suckers, up the tributary rivers to the shallows. It is during this period when large numbers of fish are especially vulnerable to netting techniques. Freshwater mussels may also have been gathered at the same time fish were to supplement the diet. The few turtles at the site probably were gathered for technological purposes with food being a secondary purpose. The snapping and softshell turtles were probably killed for food, but the three remaining species—box, painted, and Blanding's turtles—had been made into rattles (the former) and bowls (the latter two).

Three types of nuts—hickory, black walnut, and butternut—contributed 13% to the reconstructed diet and undoubtedly a great deal more to the actual diet. Nine-tenths of the nut meat is shagbark hickory, which is often considered to be the best tasting of the three and is the most nutritious. The tree, *C. ovata*, was probably abundant in the oak forests near Hadfields Cave as it is a major component of the white oak forest (Curtis 1959). It has been pointed out that the nut remains may be considerably underrepresented among all of the food remains. If it is assumed that five times as many nuts were consumed as were carbonized, then this dietary reconstruction would have given them about 49% of the total diet. Of course, a full accounting of the actual diet would also increase the contribution from animals. But the motive for this digression is to demonstrate that the 13% estimate for the nut meat in Table 26 is unrealistically low.

One beneficial result of a dietary reconstruction is the potential for estimating the number of days a site was occupied. This would first require prediction(s) of how many people may have occupied a site. Then these predictions would have to be converted to a minimum standard daily calorie requirement for the group and finally divided into the total calories reconstructed for the site. The resulting number of days would be a very rough estimate of the amount of time a site was occupied. Substituting several predictions of the number of occupants would provide alternate lengths of occupation, which could then be compared with the actual stratigraphy and cultural debris to aid in developing inferences about the settlement patterns of a people.

A summary of several predictions of the length of occupation at 13JN3 is presented in Table 27. The table shows variations in length of occupation resulting from changes in three variables:

(a) Two estimates of the numbers of occupants are modeled after band level social organization: (1) six members: grandfather, husband, wife, two children, and a juvenile son, and (2) nine members: grandfather, two brothers and their wives, two children, and a juvenile son and daughter.

(b) Two estimates of the minimum standard daily calorie requirement for maintaining the health of the group are: (1) the caloric requirements according to each age group and six of the individuals from Spector (1956:195), and (2) an average daily requirement for all people of the world from Harrison et al. (1964:415).

(c) Three estimates of the total number of calories available from the food remains recovered at 13JN3 are: (1) the original calculated total of 3,077,973 calories; (2) an extrapolated total, 5,351,711 calories, which includes an additional one-quarter of the calories from animal foods to compensate for the exclusion of cooked meat from these calculations and five times the calculated number of nuts; and (3) a second extrapolated total, 7,357,371 calories, with the one-quarter additional meat calories and ten times the number of nuts.

The resultant occupation lengths (Table 27) vary from a low of 151 days for nine people to 256 days for six people and the original calculation of 3,077,973 calories. The highest estimates are 361 and 613 days for nine and six people respectively and 7,357,371 calories. The faunal and floral remains almost universally indicate a fall-to-spring seasonal occupation, or about 150-180 days between the first of October and early or late March. Returning to the ceramic analysis, the two ware groups at the site are assumed to have been deposited by at least two different groups of people. Thus, the highest estimated stay of 613 days, or three to four visits by six people for the seasonal duration just indicated, is one alternative which would account for these variations in ceramic types.

One additional inference is available to modify this hypothetical reconstruction to a more realistic condition. The Hadfields site may have been one of several wintering sites for Woodland peoples in this region. A band of six to nine people could have moved from site to site, exploiting the local resources for only a few weeks to one month at a time, and yet still have maintained a specific territory to which they would return year after year. A segmented seasonal settlement pattern such as this would account for sites, such as 13JN3, which exhibit limited seasonal occupations and a wide variety of cultural artifacts (projectile points, stone tool manufacturing debris, scrapers, awls, ceremonial items, etc.). Such artifacts appear to suggest extensive occupation by family units on several occasions.

TABLE 26
Available Calories Based on Hadfields Food Remains
(raw food values)

Species[*]	Species Weight (lbs.)	(gm.)	Cal./ 100 gm.	Total Calories	%		
Mammals							
Didelphis marsupialis	8.5	3,855	143	5,513	0.2		
Sylvilagus floridanus	14	6,350.3	135	8,573	0.3		
Castor canadensis	192.5	87,316	161	140,580	4.6		
Ondatra zibethicus	3.3	1,496.8	99.5	1,489	—		
Procyon lotor	140	63,502.8	165.5	105,097	3.4		
Cervus canadensis	350	158,757.2	126	200,034	6.5		
Odocoileus virginianus	2600	1,179,339	126	1,485,967	48.2		
All Others	841.75	381,811	138	526,899	17.1		
					Mammals	80.3%	2,474,152 calories
Birds							
Branta canadensis	5.6	2,540.1	188	4,775	0.2		
Anas platyrhynchos	1.75	793.8	131	1,040	—		
Anas carolinensis	.75	340.2	131	446	—		
Bucephala clangula	1.8	816.5	131	1,070	—		
Mergus merganser	2.1	952.5	131	1,248	—		
Tympanuchus cupido	18	8,164.6	179	14,615	0.5		
Bonasa umbellus	3.0	1,360.8	168	2,286	0.1		
Colinus virginianus	.26	117.9	168	198	—		
Meleagris gallopavo		30,844.2	179	55,211	1.8		
Ectopistes migratorius	26	11,790	205	24,170	0.8		
All Others	10.8	4,898.8	174	8,524	0.2		
					Birds	3.6%	113,583 calories

Fish						
Catostomus sp.	25.38	11,512.2	104	11,973	0.4	
Moxostoma sp.	75.5	34,246.2	104	35,616	1.2	
Hypentelium sp.	13.6	6,168.9	104	6,416	0.2	
Cyprinidae	31.25	14,174.8	145	20,553	0.7	
Ictaluridae	2.5	1,134	98	1,111	—	
Ictalurus sp.	.8	362.9	84	305	—	
				Fish	2.5%	75,974 calories
All Turtles	18	8,164.7	111	9,063	0.3	
				Turtles	0.3%	9,063 calories
All Mussels	13.17	5,987	68	4,069	0.1	
				Mussels	0.1%	4,069 calories
Seeds						
Carya ovata	—	34,954.6	715	249,927		
Juglans nigra	—	2,688.8	672	18,068		
Juglans cinerea	—	810.9	679	5,506		
Nut spp. (all above)	—	17,849.5	715	127,631		
Chenopodium spp.	—	180.43	na	—		
				Seeds	13.0%	401,132 calories
				GRAND TOTAL		3,077,973 calories

*those species analysed where caloric data was available; some species calculated according to caloric values of other similar species.

181

TABLE 27
Days of Occupation at 13JN3
Based on Calories from Food Remains

Family Minimum Daily Requirements[*]	Table 26 Reconstruction 3,077,973 calories	Table 26 5X the nuts $+\frac{1}{4}$ more from meat 5,351,711 calories	Table 26 10X the nuts $+\frac{1}{4}$ more from meat 7,357,371 calories
(Spector 1956:195)			
Six Members 13,600 calories	226 days	394 days	541 days
Nine Members 20,400 calories	151 days	262 days	361 days
(Harrison et al. 1964:415)			
Six Members 12,000 calories	256 days	446 days	613 days
Nine Members 18,000 calories	171 days	297 days	409 days

[*]Examples of Minimum Daily Requirements (Spector 1956:195)

Age	Relation	Calories	Age	Relation	Calories
25	hu	2,900	25	br	2,900
25	wi	2,400	25	wi	2,400
65	grfa	2,300	25	br	2,900
10-12	so	2,400	25	wi	2,400
4-6	child	1,600	65	grfa	2,300
7-9	child	2,000	1-3	child	1,200
		13,600	4-6	child	1,600
			10-12	so	2,400
			10-12	da	2,300
					20,400

6

Subsistence and Settlement Patterns

Recently a small number of archaeologists have dealt with the reconstruction of prehistoric subsistence economy with an increasing amount of scientific sophistication. Varying degrees of success have been achieved along this avenue of research by Clark (1954), Munson et al. (1971), Chmurny (1973), Smith (1974a), Lewis (1974), and Geier (1973). In general, these works begin with analyses of prehistoric faunal and floral assemblages. They then attempt to relate these findings to an inferred seasonal subsistence cycle and the prehistoric environment as reconstructed from the earliest land survey record. This approach to the reconstruction of past lifeways is probably secure for recent prehistory, because it is grounded on ethnographers' observations of Indian tribes which were genetically related to the prehistoric groups being studied. (Three of the six studies mentioned are of Mississippian culture peoples.) However, as the peoples we study become farther removed from the present, the ethnographic parallels rapidly become related by inference rather than ancestry.

The forthcoming discussion of subsistence will not reconstruct the prehistoric patterns simply by matching the archaeological data with ethnographically documented life patterns. Such a reconstruction has been criticized by Binford (1968:13) and Harris (1968:359-61) because it narrows the variety of interpretations of past life styles. It also limits our vision of the past to presently known modes of behavior. However, the archaeologist should not be denied the vast number of specifics (for example, uses of tools and raw materials, modes of behavior, and beliefs) which are found in the ethnographic sources but cannot be inferred from archaeological finds. The ethnographic accounts can provide insights on the status of certain finds which can then be transformed into propositions to be tested with archaeological data.

Much has been made in the literature of the importance of the white-tailed deer to prehistoric peoples in the Eastern Woodlands. This animal seems to have provided up to one-half or more of their diet for the last several thousand years. There are three practical reasons for this heavy reliance on deer. First, this animal is just small enough to be transported whole by one or two men from the kill site to the occupation area. Secondly, the deer is large enough to produce not only a substantial quantity of flesh, but also grease, sinew, bone, antler, hides, and a multitude of other resources. Finally, Dahlberg and Guettinger (1956:14-15) have estimated that the prehistoric population of this animal in southern Wisconsin, the oak forest/prairie mosaic, was between 20 and 50 per square mile. This figure is certainly applicable to the forested valleys of eastern Iowa, making the white-tailed deer a resource which could have been efficiently and reliably hunted by a small band of people controlling a territory of only a few square miles. The male deer is especially easy to hunt in the late fall and early winter, as this is the rutting season when he is belligerent, aggressive, and curious. Deer in general will usually yard, that is, congregate, during the harshest portion of the winter. During this time they can be predictably located and exploited by relatively few persons (Dahlberg and Guettinger 1956:145-48).

Elk and bison, although they are considerably larger than the deer, were not especially important to the occupants at 13JN3. The presence of a single bison, a juvenile, probably indicates that this species did not frequent the prairies in the vicinity of the site, or was not exploited if it did. It is difficult to explain why the elk was not exploited to the same degree as deer at 13JN3 and, for that matter, during much of the Woodland time span over the Midwest. The elk was fairly plentiful in the past (Schorger 1954), is substantially larger than the deer, and is normally found on the prairie and along forest borders (Murie 1951). This animal may have been ignored by the forest-oriented Woodland peoples simply because the deer was more readily available. Hickerson (1965:51) has further suggested that the elk was not hunted in the "buffer zone" of central Minnesota and Wisconsin because the animal was too large to carry back to camp when the camp could not be moved to the dead animal.

The raccoon and beaver also stand out as frequent components of the Woodland hunter's procurement strategy. Both were hunted for their fine pelts and savory flesh. They were taken often apparently because of a regularized behavior pattern which renders their movements predictable. The beaver usually constructs a conspicuous house and dam and moves about along a series of paths on land. To capture one is a matter of breaking into the house or snaring it along its path (cf. Quimby 1962:226). Raccoons can be efficiently hunted with dogs or, after the snow has fallen, can be tracked to their dens where several may be found together in a dormant state (Quimby 1962:223; Struewer 1943:208).

The residents of Hadfields Cave also took advantage of the turkeys, prairie chickens, and passenger pigeons which would have congregated to feed on the hazelnut and acorn masts available in the autumn. These birds would have been found in the white oak forests and oak savannas covering the bluffs and rolling hills above the Maquoketa valley. The passenger pigeon may have been taken in the spring as well, since this species is known to have nested in tremendous colonies where they were susceptible to mass extermination (Bent 1932:395; Orr 1971:41-47). According to early accounts of historic Indian hunting practices, turkeys were usually hunted during the fall or winter when they were the fattest. Turkeys form large flocks to feed on the masts of acorns at this time of year and can be easily taken using decoys, calls, or the drive (Schorger 1966:377-408).

The relatively small amount of aquatic animals recovered at the site indicates that such food resources were not a major part of the subsistence base for this fall-through-spring occupation. A few water birds would have been available in the vicinity of the site during their biannual migrations along the Mississippi flyway, but tremendous numbers of migrating birds would have been available in the Mississippi River trench just 20 miles from the site (see Appendix H). It has previously been suggested that the fish and mussels may have been taken at one time during the year, for instance, the spring. By this season the nut supplies cached for winter probably had been depleted, and, lacking the vegetable resources of the summer and fall, fish and clams would have been available as a food source. Nets must have been employed to catch the wide range of fish sizes represented by this sample (see Appendix J). Spearing may also have been used to obtain the largest specimens, but the North Maquoketa is an optimal stream for the use of a seine or dip net. Net fishing is clearly the most efficient method for exploiting the abundant fish which were available in tributaries of the Mississippi River drainage in prehistoric times (cf. Rostlund 1952; Carlander 1954).

The evidence for plant uses and importance in the diet has been discussed above, but there exist other potentially important plant food resources for which there is no evidence at 13JN3 and most other midwestern sites. The waterplants, *Nelumbo lutea* (yellow lotus) and *Sagittaria* spp. (arrowhead or duck potato), produce edible tubers which were frequently collected by the Ojibwa, Menomini, and Sauk-Fox (Densmore 1928:320; Smith 1932:407, 1933:105). Both are available in the autumn and winter, and yellow lotus can also be eaten in the spring. These plants are abundant in the backwaters of the Mississippi River trench and grow in the quiet shallows and marshes of its tributaries. In addition, they were often taken from the caches in muskrat and beaver houses during the winter (Smith 1933:105). The tubers of such plants, although they may have been exploited in large quantities, leave virtually no carbonized evidence in archaeological contexts aside from an occasional chance find.

Maple sugar is another potential prehistoric food resource for which there is no hard archaeological evidence. There is always the possibility of recovering evidence of the "hardware" used in sugar manufacturing at a sugaring camp. Sugar was especially important to the historic tribes of the

Great Lakes region when copper kettles were available to facilitate the production of large quantities. This resource may have been less important prehistorically for this reason (Yarnell 1964:78). Sugar can be made from the sap of many trees—for instance, *Acer saccharum* (sugar maple), *A. saccharinum* (silver maple), *A. negundo* (box elder), *Juglans nigra* (black walnut), and *J. cinerea* (butternut)—all of which were present in the vicinity of Hadfields Cave. Woodland peoples had a variety of bark containers and ceramic vessels which would accommodate the boiling of sap to produce syrup and sugar. The time of sap flows, March and April, would have been an especially propitious time to produce sugar if the winter caches of food were running low. Therefore, the potential of sugar should not be overlooked in the prehistoric diet; seven Chippewa Indians, described in Quimby (1962:228), produced 1,900 pounds of maple sugar and 36 gallons of syrup, and eight Indians consumed 300 pounds of sugar in one month during the spring!

Wild rice is another plant which might have been expected to occur in larger numbers at this site where there were only five grains. The rice plant probably did not grow in significant quantities in the North Maquoketa valley but would have been available along the quiet shores and in the backwater lakes of the Mississippi and other large rivers. The meager evidence for wild rice in archaeological contexts in the northern United States could indicate that it was not as heavily utilized prehistorically as it was by historic Indian tribes (cf. Jenks 1900). Conversely, the paucity of this plant may only be a function of not excavating in the right places, that is, the ricing stations. It would appear, however, that rice was not important to the peoples of 13JN3, for it is difficult to explain why an important commodity such as corn was found in the midden while wild rice was practically absent. Both would have been brought to this cave to supplement winter food caches after having been hulled and parched at the previous living site where they had been gathered.

The potential alternatives to wild rice, as the major plant resources gathered in the fall for winter consumption, are the hickory nut, black walnut, and butternut. This, predictably, may be the case for the Woodland peoples in eastern Iowa, Illinois, and north into the Driftless Zone of Wisconsin. Nuts are far more nutritious than rice and can be gathered in the forests where the bands winter. The acorn seems to have been only sporadically exploited, despite the fact that oak trees dominated the prehistoric forests around 13JN3. This nut may have been shunned because it must be leached of its naturally bitter and astringent properties. The hazelnut, on the other hand, is particularly palatable in its raw form, was available in the forests around the site, and appears in small numbers at 13JN3.

Since hazelnuts and many animals appear to be underrepresented at 13JN3, it seems plain that the cave's residents were fairly selective in the foods they hunted and gathered. A rough estimate can be made of the resources available but only partially exploited by prehistoric peoples around the site. Shelford's (1963:28) estimated animal population for a typical 10 mile^2 area of the temperate deciduous forest biome includes: 100-840 deer, 10,000-20,000 squirrels, five black bears, and probably more than 200 turkeys. His estimates for the maple-beech-hemlock forest of northern Ohio, one with considerably less groundcover than the oak-hickory forest, would also contain 3,000 cottontail rabbits, 1,200 raccoons, and 1,000 woodchucks (1963:47). Not considered in these figures are the elk, prairie chicken, grouse, beaver, muskrat, and a host of other animals, many of which are present in the Hadfields fauna. As for the available nut resources, Zawacki and Hausfater (1969: Table 11) have estimated the yearly minimum per square mile nut yields of lower Illinois River upland forest as: 2,055 bushels of burr and white oak acorns, 6,510 bushels of red and black oak acorns, 76 bushels of butternuts, and 29,546 bushels of hickory nuts (three species). Their estimate for the butternut is undoubtedly too low for eastern Iowa, and the yields for black walnut may have been similar to or slightly lower than that for butternuts. Their estimates for maximum yields of all the above species range from two to 15 times higher.

A review of the minimum counts of every species of plant or animal found at 13JN3 demonstrates that the numbers of prehistoric remains do not come close to equaling the carrying capacity of the forest biomes tabulated above. Additionally, it is important to note that the Hadfields Cave occupation represents at most only a 20-month stay at the site, and this was only intermittent over a period of ca. 500 years. If additional occupation areas were found near 13JN3 and represented the same time period, the food resources evidenced in all combined sites probably would fall far short of the available biomass for a 10 mile^2 region of that area. We are left with the conclusion that food resources were selectively exploited to the virtual exclusion of some.

Considering this vast abundance of wild resources it may seem curious that the Hadfields people also made use of cultigens. The cultivation of maize, however, may have arisen from adaptations made in an earlier time than the Woodland period and not as a prerequisite for maintaining a subsistence base. This earlier adaptation to maize agriculture was first discussed by Linton (1924) in an article of surprising foresight. He proposed that Indians of the eastern United States were preadapted for maize agriculture borrowed from Mexico, and that maize was added to an indigenous cultivation system. Linton made the point that maize agriculture in the Eastern Woodlands was marginal, and that because of the considerable abundance of wild resources the cultivation of maize was slow to come into widespread use. Subsequently the idea of a preadaptation for maize was more elaborately developed by Fowler (1971) in his Eastern

Agricultural Complex. The concept being borrowed here from Linton and Fowler is that the domesticate, maize, was merely grafted onto an existing practice of relatively leisurely cultivation by Early Woodland peoples. This form of agriculture continued to be practiced into the Late Woodland period in eastern Iowa for a supplemental food resource.

The notion of a Late Woodland diffuse hunting and gathering economy supplemented by leisure agriculture is somewhat at odds with the opinion that during the previous Middle Woodland period there was a shift from a diffuse to a focal economy due to the increased input of intensified maize agriculture. Cleland (1966:66-67) argues that two subsistence variants found in the Midwest show trends toward a focal subsistence economy: (a) summer and fall wild plant resources became the focus of Struever's (1964:87-106) Illinois riverine adaptation and at the Schultz site in Michigan, and (b) larger game animals represented the focus of the Illinois and Ohio Middle Woodland and at the Spoonville site in Michigan.

> This type of faunal assemblage is thought to signal the beginning of a new focal economy in which heavy reliance is placed upon food production. . .This pattern is intensified in later cultural developments in the same areas. Perhaps a date of AD 200 would be a reasonable estimation of the earliest appearance of this kind of adaptive pattern, although it may have become established slightly earlier in the area south of the Great Lakes. [1966:67]

This same opinion is expressed by Cleland and Kearney (1967:45-47) for the Late Woodland Chesser Cave site in Athens County, Ohio. Here a winter occupation by a small band left deposits of ungulates which were calculated to have yielded about 75% of the total available meat in the diet. On this evidence alone, for no corn was found at the site, the authors inferred that ". . .Chesser Cave was a winter hunting and habitation site of a small group of people who were, to a great extent, subsisting upon venison and perhaps stored cereal food," that is, "a winter hunting encampment of agricultural peoples" (1967:47, 46).

The arguments presented above may not apply to Woodland peoples in northeast Iowa. One substantial argument is available against the development of focal economies dependent on an agricultural base by the late Middle Woodland period. It is that, although maize was cultivated during Middle Woodland times (cf. Struever and Vickery 1973), the numbers of kernels and cobs which have been found in Middle Woodland contexts are not comparable to the tremendous numbers being found in occupation areas of the Mississippian, Oneota, and Plains Village cultures—all historically documented, intensive agriculturalists (cf. Cutler and Blake 1973). The evidence for intensive agriculture in the pre-A.D. 800 Eastern Woodlands does not presently exist. Ample data indicate that maize may have been an integral part of the agricultural complex, which was a small part of the seasonal subsistence cycle of Woodland peoples in eastern America. Part of this latter argument is implicit in the term *simple mud-flat horticulture* coined by Struever (1964; 1968b; Struever and Vickery 1973:1211) to describe the subsistence base of the Hopewell culture of Illinois. This term provides the flexibility necessary to explain the variations in modes of subsistence and reliance on cultivated products which seem to characterize the Woodland cultural manifestations.

> It is argued that a low-level, technologically simple cultivation was an important feature conditioning the degree to which Middle Woodland expressions in different locales underwent shifts to higher levels of complexity exemplified in Hopewell mound cemeteries, in the products exchanged in the Interaction Sphere and in evidence for expanding populations. [Struever and Vickery 1973:1211]

Struever and Vickery here seem to infer that simple mud-flat horticulture was the dependable subsistence base which made possible an expansion of population, lines of intercommunication and exchange, and ceremonial practices requiring substantial inputs of non-productive (in a subsistence sense) labor. Again, this has yet to be archaeologically demonstrated, but this type of low-level adapted, mud-flat agriculture is also the type envisioned for the Hadfields site's occupants. It is a "leisurely" mode of cultivation which could be slotted into the seasonal round of hunting and gathering.

The model of mud-flat agriculture for post-Hopewellian Woodland groups seems an appropriate fit to Hall's (1973:37) idea that the genetic adaptation of Eastern Complex corn may have taken place in small, isolated corn plots scattered throughout the upper Mississippi River drainage (see chapter 5). Implicit in his argument is that the qualities which distinguish Northern Flint as a variety adapted to the northern Midwest were probably the unintentional result of isolating corn plots in the gradual northward drift of the practice of cultivation among Woodland groups. Maize, of course, was only one of the component crops in this system, but the one which demanded the greatest care to insure maturation. Other apparent cultigens—sunflowers, cucurbits, and chenopods—require less scrutiny during the growing season and are admirably suited for mud-flat agriculture.

Seasonal Round

The winter occupation of 13JN3 has been mentioned several times, but one-half or more of the year was spent at some other location. In building a model which accounts for the array of food remains found at this site and a seasonal round of hunting and gathering, it will be useful to look at a few of the seasonal patterns described by ethnographers for historic tribes of the Eastern Woodlands. This does not necessarily propose any genetic relationship between the prehistoric Woodland peoples of eastern Iowa and tribes in the ethnographic accounts. Rather, historic narratives can provide insights which suggest what the most common seasonal settlement patterns were for early historic tribes, and how these patterns contributed constructively to the annual success of the subsistence quest.

190

During the early exploration and fur trading period in North America (ca. A.D. 1615-1750) many narratives relate that, while tribes living on the prairies were generally sedentary agriculturalists and bison hunters, the Great Lakes Indians tended to be semi-sedentary, splitting into hunting bands after the summer crops were in (Brown 1965:32-33). The Great Lakes pattern was generally noted over much of the upper Midwest. In Eaton County, Michigan, the local Indian groups (possibly Pottawattamie) spent the early spring in the maple forests making sugar and the warmer months in the oak openings raising crops and gathering berries (Foote in Cleland 1966:75). Peter Pond (1933:40), writing in the mid-eighteenth century of the Sauk village on the Wisconsin River about 40 miles below Portage, Wisconsin, stated that:

> In the fall of ye Year thay Leave these Huts [long house with several families-ed.] and Go into the Woods in Quest of Game and Return in the Spring to thare Huts befou(r) Planting tim. . .the women Rase Grat Crop of Corn Been Pumkens--Potatoes Millans and artickels. . . .[sic]

Pond also said the same of the Ottawa living to the north of the Sauk (1933:32). Alanson Skinner (1921:84) indicated that the Menomini living on the Green Bay shore of Lake Michigan scattered into family units up the tributary streams to pass the winter and congregated in summer in large fishing villages along the lake shore. Walter Hoffman outlined the Menomini seasonal subsistence cycle as follows: maple sugar and fish were eaten in the spring, fish and game in the summer, wild rice and corn in the fall, and fish, game, and some rice during the winter (Morse in Hoffman 1896:290). Hickerson said that the Sioux and Chippewa villages of central Minnesota and Wisconsin functioned from late spring to early fall, and the remainder of the year was spent in more scattered bands. (Note: Hickerson [1965:44] defined *band* as comprising between 75 and 100 persons, probably implying a social-organizational term.)

The seasonal cycle of the historic Illini, Sauk, and Osage residing on the eastern extremity of the Prairie Peninsula is known in some detail from several sources collated in Brown (1965:69). The occupation of the semi-permanent villages began in March after the winter bison hunt. Hunting progressed on an individual basis from this village until the crops were planted in May. After the June hoeing the village was abandoned to a few women who cared for the crops while the remaining villagers departed to hunt bison. In July the village was reoccupied by all, and from late August through September the crops were harvested and stored. The villagers then dispersed into scattered wintering lodges.

A detailed seasonal cycle is available in the writings of Alexander Henry, who lived with a family-band of seven Chippewa Indians in the northern lower peninsula of Michigan in 1763-64 (Quimby 1962). His narrative opens in June with the Indian family living at a large village site on Mackinac Island. This month was the only time of year when this family was hungry. Later in the summer the family hunted wild fowl and fished at small sites in the Straits of Mackinac. For the three months of autumn this band moved inland and subsisted on maize they had purchased and on raccoon, beaver, wild fowl, and fish. Their two-month winter encampment was in the interior of the lower peninsula, where they lived on the flesh of the animals they killed for furs—primarily beaver, otter, porcupine, raccoon, and elk. By March they had returned near the Lake Michigan shore and spent one month at a sugaring camp producing and consuming maple sugar. By the time this party had returned to the Straits of Mackinac in the following summer, they had accumulated a large quantity of furs for trade and still carried a supply of bear grease, meat, and sugar left over from the winter hunt and spring sugaring activities.

Woodland sites where the biological data have been analyzed for evidence of seasonal exploitation are rather few and far apart in the Midwest. But in cases where there is prehistoric information available, some interesting parallels exist with the ethnographic examples just presented. Beginning well beyond the Iowa region, the occupation of the Late Woodland Chesser Cave site in Ohio has been labeled as a winter hunting encampment of agricultural peoples (Cleland and Kearney 1967:46-47). The Summer Island site in the mouth of Bay de Noc in Lake Michigan has been identified by Brose (1970:148) as a "major spring-summer occupation for harvesting sturgeon." The Mero site on Green Bay (Mason 1966:29-195) has been described by Cleland (1966) as a small group summer occupation. Together the Mero and Summer Island sites are analogous to part of the seasonal cycles represented by Skinner for the Menomini (1921) and Quimby for the Chippewa family (1962)—the spring-summer village fishing site and the late summer fishing and hunting site for the family-band.

In Wisconsin the Sanders sites (47WP26 and 47WP70), described by Hurley (1970, 1975) as large village sites of the Effigy Mound Tradition, have been identified as spring-through-fall occupations on the basis of the fauna present (Lippold 1971). At the Brogley rock shelter (47GT156) a seed analysis (Tiffany 1974:26) indicates a probable autumn-through-winter occupation for the generalized Woodland levels. Mayland Cave in the central Driftless Zone of Wisconsin was another small cave occupied A.D. 900-1300 (Storck 1972). The author suggests that Mayland Cave was visited intermittently throughout the year by hunting bands, primarily Woodland peoples, but was inhabited most extensively in the fall and winter. Storck further indicated that the white-tailed deer was the most important animal in the diet.

A fairly detailed reconstruction is available for the seasonal occupations of the Scovill site, Fulton County, Illinois, a Weaver component in the Spoon River valley (Munson et al. 1971). Based on floral and faunal evidence, the authors have reconstructed the seasonal habitations as follows: a brief occupation in the late spring and early summer to plant crops, fish, and gather mussel; a late summer-early fall occupation to gather nuts, harvest their modest crops, and hunt deer and turkey; a final occupation in early to midwinter to consume stored crops and hunt deer and turkeys. The authors note that Scovill was not occupied during the early spring and autumn, the peak periods of bird migrations along the Illinois River valley. This continual reoccupation of a single semi-permanent site, alternating hunting forays with the activities of cropping, is distinctly similar to the periodic seasonal movements of the Illini, Sauk, and Osage described in Brown (1965:69).

The preceding materials have shown that considerable continuity can be found between certain specific ethnographic accounts and archaeological data regarding seasonal exploitation of wild food resources. In returning this discussion to the Hadfields site and the inferred seasonal movements of its residents, any reconstruction is hampered by the absence of chronological continuity with the ethnographic present. In addition, we are plagued by our lack of knowledge concerning the social systems and obligations which are characteristic of interacting bands, in this case, Woodland peoples of the Intermediate period in eastern Iowa. The aim of this discussion is to develop an interpretive model of the annual seasonal round into which the Hadfields data will fit comfortably, which can be tested with excavations, and which will complement theories which have been advanced about the structure of the Late Woodland social systems in this area.

Hadfields Cave was regularly occupied beginning in the fall of the year. If an extended occupation was planned by its occupants, it would be necessary to arrive around the first of October, plus or minus a week or two. A substantial food resource is available in the nuts which ripen and drop in September and October. As man must compete with squirrels and larger animals for the mast supply, it would be necessary to harvest the nuts as they fell. Occupation at 13JN3 continued through most of the winter with subsistence based primarily on cached nuts and land animals hunted in the vicinity. The ethnographic references cited here virtually all agree that land animals were an indispensable winter food resource, although supplementary foods varied from wild rice to maize to nuts.

It is difficult to estimate the month of late winter or early spring when Hadfields Cave was abandoned for the warmer seasons of the year; few archaeological data are applicable to the problem at hand. Relatively small numbers of fish and mussels are present at the site, yet they may have been an important spring food resource. This is the season when many fish spawn in small tributary streams and are vulnerable to mass collecting, as evidenced at this site in the small sizes of fish. Mammals may also have been taken at this time if this resource had not already been exhausted by winter hunting activities. Wild fowl make one annual migration throughout the spring, although it probably would have been necessary for the Hadfields residents to journey to the Mississippi River trench to exploit this resource in any significant quantity. Yarnell (1964:79) has indicated that some plants may have provided large potential food resources at this time of year: maple sugar in March and April, subterranean tubers throughout the spring, and greens in late spring and early summer. Of course these three plant resources have little potential for being carbonized and recovered archaeologically, and we are practically without means to identify and quantify their importance prehistorically.

The spring and early summer are widely known to have been the most marginal portions of the year for Indian subsistence. The preceding food resources are found in a variety of locales in eastern Iowa and along the Mississippi. It may have been necessary for a small family-band to visit a number of locations during the spring to acquire sufficient nourishment to last through August. Small sites where specialized food gathering took place may be scattered along all of the streams and rivers of eastern Iowa in a manner similar to that outlined by Quimby (1962:232-37) for Michigan.

In May the wintering bands probably congregated at a village site near land suitable for mud-flat cultivation. The congregating of bands into larger village units has been proposed by Mallam (1975: Hypothesis II) as the portion of the seasonal cycle which functioned as an integrative mechanism of the Effigy Mound culture. At this time village bands gathered to bury their dead and construct effigy mounds. Mallam has focused his attention on the Mississippi River trench as the locus of the Effigy Mound summer villages, but this discussion is intended to be general enough to include the Intermediate period as well as the Late Woodland period beyond the Driftless Zone in Iowa. Thus, these summer villages may be found along many of the larger rivers of Iowa—the Cedar, Iowa, and Des Moines, as well as smaller rivers with broad floodplains such as the lower portion of the South Maquoketa, the Skunk, and the Wapsipinicon Rivers. The primary function of such villages may have been as a social integrative mechanism, but cultigens probably were raised at these sites to supplement the winter food supply and add a touch of variety to the diet. Crops would have been planted by late May or early June. However, as Brown (1965) has indicated for the historic tribes of Illinois, summer hunts may have taken many members away from the village while the crops were growing.

One potential conflict is evident in the seasonal cycle as outlined. While maize requires up to about 90 days to reach maturity and at least an additional month to field dry, the nut harvest, which apparently took place at the small wintering sites, would overlap the final drying stage of field corn. This time schedule for ripening maize has been borrowed from the Pawnee type of corn (Will and Hyde 1917:118-19), a tall variety adapted to the relatively longer growing season of the Kansas/Nebraska border region. The traits which distinguish Northern Flint as a rapidly maturing variety, like that grown by the Hidatsa (Wilson 1917), were theoretically only beginning to appear in the varieties cultivated by the Intermediate period peoples of eastern Iowa. The corn of this time period may have been allowed to ripen and dry in the field.

> . . .the Pawnees returned from their summer hunt about September 1, and at once began to roast and dry corn that was in the milk. From morning to night the women and children were in the patches, gathering fuel, making fires, picking, roasting, and drying corn. This was called roasting-ear time. [Dunbar in Will and Hyde 1917:118-19]

Immature corn could be prepared for storage either by boiling, shelling, and sun drying, as the Hidatsa did (Wilson 1917:39-41), or by first roasting it in the husk over hot coals and then boiling and drying the corn as the Pawnee did (Will and Hyde 1917:116-23). Green corn may have been processed by Woodland groups in this manner. In this way crops would have been gathered for storage in time for the fall nut harvest.

Subsistence-Settlement and Social Patterns

This discussion has reached the point where it is feasible to consider a model for the social and settlement patterns of the peoples inhabiting the Hadfields site. Such a model must necessarily be molded from the previous analysis of the subsistence base. But first it is important to state that it is possible to build a model of social and settlement patterns of Intermediate and Late Woodland period peoples because enough cultural coherence can be found to establish norms of behavior which describe a regularized routine in their lives. It would seem that we can establish a distinct Late Woodland life style by accepting two premises. The first begins with the major subsistence base which seems to have been wild foods, that is, a set of resources which required periodic movements of the group to live comfortably. Hunters and gatherers following a seasonal collecting cycle would be distributed in bands, and the social cohesion between bands would be minimal. Thus, we should look for integrative mechanisms which unify these dispersed bands into a single culture. Premise two is that the Woodland groups being discussed here were characteristically conservative toward the adoption of new modes of behavior (and beliefs) which would tend to alter their life style. This resistance to change may or may not be reflected in the artifactual remains, but it is most clearly evident in the persistent pursuit of a basic hunting and gathering economy which can be traced back in time to the Archaic period.

The subsistence base of the Hadfields people was, in Cleland's terms (1966:42-45), a diffuse economy. Intensive Harvest Collecting (Struever 1968) probably more precisely describes their economy: a focal use of several resources diffused throughout the seasonal cycle (cf. Mallam 1975:

Hypothesis IV). A diffuse type of economy subsumes several restrictions as noted by Cleland (1966:44). It is confined by the available natural resources but requires a substantial degree of mobility to efficiently exploit specific food sources as they mature. Additionally, it is difficult for small groups with a diffuse economy to fully absorb large food surpluses when they occur. Therefore, a high percentage of the potentially usable food may remain unexploited by hunters and gatherers in a given territory.

Recently, a number of authors have proposed models for a settlement system which would fit a diffuse subsistence base. Hurley (1970) suggested the Effigy Mound peoples had a central-based wandering type of settlement pattern (Steward 1948; Meggars 1956) which included large summer villages, such as the Sanders and Bigelow sites he excavated. Storck (1972:411-12) was more specific with his suggestions:

> The subsistence was probably largely if not entirely based on hunting, gathering, and fishing. . .There is some evidence that family groups probably congregated into larger social units at mound groups for ceremonial and burial activities. . .The majority of mound groups, however, were probably constructed by small groups of related families and the Effigy Mound population may have been fairly dispersed throughout most of the year.

Some of the ideas inherent in the inferences of Hurley and Storck have been expanded by Mallam (1975) in developing his model which explains the structure of Effigy Mound manifestations in northeastern Iowa (cf. Logan 1959:379-80). Mallam has taken into account the cultural ecology of this region in Iowa. His model of the subsistence-settlement patterns relates the seasonal cycle of resource utilization to the dynamics of Effigy Mound culture. To quote but a small portion of Mallam's reasoning:

> With the establishment of a form of Primary Forest Efficiency in northeastern Iowa, a successful and complex cultural system predicated on hunting and gathering was achieved. In terms of social organization this was a flexible and fluid system characterized by coalescence and dispersal of social groups in response to seasonal occurrence and density of natural resources. The basic social unit was probably the nuclear family which operated relatively independent of other family groups throughout most of the year. [1975:58]

> These nuclear families seasonally merged into larger social groupings at the respective mound complexes for the purpose of collective exploitation of natural resources in the Mississippi trench and other ecologically rich areas. [1975:68]

Testing this model will require extensive excavations in sites representing occupations during every season of the year. But for the present the occupation at Hadfields Cave seems to show good evidence for recurrent winter habitations by small family-bands. There are references in the ethnographic sources to a system of band-oriented subsistence. Dwight Goss (in Cleland 1966:74) said of the Chippewas, Ottawas, and Pottawattamies in the lower peninsula of Michigan, "In autumn an entire family, and sometimes two or three families together, would leave the villages and wander up the small streams into the forests of the interior for their winter's hunt, and they would generally camp in or near a bunch of maple trees in order that they might make sugar in the spring." Hickerson wrote of the Chippewa:

> . . .[they] were farmers, hunters, and fishermen. . . . In the late 18th century, those whose winter hunting grounds were in the heart of the lower peninsula appeared to have been organized for the winter season in extended family hunting bands. These aggregates were larger than the family territorial units of the northern Chippewa and appear to have constituted temporarily detached segments of large, permanent summer villages on the lakes of Huron and Michigan shores to the north. [1962:2]

It would be possible to cite many more authors who noted that subsistence in aboriginal Indian cultures was inexorably linked to the social organization. The point of this, however, is that although food acquisition may have been largely the exclusive domain of individualized family bands of the post-A.D. 300 Woodland life style, a conglomerate of these bands in the Driftless region of Iowa can be identified as a single cultural unit. That is, we can suggest a generalized group of people sharing roughly the same ceramic and artifactual traits as well as a similar economic pattern—in short, a series of periodically interacting family-bands.

7

CHRONOLOGICAL, GEOGRAPHICAL, AND THEORETICAL CONSTRUCTS

It would not be possible to deal satisfactorily with the Intermediate and Late Woodland period populations without first considering what impact the Illinois Havana Tradition (Struever 1964, 1968b; Brown 1964; Griffin et al. 1970:5-9) and Hopewellian Interaction Sphere (Struever 1964; Brown 1964) had on the Middle Woodland period peoples of Iowa.

The intricacies of the distribution and stylistic variations of the Iowan Havana ceramics have not been detailed in this volume, nor could such discussions have been reasonably included in view of the lack of evidence for this period at 13JN3. Nevertheless, this writer can suggest a number of trends which characterize the cultural manifestations of this time period. These intuitions stem directly from a perusal of the Keyes collection and survey and testing operations at Pleasant Creek Reservoir, Palo, Iowa (Benn n.d.).

Evidence for both the Hopewell Interaction Sphere (Caldwell 1964; Struever 1964, 1968a) and Havana Tradition in Iowa is explicit and widely recognized. However, the two manifestations contrast sharply in their real geographic distributions and apparent influences on indigenous populations. The sway of the Hopewellian mortuary cult, as symbolized by its Interaction Sphere, is assumed to have influenced only those populations living along the Mississippi River trench in Iowa. It is only along this great river that significant concentrations of classic Hopewellian artifacts and burial cult assemblages have been recovered—for example, Effigy Mounds National Monument (Beaubien 1953b), the Wolfe site (Straffin 1971), and the Toolesboro sites (Scholtz 1960). On the other hand, the Havana Tradition seems to pervade the whole of eastern Iowa until A.D. 300-400. Havana-like materials, both lithic and ceramic, can be located in the collections of a large percentage of sites of all time periods, suggesting that this was the first major ceramic bearing culture to expand territorially and numerically across the state.

The precise nature of the Havana horizon west of the Mississippi trench is not known, for no significant assemblages representing this time period have been analysed. Havana-like sherds are common in the rock shelter site collections from Jackson and Linn Counties (cf. Logan 1959), and a number of open sites are known—and rumored—to exist in this portion of the state. At least two extensive sites of this nature, 13LN44 and 13LN133, were tested in the Pleasant Creek Reservoir. The exact classification of these manifestations, whether as an Iowa variant of the Havana Tradition or a completely separate tradition of the Iowan Middle Woodland, must await the thorough analysis of both complexes (Cedar Ware, Benn and Thompson 1977). At this point it can only be said that there are extraordinary similarities between the Iowan and Illinoian remains, although the former are usually manufactured from indigenous raw materials and not imported into the state.

Having recognized the potential existence of a ubiquitous Havana horizon in eastern Iowa, it is important to establish those fundamental aspects of culture which differ in the Middle Woodland, Intermediate, and Late Woodland periods. The most evident of these differences is manifested in the progression of ceramic types. However, more basic than the turnover in popular ceramic motifs is the technological evolution in pottery production, observable with the advent of Linn and Weaver Wares and later in Madison Ware. In the foregoing wares there are distinct trends toward thinner, denser walls and more globular vessel forms. In addition, there is a lesser degree of regional uniformity in decorative motifs and a proliferation of individualized inventiveness in ceramic designs.

Another aspect of fundamental change between the Middle and Late Woodland periods involves an increasingly fragmented settlement pattern for the latter time. The Intermediate period may be included with the pattern of the former time period, but only when considering the area outside of the Driftless Zone limits. Practically no evidence is presently available for reconstruction of settlement patterns within the Driftless Zone for any time horizon. In areas such as the Pleasant Creek valley in Linn County, the Middle Woodland period sites have widespread, abundant village debris—sherds, skin processing tools, projectile points, fire-cracked stone—indicating relatively stable occupations with several structures. The contrasting Late Woodland period components in this same valley have only sparse scatters of debris. The reverse seems to have been true for the rock shelters of eastern Iowa; the Intermediate and Late Woodland period habitations of these smaller sites are typically more intensive than the preceding Middle Woodland levels.

Whether this broad generalization involving a modest shift in settlement patterns will be demonstrated in the future will depend on more extensive site surveys of entire valleys and drainage systems. Similar kinds of changes in settlement patterns have been postulated for the same time period in the Illinois River valley. Fowler has suggested that these changes may have taken the form of a population redistribution:

> Following the Hopewellian Interaction there seems to have been a cultural decline in the area. This decline took place in the sense that all areas were no longer tied together by the tomb-burial cult, its attendant ceremonialism, and the common fine goods associated with this practice. There seems to have been a return to regionalism in that the local ceramic traditions continued on. That this decline took place also in settlement size, population, and other facets of culture is sometimes implied but little data bearing on this is known. As a matter of fact, there may have been a population increase in this period over the Hopewellian Interaction. There is some evidence that corn can be associated with these post Hopewellian or Late Woodland settlements throughout the entire area. [Fowler 1971a: 398]

Kenneth Farnsworth in a survey report on the Macoupin valley presents a more specific hypothesis following these same lines. He recovered evidence for Middle Woodland settlements in the region *only* for the A.D. 100-400 time period. Farnsworth also found evidence for settlements moving from valley bottoms to bluff crests, and he infers that this movement represents a shift toward isolated farmsteads and mobile slash-and-burn agriculture (1973:26-29):

> Since backwater-lake fish populations and migratory waterfowl served as fundamental subsistence resources for Illinois Valley Middle Woodland peoples, we should expect that if breakaway groups entered Macoupin Valley, forsaking basic aquatic resources previously available to them, significant restructuring of subsistence and interrelated social subsystems of culture would be forced.

> In making such a move, these individuals lost fundamental fish and wildfowl resources for which other foods had to be substituted. *Only one subsistence item known to them could offer comparable productive potential: corn.* [emphasis his]

Taking a cue from Farnsworth for the case in Iowa, we may substitute two additional adaptations in place of corn agriculture in the above quotation. In the first instance the existence of a formal structure of hunting territories, established at the band level, would mitigate against overextending the limits of the regional carrying capacity during periods of population redistribution. Secondly, Iowa in A.D. 300, unlike Illinois, *may* have been a frontier area in the sense that great expanses of central Iowa were underpopulated relative to the eastern sections of the state. Thus, it is hypothesized that an excess population may have been relieved by a gradual westward expansion during the late Middle Woodland and succeeding periods. Evidence for a westward expansion can be seen in the similarity between Minotts and Maples Mills ceramics.

Returning to the termination of the Havana Tradition, it has become widely recognized by those concerned that the dissipation of Hopewell does not signal the beginning of a general cultural decline in the Midwest. For peoples in Iowa the term decline has no relevance, since the Hopewellian burial cult was not developed in regions west of the Mississippi trench. Instead, the Intermediate period seems to have been a time of population reshuffling and restructuring of social interactions. One common thread in many of the investigations from the cultural "centers" of Illinois and Ohio suggests that in moving from Hopewell to Late Woodland cultural systems, societies shifted from large villages and a ranked social hierarchy to smaller, economically independent units of an egalitarian nature. While such a generalization may be difficult to demonstrate, even for the relatively integrated Illinois River valley cultures, it is virtually impossible to apply to the presently known cultural entities of eastern Iowa. The recognized changes for the time period—Middle to Late Woodland—which were outlined in the previous paragraphs must suffice for the present discussion.

A certain degree of cultural uniformity can also be identified throughout the progression of societies in Iowa from Middle to Late Woodland periods. For instance, the standards of subsistence remained very conservative—hunting and collecting supplemented by sporadic cultivation of domestic and wild plant species. There is at present no evidence for the development of intensive corn agriculture among Woodland groups as it existed in the Oneota, Glenwood, and Mill Creek cultures. Another example of cultural continuity in a chronological dimension involves the persistent use of burial mounds which also function as societal integrative mechanisms (cf. Mallam 1975: Hypothesis II). This situation is especially visible in northeast Iowa, where there is a gradual transition from the construction of conical mounds with prepared tombs and elaborate grave goods to the extensive use of animal effigy mounds.

Content and Social Structure of the Intermediate and Late Woodland Periods

The inference that Woodland Indian societies were organized primarily into fluid bands has been in the literature for decades. This notion was applied by Paul Radin (1923:185-203) to the Wisconsin Effigy Mound manifestation. Clark Mallam (1975: Hypotheses I and II) has added substantial depth to this inference, suggesting that the Iowa effigy mounds functioned as totemic symbols for loosely related lineages and as devices for bringing self-sufficient bands together on a periodic schedule. It is quite clear that there is considerable time depth for the presence of both band social organization and integrative mechanisms among such bands (for example, Kinietz 1965:117-20, 317-29). It is also noteworthy that integrative mechanisms have been intensively prescribed for the Havana Hopewell Interaction Sphere as well. For example, in searching for elements of Havana culture which functioned as mechanisms for communication, Hall states:

Other elements which could have been involved in the interaction mechanism were the use of fictions of kinship and the inviolability or sacredness of certain occasions or precincts for purposes of interpersonal and intertribal exchange . . . , and possibly also the use of honorific weapons of special manufacture to validate peaceful intergroup relations. [1973:12]

Thus, if integrative mechanisms were built into Havana culture in varying degrees, it is not especially imaginative to see such mechanisms changing form but not function in the Intermediate and Late Woodland periods.

An interesting ethnographic parallel for the Iowa settlement system after A.D. 300 is provided by the 17th-century Chippewa, as reconstructed by Hickerson (1962:83, 95). The Chippewa were hunters and gatherers with a social and economic system based on self-sufficient nuclear family units occupying contiguous territories under the ownership of autonomous patrilineal totemic kindreds. The family-bands were separated in hunting grounds for most of the year, congregating at summer fishing stations to renew acquaintances and establish lineage bonds. For such a system to be visualized in northeast Iowa during the Late Woodland period, one need only infer that the summer gatherings were promulgated for the purpose of building effigy mounds. Mounds would have symbolized both the cooperative identity of the lineage for whom the mound was constructed and the network of mutual reciprocity, if, indeed, lineages exchanged responsibilities for burying their respective members (cf. Radin 1923:201).

Before proceeding it is important to confront the definition for *band* employed here. This discussion follows the lead of Williams (1974:25) in utilizing band as a term for human residence units:

> It will designate the group of families currently camping together and cooperating—or at least companionate—in daily economic and social activities. Used in this sense we can speak of a band as splitting into two or more bands during some part of the year and amalgamating into a single, larger band at other times.

Williams is using the term band specifically in the context of hunting and gathering cultures. We can consider that the Effigy Mound peoples also subsisted by hunting and gathering, although crops were cultivated at the summer residences.

Let us turn now to a consideration of subsistence patterns. A number of moderately contrary statements have been put forth to describe the general patterns of prehistoric people's shifting subsistence base in the upper Midwest. Our interest here should be in recognizing the merits of each generalization as it was induced from a data base. Initially we have Storck's statement, "There is clearly no indication, either in the variety of species obtained or in the relative importance in the diet, that the hunting economy of Archaic peoples, at least as represented at rock shelter sites, was any more diversified than that of Late Woodland Effigy Mound peoples" (1972:383). The data base for such a statement is firm, for the comparison has been drawn from three Driftless Zone rock shelter sites with substantial faunal assemblages. Of particular interest is Storck's parallel between the subsistence base of the Effigy Mound Tradition and the Archaic, a relationship which had been recognized previously by Wittry (1959).

The interval between Late Woodland and Archaic has been documented to some degree with a comparative study of Middle and Late Woodland site faunal assemblages by Lippold (1971). The data base for this study was occasionally quite thin, since approximately one-half of the reported sites were represented by low numbers of bone elements. In her summary statement Lippold concludes that Late Woodland sites tended to be seasonal collecting stations with a low species diversity (1971:152, 158). Middle Woodland sites had both seasonal and long-term occupations and usually contained a greater species diversity as well as larger numbers of elk. The first inference, that of the existence of longer-term Middle Woodland occupations, has been alluded to in this discussion. Her remaining inference, that Late Woodland species diversity is lower than Middle Woodland, is largely negated by a comparison of three additional faunal assemblages in the Driftless Zone. The diversity of animal species at Millville, an open Middle Woodland site in Grant County, Wisconsin (Pillaert 1969), is as great as that at Mayland Cave (Storck 1972), a Late Woodland site, or at Hadfields Cave.

The preceding discussion terminates inconclusively. However, the degree of difference in species diversity and numerical variation in the above faunal reports is quite small. The contrast between total numbers of species appears slight when compared to the fauna from Paleo-Indian or historic fur trapping sites. In short, the levels of change visible among the Archaic, Middle, and Late Woodland faunal assemblages in the upper Midwest appear to have low potential for explaining culture change during these time periods.

Turning to an evaluation of the contribution vegetable products made to the diet, similar conclusions will be reached. Quantified evidence for the use of plants is almost nonexistent, excepting the recent publication of the Brogley site seed analysis (Tiffany 1974) and the paleobotanical analysis in this volume. In the absence of comparative information any statements made here are necessarily speculative. Tiffany (1974:27) has presented a single comparison between the Archaic and generalized Woodland levels at Brogley: that the Woodland levels contain a narrower range of weed species and fewer nuts than do the Archaic levels. He has further speculated that cultigens—corn and sunflowers—may have been substituted for wild plant seeds. However much Tiffany's interpretations may agree with those from farther-ranging seed analyses (for example, Allison 1972), they are not complemented by the findings at Hadfields Cave. The diet of the Hadfields residents is suggested to have been 30-50% seed foods, the majority of which were nuts, and cultigens. Future work will probably confirm the contention that a switch to intensive agriculture, or more generally, the restructuring of a diffuse subsistence economy to a focal economy, occurred only when Woodland peoples underwent a process of "Mississippianization." This process of culture change culminated in the appearances of the

Oneota, Mill Creek, and Glenwood manifestations with a parallel dissipation of diffuse Woodland subsistence patterns.

The arguments favoring the existence of a family-band social organization and diffuse subsistence base for the Intermediate and Late Woodland peoples inhabiting 13JN3 have been presented in this volume. In a series of hypotheses Mallam (1975) has realized both patterns and their relationships to the environment of northeast Iowa for the Effigy Mound manifestations. His processes of interpretation take the following forms:

> Throughout the year natural resources were abundant but only on a seasonal basis. . . None of these zones were entirely adequate for larger numbers of hunters and gatherers, but collectively and systematically exploited on a seasonal and cyclical basis they could have supplied a profusion of natural resources, sufficient to support a number of human communities. [1975:56-57]

> During the spring, summer and fall periods, the abundance and density of natural resources of the Mississippi trench expedited large social groupings. [1975:60]

> During the winter months, the Mississippi trench became a barrier to large scale human habitation and subsistence activities. Ecologically, the floodplain entered a state of dormancy and northerly winds, channelled through the trench, magnified the cold, making it an inhospitable area. Game animals such as bison, deer and elk sought refuge and sustenance in the sheltered valleys away from the Mississippi trench and open prairies to the west. At this time the large social groups fragmented into small nuclear family units and similarly dispersed into the protected interior of the ecotone. [1975:62]

His interpretive model also incorporates the use of territories (identified by locations of mound groups) as demarcators of the bands' seasonal movements (1975:62).

The preceding model is partially confirmed by the data from 13JN3, a winter occupation, but the model would appear to be overly deterministic in terms of the necessity for seasonal movements. Implied in the last several pages of this volume is the proposition that the diffuse subsistence pattern, which is characteristic of Late Woodland peoples throughout the Effigy Mound sphere of influence, has substantial time depth, potentially arising during the Archaic period. Indeed, given Mallam's model, we might suggest that with the advent of effigy mound construction, the established seasonal round subsistence pattern was further stabilized because territorial markers were established in the form of effigy mound complexes. Thus, one can conclude that Late Woodland peoples had a basically conservative attitude toward change, even as they had possession of mud-flat horticulture at the very least. This suggests that the people in question had stabilized in their relationships with the environment and the regional population such that there existed no significant degree of ecological or demographic pressure which would stimulate a move toward intensive agriculture and greater sedentism.

One of the major aspects of Late Woodland period society in northeast Iowa is that the primary subsistence unit was the territorially based family-band. Circumscribed territories may have served two functions for the population (Williams 1974:8-9). In one sense territories are delineated with sufficient proportions to ensure that the resource requirements of the band are provided. In actuality the minimal needs of the band are usually recovered from only a small segment of their territory, for the population of hunting and gathering societies is often considerably less than the environmental carrying capacity. This appears to be the situation evidenced by the Hadfields Cave dietary reconstruction. In peaceful societies social rules governing the boundaries and exploitation of territories are formulated through interaction among independent bands within autonomous kindreds, and by agreement or reciprocal arrangement between autonomous kindreds. This statement assumes the second function of territories—to geographically define the important kinship units of the hunting society, that is, the breeding isolates and lineage-bands (Williams 1974: Postulates III and IV). In northeast Iowa during the Late Woodland period, family-bands were equivalent to breeding isolates, and lineage-bands were aggregates of several family-bands. Theoretically the latter group should be identified by individual effigy mound complexes (Mallam 1975: Hypothesis I). The functional nature of lineage-bands probably was multidimensional. First, they would serve as exogamic kin units, thereby prescribing potential mates for lineage members (Williams 1974: Postulate V). Secondly, the maintenance of marriage alliances between lineages would promote regional peace. Thirdly, lineage identification would ensure that the autonomy of family-band territories was perpetuated through time. Finally, the need for reestablishment of inter- and intra-lineage ties and the periodic renewal of the ceremonial universe—the construction of effigy mounds and burial of the dead—would have provided the incentive for the annual congregation in summer villages.

It is argued here (and by Mallam 1975) that aggregation at summer villages had primarily an integrative function. Cultivation of domestic and wild plants certainly was pursued at these locations, but this practice was supplemental to the mainstays of hunting and collecting.

Social interaction at these summer gatherings would also provide an opportunity for exchange of information concerning popular ceramic designs. Thus, we can establish the process by which modes of ceramic decoration were formalized throughout the Effigy Mound Tradition, providing the archaeologist with sufficient attribute uniformity to designate formal types. At the same time we can assume the existence of enough irregularities in the social structure of this loose-knit, egalitarian society to explain temporary lags in the uniform acceptance or abandonment of some traits. This variance in the velocity of trait movement through societies seems to result in an increase in the proportional representation of so-called aberrant vessels in the Linn and Madison Wares of eastern Iowa.

The projectile point assemblages at 13JN3 and other Woodland sites provide added insight into a family-band oriented society. In general, projectile points are reduced in size after ca. A.D. 300, a technological change usually assumed to represent a shift to the use of the bow and arrow. This weapon is obviously well-adapted for hunting by ambush. Such an innovation would have additionally fostered the self-sufficiency of small, independent family-bands (cf. Hall 1973:54). One characteristic of projectile point complexes in northeast Iowa is the inherent diversity within types and assemblages. These differences are perhaps more than simple reflections of stylistic turnover, since there does not seem to be as much diversity in contemporary ceramic assemblages. A potential explanation for the contrast between ceramic and lithic diversity within types is provided by Williams. He notes that an obvious feature of patrilocal hunting societies is:

> ... that the "velocity" of movement of women is much greater than that of men from generation to generation. This means that any feature differentially associated with the sexes will show different spatial distributions. Specifically, items associated with females will show less local differentiation than items associated with males. [1974:107]

Applying this principal to the Hadfields assemblage, it may be deduced on purely speculative grounds that kin groups of the Late Woodland period in northeast Iowa were patrilineal and patrilocal, assuming that women manufactured pottery and men made projectile points.

Distribution of Woodland Cultures in Iowa

The spatial patterns in which man orders himself across the landscape are probably affected by at least four factors: the political and economic makeup of his societies, individual personalities within those societies, the carrying capacity of the environment for any given mode of subsistence, and geographic features. The first two factors, particularly the latter, obviously present problems of reconstruction for the archaeologist. Three of these four, however, have been specifically analysed in this volume. At this point we are able to evaluate the impact of the three factors on Woodland population distributions in Iowa, as well as fabricate a model which begins to explain the movement of some cultural traits with high archaeological visibility.

The area of first consideration will be the region of northeastern Iowa, for a large part of the preceding discussions is directly applicable to this area. This heavily dissected area can be recognized as a unique culture area of the state for at least the Late Woodland period and probably earlier as well. The periphery of this region may be roughly identified as the Maquoketa River drainage on the west and the Mississippi trench to the east. The two most prominent geographic features are a well-developed dendritic pattern of drainage, which scatters the climax vegetation into a mosaic of contrasting micro-environments, and the east-west orientation of rivers and streams. Both of these features are clearly complementary to the social/subsistence patterns inferred for Effigy Mound peoples. The abruptly dissected drainages of the Driftless Zone would have provided hundreds of protected valleys where wintering family-bands would have defined their territories. The drainage systems running west to east could have offered routes for seasonal movement between wintering territories and the summer villages in the broader river valleys such as the Mississippi. Present archaeological evidence partially confirms the hypothetical reconstruction of the typical settlement pattern—wintering sites such as Hadfields Cave and others in the interior and practically all of the known Effigy Mound complexes along the Mississippi and its larger tributaries.

To digress for a moment, a similar pattern of seasonal movement may be implied for the Wisconsin Effigy Mound culture. However, one should not expect the Wisconsin sites to show the high degree of linearity which is evidenced in Iowa. Because effigy mounds are distributed over a far larger area in Wisconsin, an area which has much more complex drainage patterns, we can speculate that Wisconsin effigy mound groups would be centers in a truer sense with family-band wintering territories scattered in a more inclusive arc around a center.

Returning to Iowa and the region to the west of the Driftless Zone, two fundamental reasons justify distinguishing this area culturally from northeast Iowa. First, the ceramic styles in east-central and central Iowa are strongly influenced by ceramic traditions of the Illinois River Valley. This notion holds for the Middle Woodland, Intermediate, and Late Woodland periods, as outlined in the section on ceramics in this study. In contrast, pottery in the Driftless Zone is related to some Wisconsin types and also contains a number of very localized styles. The implication that the central sections of Iowa were directionally influenced from Illinois is intended to assume both the actual movement of Woodland groups as well as the diffusion of horizon styles. The second justification for identifying two cultural areas in eastern Iowa is that there were few, if any, effigy mounds constructed outside the Driftless Zone (Fig. 66). Implicit in this fact is the inference that the structured interrelationships between family- and lineage-bands, for which the building of effigy mounds functioned as an integrative mechanism, were not developed to the same degree among populations beyond the Driftless Zone.

It is being suggested that the great expanse of east-central and central Iowa was effectively a frontier zone between the Middle Woodland and early Late Woodland periods. Such a notion assumes that a population growth and expansion occurred during the Middle Woodland period in Illinois, and that no major cultural traditions coalesced in the Iowa area. While the first assumption is probably viable, the latter one can be accepted only in the absence of contrary evidence. The major river systems of Iowa flow to the southeast, with the exception of those in the Driftless

Zone. Iowa's major rivers merge with the Mississippi immediately to the northwest of the central Illinois River valley and the Spoon River, the focal region of the Woodland cultural developments in Illinois. Thus, the topographical features of central and eastern Iowa are oriented in the proper direction to provide important river valley routes for the movement of populations and the diffusion of cultural influence through a sparsely populated Iowa frontier. The fact that Effigy Mound culture is found only in northeast Iowa may be a function of both geographic and social factors.

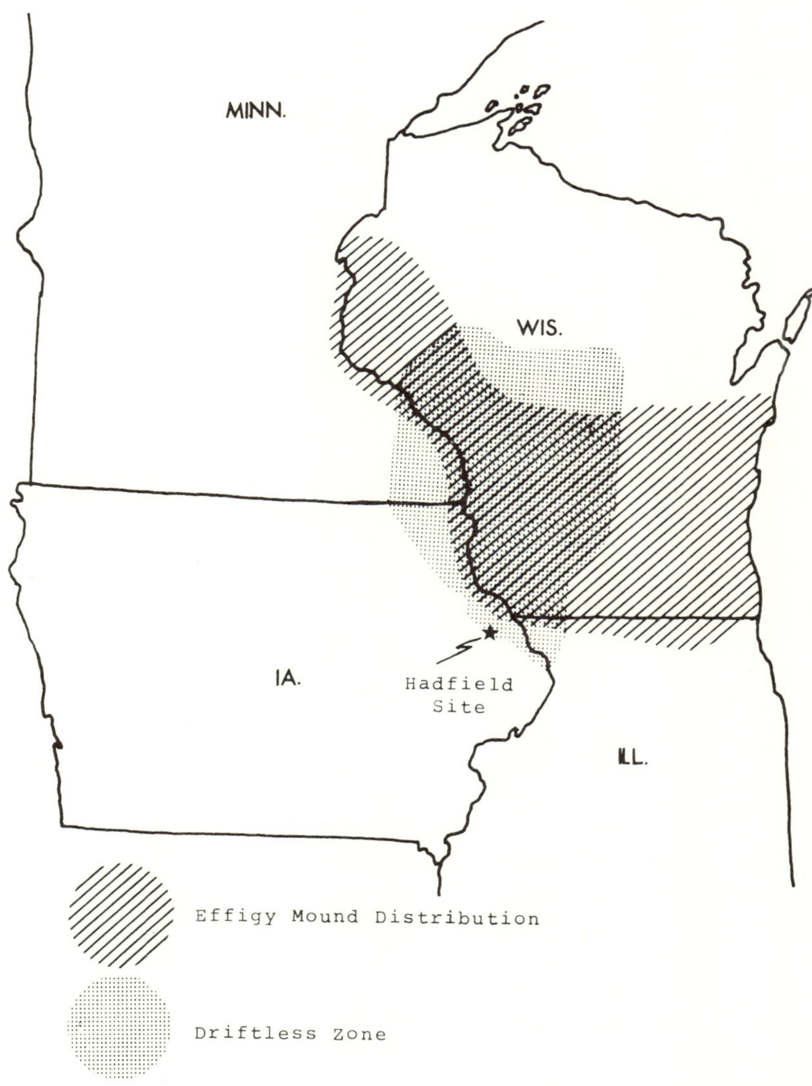

Fig. 66. Distribution of the Effigy Mound Tradition and the Driftless Zone.

In an environmentally deterministic sense the Effigy Mound Tradition was confined to the dissected portion of the state and stopped short of spreading beyond the limits of the easterly-flowing streams and rivers. The cultural explanation has already been alluded to—that the societal integrative mechanisms failed to incorporate peoples beyond the narrow enclave along the Mississippi River into the Effigy Mound cultural sphere of participation.

Terminology

Mallam (1975:66) has nominated Caldwell's (1964) concept of the Interaction Sphere to describe the manifestations of the Effigy Mound culture in the upper Mississippi River region. In speaking of the periodic gatherings of family-bands at their effigy mound complexes and the occasional supra-gatherings of lineage-bands at one large complex, he states, "Maintenance of contact...was a prerequisite factor in perpetuating a stable hunting and gathering cultural system in northeastern Iowa. Sociocultural integration at this level, involving participation of members of the various complexes, would constitute an interaction sphere" (Caldwell 1964). Although Mallam's concept of the social integrative mechanism of Effigy Mound essentially fits the inferences developed in this section, this writer would differ with his application of the interaction sphere concept. It would seem that Effigy Mound culture has a comfortable match in the term *tradition* (Willey and Phillips 1958:37) which has been used in this situation by Hurley (1970). In Effigy Mound culture there is a "...temporal continuity represented by persistent configurations in single technologies or other systems of related forms," that is, a tradition (Willey and Phillips 1958:37). This writer does not see an interaction sphere for this culture, that is, "...the areal matrices of regular and institutionally maintained *intersocietal* articulation" (Binford 1965:208; emphasis mine). The interaction evidenced in the effigy complexes apparently was on a band and/or village level. This type of interaction must be implied in the term tradition if the primary artifact configurations are to be genetically similar.

The concept *interaction sphere* may be more applicable to the group of Intermediate and Late Woodland period manifestations, of which the Effigy Mound Tradition is the major portion in the upper Mississippi River region. Archaeological entities which may be considered for membership in this sphere include the relatively unknown Late Woodland complexes in the northern one-third of Illinois, Maples Mills or Tampico of central Illinois, Late Woodland in Minnesota, and an unknown quantity to the west and south of the Driftless Zone in Iowa. These groups have not been sufficiently investigated by the archaeologists, but each appears to embody enough configurational identity in their complexes to warrant some temporal and cultural term in the nomenclature of Willey and Phillips. Despite the present uncertainty of identities, these several Woodland manifestations appear to have a number of characteristics in common. Together, these characters intimate the existence of an interaction sphere. One such characteristic is the widespread inauguration of the bow and arrow as the major hunting weapon, as evidenced in the appearance of small side-notched and triangular projectile points. Another is the generalized use of cordage as the primary applique in the zoned rim designs of Late Woodland period vessels. A third is the persistent use of burial mounds—effigy, linear, or conical—as a major mode of interment. The fourth characteristic is typified by the Woodland peoples' coexistence with the relatively sweeping social and institutional changes manifest in the general developments associated with Mississippian culture. Apparently the integrative mechanisms, which acted as the cohesive agents binding together the independent social-subsistence units of the Woodland life style, mitigated against the encroachments of the more sedentary Mississippian way of life. A fifth and final characteristic, probably the functional heart of an interaction sphere, is the hypothetical existence of family-band territories among Woodland peoples.

The motive for introducing any taxonomic terms, such as *interaction sphere*, is that we are faced with a very real dilemma in attempting to classify apparently autonomous, band-oriented Woodland societies. Just as the integrative integrity of the archaeologist's classificatory units is inversely proportional to the increase in distance between contemporary cultural entities (cf. Mason 1970: 802), so is the integrative integrity of established classificatory units made more superficial by applying them to hunting and gathering societies. Classification has the purpose of congealing a fluid mass of data in convenient units that are useful to the investigator. The ever-present problem faced by this writer as well as other investigators is to gain sufficient command of the evidence for Woodland societies in eastern Iowa such that we can formulate a classificatory structure which is thought to represent the "real" aboriginal relationships.

The terms *Early, Middle,* and *Late Woodland,* generally identified with James B. Griffin (1952b), have been employed extensively here as chronological periods. Occasionally they have also been used to designate culture type, a usage which Mason (1970: 814) argues should be made very explicit. However, to utilize these terms as stages of linear or evolutionary development clearly confuses their integrity as homogeneous classificatory units.

The foregoing effort to utilize *interaction sphere* is an attempt to recognize the structural uniformity and similar content of Late Woodland period hunting and gathering societies in the upper Mississippi region. The usage of this term, *Late Woodland Interaction Sphere*, assumes that there was no defined focus, a type area from whence all definitive traits diffused. Rather, a loosely integrated system of interrelated societies is envisioned, with specific cultural continuity existing between adjacent populations and only the most general continuity present across the entire system.

Culture traditions, in the Willey and Phillips (1958) sense, have been identified within the Interaction Sphere. At this taxonomic level, the archaeologist must necessarily recognize the significance of his artifact typologies within broad geographic and chronological dimensions. The Effigy Mound Tradition is the single most established Late Woodland period entity now in the literature (cf. Baerreis 1966:126; Hurley 1970), although the Maples Mills complex of central Illinois is a potential candidate.

Proceeding to the next lower step in the taxonomic hierarchy, the phase, we arrive at a taxon which is the very heart of the cultural/chronological classification system. The phase has not yet been applied in lending order to the archaeological manifestations of eastern Iowa. Logan's dissertation (1959), the definitive and only comprehensive study of the prehistory of this region, was conceived within the bounds of the Midwestern Taxonomic System (McKern 1939). Due to the fact that many known prehistoric complexes in eastern Iowa have not been sufficiently described and delimited, the process of transforming Logan's foci to the modern system of phases will inevitably result in future classification problems. For this reason the foci defined by Logan will be reviewed here with the goal of identifying potential conflicts which may arise during and after the turnover of taxon units.

The use of established time periods—Early, Middle, and Late Woodland—implies some degree of temporal and cultural relativity to a single, widely recognized constant, the Hopewellian cult. While this author is not opposed to the ubiquitous presence of Hopewell or Havana as a chronometric mainstay for the Woodland periods in the Midwest, our system of cultural classifications will suffer in terms of clarity if newly recognized cultural entities are always defined relative to an assumed cultural constant. This criticism is especially relevant when analysing an autonomous society existing at the periphery of an assumed sphere of influence: for example, Laurel culture relative to the Havana Tradition (Mason 1970). For the Middle Woodland time period in Iowa, the presence of the Havana Tradition immediately to the east has clearly determined our definitions of ceramic types and cultural classifications. In his classification of northeast Iowa pottery, Logan (1959) opted to use Havana Ware, particularly the Naples Stamped type, as the formal name for Iowan pottery of this time period. Although the large majority of this pottery impressionistically seems to fit into the Havana Ware typology, practically all of these vessels were locally produced and often exhibit stylistic variations which depart from formal type definitions. The ultimate question is whether we should continue to utilize the Havana Ware types, or whether a new Iowan ware category should be developed to recognize the geographic and cultural displacement of central Iowa (Benn and Thompson 1977) from the Illinois River valley.

This open questioning of the status of Havana Ware in Iowa leads directly to a consideration of the McGregor and Allamakee Foci named by Logan (1959:307-308). The former identifies a number of Hopewell cult burial mounds in northeast Iowa, and the latter, a contemporary of the Nickerson Focus (Bennett 1945:113-22) in Jo Daviess County, Illinois, is a manifestation related to the Weaver complexes in Illinois. Neither of these Iowa foci has been investigated since Logan's work, making it impossible to evaluate their present classificatory integrity or increase their areal scope to incorporate additional assemblages, such as the one at Hadfields Cave. The apparently close relationships between the McGregor and Allamakee Foci and comparable complexes in southwestern Wisconsin will also require analysis prior to the permanent establishment of the Iowa foci in terms of phases.

The term *Intermediate period* is employed in this volume to represent the interval ca. A.D. 300-650. The cultural taxons roughly corresponding to this time span in the southern Illinois River valley have been termed the White Hall Phase by Struever (1968) and the Weaver Phase in the central Illinois valley (Griffin et al. 1970). However, in many portions of the upper Mississippi region there are no secure cultural entities defined for this period, excepting the Allamakee Focus. While the lingering influence of the Havana Tradition is still evident during this time, Havana decorative styles were dissipating along with the thick-walled, bag-shaped vessel form. A few selected elements of the Havana ceramic sphere were incorporated into the new types of pottery. A broad, general shift toward thinner vessel walls, denser paste, and more localized concentrations of distinctive decorative styles reflect this newer ceramic tradition. In short, the use of *Intermediate period* expressly states that this was a time of transition not to be confused with the Middle Woodland period, a time when the influence of the Havana Tradition was paramount in the upper Mississippi region. Other characteristics—changeover to the bow and arrow, the florescence of maize agriculture, and changing settlement patterns—also contribute to the recognition of this period as a time of transition. The future of the Intermediate period as a useful chronometric term is dependent on new conclusive research on the contents and social nature of Illinois Weaver and all of the other unknown societies which are contemporary with it.

A large portion of the discussion in this study has been directed toward establishing the presence of two Late Woodland cultural entities in east-central and northeast Iowa. The first of these entities, represented best by the upper component at 13JN3 containing Madison Ware and more generally by the Effigy Mound manifestation, is confined to the Driftless and Drift Border Zones of northeast Iowa. The existence of this culture unit was recognized by Logan (1959:334) but was not formally named in his study. Minotts Focus, Logan's second classificatory unit (1959:333-34), is identified with Late Woodland complexes of east-central Iowa showing the apparent influence of Illinois Maples Mills. A comprehensive analysis of prehistoric materials in the Keyes collection would undoubtedly confirm the utility of transforming this unit to Minotts Phase. However, this writer does not foresee its continued incorporation with the Effigy Mound Tradition, as Logan did in placing Minotts Focus in the Effigy Mounds Aspect (1959). We should continue to place heavy emphasis on the existence of effigy mounds and the integrative social mechanisms implied by their presence as some of the very few unifying factors of this rather amorphous tradition. Minotts Phase may be described with our present knowledge as a regional sequence (Willey and Phillips 1958:23), for it appears to be quite diffused throughout east-central and central Iowa. A special problem to be faced in future work with this phase will be describing its interactions with the Effigy Mound Tradition immediately to the northeast. The zone of interface for these two phases may be as much as one county wide—for example, Jackson, Jones, and Delaware Counties— and sites in this zone may exhibit mixed components representing both phases.

The Keyes Phase

The Late Woodland complexes in the Driftless Zone of northeast Iowa are here named the *Keyes Phase.* This gesture seems appropriate, for Charles R. Keyes was the first and foremost collator and classifier of Iowa prehistory. In applying Keyes' name to this manifestation we not only recognize his important contributions, but the term Effigy Mound as shorthand reference for Late Woodland culture can now be discarded. The range and scope of the Keyes Phase has been one of the central issues of this volume. It is certain that a large number of components will fit into this phase, although relatively few of these are presently known. All of the existing and destroyed effigy mounds in Iowa (Fig. 66, +54 mound complexes; also Mallam 1975) are included here along with unknown numbers of conical and linear mounds, hundreds of open sites, and many small rock shelter sites. Artifactual remains for this phase vary to some degree. Madison Fabric Impressed is the major pottery type by an overwhelming margin with only a small proportion of Madison Plain sherds in several variations also present. Triangular projectile points seem to dominate in many lithic assemblages, but a wide variety of larger forms are present early in the sequence.

The Keyes Phase is viewed as a component of the Effigy Mound Tradition, the first phase to be formally named for this tradition. It is possible that the northern extent of the Keyes Phase may eventually be recognized as terminating in Minnesota; however, the present void of evidence precludes even a preliminary determination in this question. The naming of this phase is not adjudged to be conflicting with Hurley's Early, Middle, and Late Effigy Mound periods (1970:353-99). His ordering of sites into these time intervals appears to have been accomplished relative to two criteria: radiocarbon dates and ceramic seriation. In another sense there is justification for questioning the actual integrity of the first and last of Hurley's periods. The evidence for the first, ca. A.D. 300-700, is debatable due to the quality of the radiocarbon evidence as well as on typological grounds. As for the final period, ca. A.D. 1100-1642, there is virtually no *hard* evidence for the existence of the Effigy Mound Tradition after roughly the thirteenth century. Some data are available for the transition between Woodland and Oneota culture types. If a true condition of culture change is represented by this transition, then we should recognize this in phases or subphases of the Effigy Mound Tradition and/or the Late Woodland Interaction Sphere with temporal and spatial dimensions.

Future investigations may expose the need for creating subphases (Willey and Phillips 1958:24) within the Keyes Phase. No sense of urgency presently exists in this direction due to the paucity of definitive data, but it is reasonable to anticipate our alternatives. The position of the Lane Farm complex in our cultural classificatory system, relative to its inclusion or exclusion from the Keyes Phase, will ultimately determine what horizon initiates that phase. If Lane Farm is eventually incorporated into the Keyes Phase, it will necessarily be included as the earliest subphase. Inclusion of Lane Farm could place the initial horizon of the Keyes Phase in the sixth century, and its exclusion would move the beginning date up to the seventh century. The alternative to including the Lane Farm manifestation in the Keyes Phase is placing it within Logan's Allamakee Focus. The termination of the Keyes Phase is unclear because of the absence of archaeological evidence. A dissipation of the upper Mississippi River region Effigy Mound Tradition by the fourteenth century does not seem unreasonable.

References

Adler, Kraig
1968   Turtles from Archaeological Sites in the Great Lakes Region. *Michigan Archaeologist* 14(3-4):147-63.

Agogino, George A., and W. D. Frankforter
1960   A Paleo-Indian Bison-kill in Northwestern Iowa. *American Antiquity* 25(3):414-15.

Alex, Robert A.
1968   *The Rock Run Shelter: A Stratified Woodland Site in East Central Iowa.* Masters thesis, Department of Anthropology, University of Iowa.

Allison, April
1972   Plant Remains. In The Schultz Site at Green Point, edited by James Fitting. *University of Michigan, Museum of Anthropology Memoirs* 4:77-85.

American Ornithological Union
1957   *Checklist of North American Birds* (fifth ed.). Baltimore.

Anderson, Adrian D.
1971a   Review of Iowa River Valley Archaeology. In Prehistoric Investigations. *Office of State Archaeologist of Iowa, Reports* 3:1-23.

1971b   The Late Woodland Walters Site. In Prehistoric Investigations. *Office of State Archaeologist of Iowa, Reports* 3:24-52.

Anderson, Duane C.
1974   Cherokee Sewer Site (13CK405): Lithic Analysis. In The Cherokee Sewer Site (13CK405): A Preliminary Report of a Stratified Paleo-Indian/Archaic Site in Northwestern Iowa. *Journal of the Iowa Archeological Society* 21:57-92.

Baby, Raymond S.
1961   A Glacial Kame Wolf Mask-Headdress. *American Antiquity* 26(4):552-53.

Baerreis, David A.
1953   Blackhawk Village Site (DA5), Dane County, Wisconsin. *Journal of the Iowa Archeological Society* 2(4):5-20.

1966   Early Salvage Excavations in the Madison Area, Dane County, Wisconsin. *The Wisconsin Archeologist* 42(2):101-131.

1968   Artifact Description: Bone, Stone, and Shell. In Climatic Change and the Mill Creek Culture, Part I. *Journal of the Iowa Archeological Society* 15:107-191.

Baerreis, David A., and Reid A. Bryson
  1956 Climatic Episodes and the Dating of the Mississippian Cultures. *The Wisconsin Archeologist* 46(4):203-220.

Baerreis, David A., and Robert Nero
  1965 The Storage Pits of the Dietz Site and Their Contents. *The Wisconsin Archeologist* 37(1):5-18.

Baerreis, David A., et al.
  1970 Environmental Archaeology in Western Iowa. *Northwest Chapter of the Iowa Archeological Society Newsletter* 18(5):3-15.

Baker, Frank Collins
  1923 The Use of Molluscan Shells by the Cahokia Mound Builders. *Illinois State Academy of Science Transactions* 16:328-34.

Bastian, Tyler
  1962 Some Additional Data on the Beloit College Mound Group (RO15). *The Wisconsin Archeologist* 43(3):57-64.

Beaubien, Paul L.
  1953a Culture Variation within Two Woodland Mound Groups of Northeastern Iowa. *American Antiquity* 19(1):56-66.

  1953b Some Hopewellian Mounds at the Effigy Mounds National Monument, Iowa. *The Wisconsin Archeologist* 19(1):125-38.

Behm, Jeffrey, and Alaric Faulkner
  n.d. *Thermal Alteration of Hixton Quartzite.* Paper presented at the Midwest Archaeological Conference, Milwaukee, Wisconsin, October 12, 1974.

Bellrose, Frank C.
  1968 Waterfowl Migration Corridors East of the Rocky Mountains in the U.S. *Illinois Natural History Survey Biological Notes* 61.

Bellrose, Frank C., and Robert D. Crompton
  1970 Migrational Behavior of Mallards and Black Ducks as Determined from Banding. *Illinois Natural History Survey Bulletin* 30(3).

Bender, Margaret M., Reid A. Bryson, and David A. Baerreis
  1968 University of Wisconsin Radiocarbon Dates IV. *Radiocarbon* 10:161-68.

  1969 University of Wisconsin Radiocarbon Dates VI. *Radiocarbon* 11(1):228-35.

  1970a University of Wisconsin Radiocarbon Dates VII. *Radiocarbon* 12(1):335-45.

  1970b University of Wisconsin Radiocarbon Dates VIII. *Radiocarbon* 12(2):640-43.

216

1971 University of Wisconsin Radiocarbon Dates IX. *Radiocarbon* 13(2):475-86.

1973 University of Wisconsin Radiocarbon Dates XI. *Radiocarbon* 15(3):611-23.

Benn, David W.
1974a Seed Analysis and Its Implications for an Initial Middle Missouri Site in South Dakota. *Plains Anthropologist* 19(63):55-72.

1974b Annuli in the Dental Cementum of White-Tailed Deer from Archeological Contexts. *The Wisconsin Archeologist* 55(2): 90-98.

n.d. *Archaeological Remains in the Pleasant Creek Reservoir, Iowa.* Unpublished report of the 1974 survey and testing by Luther College for the State Conservation Commission of Iowa. Manuscript on file at the Office of State Archaeologist of Iowa.

Benn, David W., and Dean M. Thompson
1977 The Young Site, Linn County, Iowa, and Comments on Woodland Ceramics. *Journal of the Iowa Archeological Society* 24:1-61.

Bennett, John W.
1945 *Archaeological Explorations in Jo Daviess County, Illinois.* University of Chicago Press, Chicago.

Bent, Arthur Cleveland
United States National Museum Bulletins

1923 Life Histories of North American Wild Fowl. 126: Part I.

1925 Life Histories of North American Wild Fowl. 130: Part II.

1932 Life Histories of North American Gallinaceous Birds. 162.

1937 Life Histories of North American Birds of Prey. 167: Part I.

1938 Life Histories of North American Birds of Prey. 170: Part II.

1942 Life Histories of North American Flycatchers, Larks, Swallows and Their Allies. 179.

1958 Life Histories of North American Blackbirds, Orioles, Tanagers, and Their Allies. 211.

1946 *Life Histories of North American Diving Birds.* (reprint of *Bulletin* 107). Dodd, Mead, and Company, New York.

Benton, Allen H.
1955 Observations on the Life History of the Northern Pine Mouse. *Journal of Mammology* 36(1):52-62.

Binford, Lewis R.
1963   A Proposed Attribute List for the Description and Classification of Projectile Points. In Miscellaneous Studies in Typology and Classification. *University of Michigan, Museum of Anthropology Anthropological Papers* 19:193-221.

1965   Archaeological Systematics and the Study of Culture Process. *American Antiquity* 31(2):203-210.

1968   Archeological Perspectives. In *New Perspectives in Archeology*, edited by Sally R. Binford and Lewis R. Binford, pp. 5-32. Aldine Publishing Company, Chicago.

Black, Meredith
1963   The Distribution and Archeological Significance of the Marsh Elder *Iva Annua* L. *Papers of the Michigan Academy of Sciences, Arts, and Letters* 48:541-47.

Bradley, Alice V.
1942   *Tables of Food Values*. Manual Arts Press, Peoria, Illinois.

Branson, Bradley A.
1962   Comparative Cephalic and Appendicular Osteology of the Fish Family Catostomidae. Part I, *Cycleptes Elongatus* (Lesueur). *Southwestern Naturalist* 7(2):81-153.

Brose, David S.
1970   The Archaeology of Summer Island: Changing Settlement Systems in Northern Lake Michigan. *University of Michigan, Museum of Anthropology Papers* 41.

Brown, James A.
1964   The Northeastern Extension of the Havana Tradition. In Hopewellian Studies, edited by J. R. Caldwell and R. L. Hall. *Illinois State Museum Scientific Papers* 12(4).

1965   *The Prairie Peninsula: An Interaction Area of the Eastern United States*. Ph.D. dissertation, Department of Anthropology, University of Chicago.

Buell, Murray F., and John E. Cantlon
1951   A Study of Two Forest Stands in Minnesota with an Interpretation of the Prairie-Forest Margin. *Ecology* 32(2):294-316.

Caldwell, Joseph R.
1962   Eastern North America. In *Courses Towards Urban Life*, edited by Robert J. Braidwood and Gordon R. Willey. Aldine Publishing Company, Chicago.

1964   Interaction Spheres in Prehistory. In Hopewellian Studies, edited by Joseph R. Caldwell and Robert L. Hall. *Illinois State Museum Scientific Papers* 12:133-43.

218

Caldwell, Warren W.
  1961   Archeological Investigations at the Coralville Reservoir, Iowa.
         Bureau of American Ethnology, River Basin Surveys Papers 22,
         Bulletin 179:79-148.

Callen, Eric O.
  1967   Analysis of the Tehaucan Coprolites. In *The Prehistory of the
         Tehaucan Valley*, edited by Douglas S. Byers, pp. 261-89.
         University of Texas Press, Austin.

Canada Department of National Health and Welfare
  1951   *Table of Food Values Recommended for Use in Canada.*
         Nutrition Division, Department of National Health and
         Welfare, Ottawa, Canada.

Carlander, Harriet Bell
  1954   *A History of Fish and Fishing in the Upper Mississippi River.*
         Upper Mississippi River Conservation Committee.

Carr, Archie
  1952   *Handbook of Turtles.* Vail-Ballou Press, Inc., Binghamton, New
         York.

Casteel, Richard W.
  1974   A Method for Estimation for Live Weight of Fish from the Size
         of Skeletal Elements. *American Antiquity* 39(1):94-98.

Chmurny, William W.
  1973   *The Ecology of the Middle Mississippian Occupation of the
         American Bottom.* Ph.D. dissertation, Department of An-
         thropology, University of Illinois.

Clark, J. G. D.
  1954   *Excavations at Starr Carr: An Early Mesolithic Site at Seamer,
         near Scarborough, Yorkshire*, with palynological contributions
         by D. Walker and H. Godwin. Cambridge University Press,
         Cambridge.

Cleland, Charles G.
  1966   The Prehistoric Animal: Ecology and Ethnozoology of the Upper
         Great Lakes Region. *University of Michigan, Museum of
         Anthropology Anthropological Papers* 29.

Cleland, Charles E., and Joan Kearney
  1967   The Vertebrate Fauna of the Chesser Cave Site, Athens County,
         Ohio. In *Studies in Ohio Archaeology*, edited by Olaf H. Pruffer
         and Douglas H. McKenzie. Western Reserve University Press,
         Cleveland.

Coe, Albert E.
  MS   Letter, dated November 5, 1934, to Charles R. Keyes. On file in
         the Keyes Collection, Iowa State Historical Society, Iowa City,
         Iowa.

MS   Two Cave Shelters, letter, dated November 10, 1947, to Charles R. Keyes. On file in the Keyes Collection, Iowa State Historical Society, Iowa City, Iowa.

Cole, Fay-Cooper, and Thorne Deuel
1937   *Rediscovering Illinois.* University of Chicago Press, Chicago.

Collins, Michael B., and Jason M. Fenwick
1974   Heat Treatment of Chert: Methods of Interpretation and Their Application. *Plains Anthropologist* 19(64):134-45.

Conrad, Henry S.
1952   The Vegetation of Iowa. *State University of Iowa Studies in Natural History* 4.

Conrad, Lawrence A., and Robert C. Koeppen
1972   An Analysis of Charcoal from the Brewster Site (13CK15), Iowa. *Plains Anthropologist* 17(55):52-54.

Cook, Sherburne F.
1975   Subsistence Economy of Scovill. *American Antiquity* 40(3):354-56.

Cooperrider, Tom S.
1962   The Vascular Plants of Clinton, Jackson and Jones Counties, Iowa, edited by G. W. Mortin. *State University of Iowa Studies in Natural History* 5.

Cornwall, J.W.
1956   *Bones for the Archaeologist.* Macmillan Company, New York.

Crane, H. R., and James B. Griffin
1961   University of Michigan Radiocarbon Dates VI. Radiocarbon 3:113. *American Journal of Science*, Yale University.

Curtis, John T.
1959   *The Vegetation of Wisconsin.* University of Wisconsin Press, Madison.

Curtis, John T., and R. P. McIntosh
1951   An Upland Forest Continuum in the Prairie-Forest Border Region of Wisconsin. *Ecology* 32(3):476-96.

Cutler, Hugh C.
1956   Corn from the Dietz Site. *The Wisconsin Archeologist* 37(1):18-19.

Cutler, Hugh C., and Leonard W. Blake
1969   Corn from Cahokia Sites. In Explorations into Cahokia Archeology, edited by Melvin L. Fowler. *Illinois Archaeological Survey Bulletin* 7:122-36.

220

1973 *Plants from Archaeological Sites East of the Rockies.* Bound photocopy, compiled at the Missouri Botanical Garden, St. Louis.

Cvancara, Alan M.
1963 Clines in three species of *Lampsilis* (Pelecypoda: Unionidae). *Malocologia* 1(2):215-25.

Dahlberg, Burton L., and Ralph C. Guettinger
1956 The White-tailed Deer in Wisconsin. *Wisconsin Conservation Department Technical Wildlife Bulletin* 14.

Densmore, Frances
1928 Uses of Plants by the Chippewa Indians. *Bureau of American Ethnology Annual Report* 44:275-398.

De Roth, Gerardus C.
1965 Age and Growth Studies of Channel Catfish in Western Lake Erie. *Journal of Wildlife Management* 29(2)280-86.

Duffield, Lathel Flay
1970 *Some Panhandle Aspect Sites in Texas: Their Vertebrates and Paleoecology.* Ph.D. dissertation, Department of Anthropology, University of Wisconsin.

1974 *Nutritional Analysis: An Aid in Reconstructing Prehistoric Diets.* Paper presented at the 39th Annual Meeting of the Society for American Archaeology, Washington, D. C., May, 1974.

Earle, F. R., and Quentin Jones
1962 Analyses of Seed Samples from 113 Plant Families. *Economic Botany* 16(4):221-50.

Elder, William H.
1965 Primeval Deer Hunting Pressures Revealed by Remains from American Indian Middens. *Journal of Wildlife Management* 29(2):366-70.

Emery, Irene
1966 *The Primary Structures of Fabrics.* Spiral Press, New York.

Erickson, James A., and William G. Seliger
1969 Efficient Sectioning of Incisors for Estimating Ages of Mule Deer. *Journal of Wildlife Management* 33(22):384-89.

Esten, Sidney R.
1931 Bird Weights of 52 Species of Birds. *Auk* 58(4):572-74.

Farnsworth, Kenneth B.
1973 An Archaeological Survey of the Macoupin Valley. *Illinois State Museum Reports of Investigations* 26.

Fenner, Gloria J.
1961   The Bowmanville Site. In Chicago Area Archaeology. *Illinois Archaeological Survey Bulletin* 3:37-56.

1963   The Plum Island Site, La Salle County, Illinois. In Illinois Prehistory I. *Illinois Archaeological Survey Bulletin* 4:1-105.

Fernald, Merritt Lyndon
1950   *Gray's Manual of Botany* (eighth ed.). American Book Company, New York.

Fernald, Merritt Lyndon, and Alfred Charles Kinsey
1958   *Edible Wild Plants of Eastern North America*, revised by Reed C. Rollins. Harper & Row, New York.

Flanders, Richard E., and Rex Hansman
1961   A Woodland Mound Complex in Webster County, Iowa. *Journal of the Iowa Archeological Society* 11(1).

Flannery, Kent V.
1967   The Vertebrate Fauna and Hunting Patterns. In *The Prehistory of the Tehaucan Valley*, edited by Douglas S. Byers, 1:132-77. University of Texas Press, Austin.

Ford, Richard I.
1973   The Moccasin Bluff Corn Holes. In The Moccasin Bluff Site and The Woodland Cultures of Southwestern Michigan, edited by Robert Louis Bettarel and Hale G. Smith. *University of Michigan, Museum of Anthropology Anthropological Papers* 49: Appendix 15:189-93.

Fowler, Melvin W.
1952   The Clear Lake Site: Hopewellian Occupations. In Hopewell Communities in Illinois, edited by Thorne Deuel. *Illinois State Museum Scientific Papers* 5(4):133-74.

1959   Summary Report of Modoc Rock Shelter, 1952, 1953, 1955, 1956. *Illinois State Museum Reports of Investigations* 8.

1971a Agriculture and Village Settlement in the North American East: The Central Mississippi Valley Area, A Case History. In *Prehistoric Agriculture*, edited by Stuart Struever, pp. 391-403. Natural History Press, Garden City, New York.

1971b The Origin of Plant Cultivation in the Central Mississippi Valley: A Hypothesis. In *Prehistoric Agriculture*, edited by Stuart Struever, pp. 122-28. Natural History Press, Garden City, New York.

Frankforter, W. D.
1959   The Hill Site. *Journal of the Iowa Archeological Society* 8:47-72.

222

Geier, Clarence R.
   1973   The Flake Assemblage in Archaeological Interpretation. *The Missouri Archaeologist* 35(3-4):1-35.

Getz, Lowell L.
   1961   Factors Influencing the Local Distribution of *Microtus* and *Synaptomys* in Southern Michigan. *Ecology* 42(1):110-19.

Gilbert, B. Miles
   1969   Some Aspects of Diet and Butchering Techniques Among Prehistoric Indians in South Dakota. *Plains Anthropologist* 14(46):277-94.

   1973   Mammalian Osteo-Archaeology: North America. *Missouri Archaeological Society Special Publication.*

Gilbert, Frederick F.
   1966   Aging White-tailed Deer by Annuli in the Cementum of the First Incisor. *Journal of Wildlife Management* 30(1):200-203.

Gilmore, Melvin R.
   1919   Uses of Plants by the Indians of the Missouri River Region. *Bureau of American Ethnology Annual Report* 33:43-154.

   1931   Vegetal Remains of the Ozark Bluff Dweller Culture. *Papers of the Michigan Academy of Science, Arts, and Letters* 14:83-102.

Grayson, Donald K.
   1973   On Methodology of Faunal Analysis. *American Antiquity* 39(4):432-39.

Griffin, James B.
   1952a Culture Periods in Eastern United States Archeology. In *Archeology of the Eastern United States*, edited by James B. Griffin, pp. 352-64. University of Chicago Press, Chicago.

   1952b Some Early and Middle Woodland Types in Illinois. In Hopewellian Communities in Illinois, edited by Thorne Deuel. *Illinois State Museum Scientific Papers* 5(3):95-129.

   1960   Climatic Change: A Contributory Cause of the Growth and Decline of Northern Hopewellian Culture. *The Wisconsin Archeologist* 41(2):21-33.

Griffin, James B., Richard E. Flanders, and Paul F. Titterington
   1970   The Burial Complexes of the Knight and Norton Mounds in Illinois and Michigan. *University of Michigan, Museum of Anthropology Memoirs* 2.

Griffin, James B., and Donald E. Wray
   1945   Bison in Illinois Archaeology. *Illinois Academy of Science Transactions* 30:21-26.

Gromme, Owen J.
  1963 *Birds of Wisconsin.* The University of Wisconsin Press, Madison.

Guilday, John E., Paul W. Parmalee, and Donald P. Tanner
  1962 Aboriginal Butchering Techniques at the Eschelman Site (36LA12), Lancaster County, Pennsylvania. *Pennsylvania Archaeologist* 32(2):59-83.

Haag, W. G.
  1948 An Osteometric Analysis of Some Aboriginal Dogs. *University of Kentucky Reports in Anthropology* 7(3).

Hall, Robert L.
  1973 *An Interpretation of the Two-Climax Model of Illinois Prehistory.* Paper prepared for the IXth International Congress of Anthropological and Ethnological Sciences, Chicago.

  n.d. *A Newly Designated Pottery Type from Northern Illinois.* Mimeographed sheets.

Hallowell, A. Irving
  1926 Bear Ceremonialism in the Northern Hemisphere. *American Anthropologist* 28(1):1-175.

Halsey, John R.
  1966 Additional Hopewell Engraved Turtle Shells from Michigan. *Papers of the Michigan Academy of Science, Arts, and Letters* 51:389-98.

Harington, H. D.
  1967 *Edible Native Plants of the Rocky Mountains.* University of New Mexico Press, Albuquerque.

Harn, Allan D.
  1973 *Cahokia and the Mississippian Emergence in the Spoon River Area of Illinois.* Paper presented at the 52nd Annual Meeting of the Central States Anthropological Society, St. Louis, Missouri, March 29-31, 1973.

Harris, Marvin
  1968 Discussion. In *New Perspectives in Archeology,* edited by Sally R. Binford and Lewis R. Binford, pp. 359-61. Aldine Publishing Company, Chicago.

Harrison, G. A., J. S. Weiner, J. M. Tanner, and N. A. Barnicot
  1964 *Human Biology.* Oxford University Press, Oxford.

Hartley, Thomas G.
  1966 The Flora of the Driftless Area. *University of Iowa Studies in Natural History* 21(1).

Hedges, James, and George W. Darland, Jr.
1963   The Scotch Grove Strath in Maquoketa River Valley, Iowa. *Iowa Academy of Science Proceedings* 70:295-306.

Herron, J. W.
1953   Study of Seed Production, Seed Identification and Seed Germination of *Chenopodium* spp. *Cornell University Agricultural Experiment Station Memoir* 320:1-23.

Hickerson, Harold
1962   The Southwestern Chippewa: An Ethnohistorical Study. *American Anthropological Association Memoir* 64(3): Part 2.

1965   The Virginia Deer and Intratribal Buffer Zones in the Upper Mississipi Valley. In Man, Culture, and Animals, edited by Anthony Leeds and Andrew P. Vayda. *American Association for the Advancement of Science Publication* 78.

Hoffman, Walter James
1896   The Menomini Indians. *Bureau of American Ethnology Annual Report* 14(1):1-238

Holmes, William Henry
1896   Prehistoric Textile Art of the Eastern United States. *Bureau of American Ethnology Report* 13:3-46.

1903   Aboriginal Pottery of the Eastern United States. *Bureau of American Ethnology Annual Report* 20:1-201.

Hubbs, Carl L., and Karl F. Lagler
1958   *Fishes of the Great Lakes Region.* University of Michigan Press, Ann Arbor.

Hunt, George T.
1967   *The Wars of the Iroquois.* University of Wisconsin Press, Madison.

Hurt, Wesley R.
1952   Report of the Investigation of the Scalp Creek Site (39GR1) and the Ellis Creek Site (39GR2). *South Dakota State Archaeological Commission, Archaeological Studies Circular* 4.

Hurley, William Michael
1966   *The Silver Creek Sites (47MO1 to 47MO5): A Complex of Five Woodland Site Localities in Monroe County, Wisconsin.* Masters thesis, Department of Anthropology, University of Wisconsin.

1970   *The Wisconsin Effigy Mound Tradition.* Ph.D. dissertation, Department of Anthropology, University of Wisconsin.

1975   An Analysis of Effigy Mound Complexes in Wisconsin. *University of Michigan, Museum of Anthropology Anthropological Papers* 59.

Jackson, Hartley H. T.
  1961   *Mammals of Wisconsin.* University of Wisconsin Press, Madison.

Jaehnig, Manfred Emil Wilheim
  1975   *The Prehistoric Cultural Ecology of Eastern Iowa as Seen from Two Woodland Rockshelters.* Ph.D. dissertation, Department of Anthropology, University of Wisconsin.

Jenkins, John T., and Holmes A. Semken
  1972   Faunal Analysis of the Lane Enclosure, Allamakee County, Iowa. *Iowa Academy of Science Proceedings* 7(3-4):76-78.

Jenks, A. E.
  1900   Wild Rice Gatherers of the Upper Lakes. *Bureau of American Ethnology Annual Report* 19:1011-1161.

Johnson, A.
  1962   *Chenopodium* as a Food in Blackfoot Prehistory. *Ecology* 43(1):129-30.

Johnson, Alfred E., and Ann S. Johnson
  1975   K-Means and Temporal Variability in Kansas City Hopewell Ceramics. *American Antiquity* 40(3):283-95.

Johnson, Paul C.
  1972   *Mammalian Remains Associated with Nebraska Phase Earth Lodges In Mills County, Iowa.* Masters thesis, Department of Geology, University of Iowa.

Jones, Volney H.
  1936   The Vegetal Remains of Newt Kash Hollow. In Rock Shelters in Menifee County, Kentucky, by W. S. Webb and W. D. Funkhouser. *University of Kentucky Reports in Archeology and Anthropology* 3(4):147-67.

Keslin, Richard O.
  1958   A Preliminary Report of the Hahn (DG 1&2) & Horicon (DG5) Sites, Dodge County, Wisconsin. *The Wisconsin Archaeologist* 39(4):191-273.

Keyes, Charles Reuben
  1927   Prehistoric Man in Iowa. *The Palimpsest* 8(6):185-229.

  1941   An Outline of Iowa Archaeology. *Iowa Academy of Science Proceedings* 48:91-98.

  1949   Four Iowa Archaeologies with Plains Affiliations. *5th Plains Conference for Archaeology, Notebook* 1:96-97.

Kivett, Marvin F.
  1952   Woodland Sites in Nebraska. *Nebraska State Historical Society Publications in Anthropology* 1.

226

Klevefal, G. A., and S. E. Kleinenberg
1969   Age Determination of Mammals by Layered Structure in Teeth and Bone, edited by D. E. Sergeant, translated from Russian. *Fisheries Research Board of Canada, Translation Series* 1024.

Knietz, W. Vernon
1965   *The Indians of the Western Great Lakes: 1615-1760.* University of Michigan Press, Ann Arbor.

Krantz, Grover S.
1959   Distinctions Between the Skulls of Coyotes and Dogs. *Kroeber Anthropological Society Papers* 21:40-42.

1968   A New Method of Counting Mammal Bones. *American Journal of Archaeology* 72(3):286-88.

Lang, R. W.
1968   The Natural Environment and Subsistence Economy of the McKees Rocks Village Site. *Pennsylvania Archaeologist* 38(1-4):50-80.

Lawrence, Barbara, and W. H. Bossert
1967   Multiple Character Analysis of *Canis lupus*, and *familiaris*, with a Discussion of the Relationships of *Canis niger. American Zoologist* 7:223-32.

Lee, Richard B., and Irven Devore (editors)
1968   *Man the Hunter.* Aldine Publishing Company, Chicago.

Leechman, Douglass
1951   Bone Grease. *American Antiquity* 16(4):355-56.

Lewis, R. Barry
1974   Mississippian Exploitative Strategies: A Southeast Missouri Example. *Missouri Archaeological Society Research Series* 11.

Lincoln, Frederick C.
1935   The Waterfowl Flyways of North America. *U.S. Department of Agriculture Circular* 342.

Linton, Ralph
1924   The Significance of Certain Traits in North American Maize Agriculture. *American Anthropologist* 26(3):345-59.

Lippold, Lois Kay
1971   *Aboriginal Animal Resource Utilization in Woodland Wisconsin.* Ph.D. dissertation, Department of Anthropology, University of Wisconsin.

Logan, Wilfred D.
1959   *Analysis of Woodland Complexes in Northeastern Iowa.* Ph.D. dissertation, Department of Anthropology, University of Wisconsin.

Low, William A., and I. M. Cowan
1963   Age Determination of Deer by Annular Structure of Dental Cementum. *Journal of Wildlife Management* 27(3):466-71.

Loy, James D.
1968   A Comparative Style Analysis of Havana Series Pottery from Two Illinois Valley Sites. In Hopewell and Woodland Site Archeology in Illinois. *Illinois Archaeological Survey Bulletin* 6:129-96.

Mallam, Clark R.
1975   *The Iowa Effigy Mound Manifestation: An Interpretative Model.* Ph.D. dissertation, Department of Anthropology, University of Kansas.

n.d.   *The Quandahl Rockshelter: An Historical and Archaeological Reconstruction.* Paper presented at the Iowa Academy of Science meeting, Dubuque, Iowa, April 21, 1971.

Manderville, M. D.
1973   A Consideration of the Thermal Pretreatment of Chert. *Plains Anthropologist* 18(61):177-202.

Martin, A. C., and W. D. Barkley
1961   *Seed Identification Manual.* University of California Press, Berkeley.

Martin, L.
1932   *The Physical Geography of Wisconsin.* University of Wisconsin Press, Madison.

Mason, Ronald J.
1966   Two Stratified Sites on the Door Peninsula, Wisconsin. *University of Michigan, Museum of Anthropology Anthropological Papers* 26.

1970   Hopewell, Middle Woodland and the Laurel Culture: A Problem in Archaeological Classification. *American Anthropologist* 72(4):802-15.

Matteson, Max R.
1958   Analysis of an Environment as Suggested by Shells of Freshwater Mussels Discarded by Indians of Illinois. *Illinois State Academy of Science Transactions* 51(3-4):8-13.

228

Maxwell, Moreau S.
1947   The Succession of Woodland Horizons in the Carbondale Area. *Illinois State Academy of Science Transactions* 40:30-35.

1951   The Woodland Cultures in Southern Illinois. *Logan Museum Publications in Anthropology, Bulletin* 7.

McCance, R. A., and E. M. Widdowson
1947   *The Chemical Composition of Foods.* Chemical Publishing Company, Inc., New York.

McGee, W. J.
1891   The Pleistocene History of Northeastern Iowa. *U.S. Geological Survey Annual Report* 11:189-577.

McGregor, John C.
1957   Prehistoric Village Distribution in the Illinois River Valley. *American Antiquity* 22(3):272-79.

McKern, W. C.
1930   The Kletzien and Nitschke Mound Groups. *Public Museum of the City of Milwaukee Bulletin* 3(4):417-572.

1939   The Midwestern Taxonomic Method as an Aid to Archaeological Culture Study. *American Antiquity* 4:301-313.

1945   Preliminary Report on the Upper Mississippi Phase in Wisconsin. *Public Museum of the City of Milwaukee Bulletin* 16(3):109-285.

McKusick, Marshall
1975   A Perspective of Iowa Prehistory 1841-1928. *The Wisconsin Archeologist* 56(1):16-54.

Meggars, Betty J. (editor)
1956   Functional and Evolutionary Implications of Community Patterning. In Seminars in Archaeology: 1955, edited by Robert Wauchope. *Society for American Archaeology Memoirs* 11:129-57.

Morse, Dan F., and Phyllis A. Morse
1963   Perforated Deer Phalanges. *Tennessee Archaeologist* 29(2):47-56.

Munson, Patrick J., Paul W. Parmalee, and Richard A. Yarnell
1971   Subsistence Ecology of Scovill, A Terminal Middle Woodland Village. *American Antiquity* 36(4):410-31.

Murie, O. J.
1951   *The Elk of North America.* Wildlife Management Institute, Washington, D.C.

Murray, Harold D., and A. Byron Leonard
1962   Handbook of Unionid Mussels in Kansas. *University of Kansas, Museum of Natural History Miscellaneous Publication* 28.

Nelson, N. C.
1917   Contributions to the Archaeology of Mammoth Cave & Vicinity, Kentucky. *American Museum of Natural History Anthropological Papers* 22(1):1-73.

Odum, Eugene
1971   *Fundamentals of Ecology.* W.B. Saunders Company, Philadelphia.

Olsen, Stanley J.
1964   Mammal Remains from Archaeological Sites: Part I, Southeastern and Southwestern U.S. *Peabody Museum of Archaeology and Ethnology Papers* 56(1).

1968   Fish, Amphibian and Reptile Remains from Archaeological Sites: Part I, Southeastern and Southwestern U.S., Appendix: Osteology of the Wild Turkey. *Peabody Museum of Archaeology and Ethnology Papers* 56(2).

Orchard, William C.
1920   Sandals and Other Fabrics from Kentucky Caves. In Indian Notes and Monographs. *Museum of the American Indian, Heye Foundation, Miscellaneous Series* 4.

Orr, Ellison
1971   Reminiscences of A Pioneer Boy, edited by Marshall McKusick. *Annals of Iowa* 7-8: Part I:530-60; Part II:593-630.

Paloumpis, Andreas A.
n.d.   *A Laboratory Manual on Fish Osteology.* Loose leaf notebook. Illinois State University, Normal.

Panshin, A. J., Carl DeZeeuw, and H. P. Brown
1964   *Textbook of Wood Technology,* volume 1. McGraw-Hill Book Company, Inc., New York.

Parmalee, Paul W.
1956   A Comparison of Past and Present Populations of Fresh-Water Mussels in Southern Illinois. *Illinois State Academy of Science Transactions* 49:184-92.

1959   Use of Mammalian Skulls and Mandibles by Prehistoric Indians of Illinois. *Illinois Academy of Science Transactions* 52(3-4):85-95.

1961   Faunal Analysis from the Zimmerman Site, La Salle County, Illinois. Appendix I, In The Zimmerman Site, edited by J. A. Brown. *Illinois State Museum Reports of Investigations* 9.

230

    1965   The Food Economy of Archaic and Woodland Peoples at the Tick Creek Cave Site, Missouri. *Missouri Archaeologist* 27(1).

    1968   Cave and Archaeological Faunal Deposits as Indicators of Post-Pleistocene Animal Populations and Distribution in Illinois. In The Quaternary of Illinois, edited by Robert E. Bergstrom. *University of Illinois College of Agriculture Special Publication* 14:104-113.

Parmalee, Paul W., and Walter E. Klippel
    1974   Freshwater Mussels as a Prehistoric Food Resource. *American Antiquity* 39(3):421-34.

Parmalee, Paul W., Andreas A. Paloumpis, and Nancy Wilson
    1972   Animals Utilized by Woodland Peoples Occupying the Apple Creek Site, Illinois. *Illinois State Museum Reports of Investigations* 23.

Peterson, Roger Tory
    1961   *A Field Guide to Western Birds.* The Riverside Press, Cambridge, Massachusetts.

Pillaert, E. Elizabeth
    1969   Faunal Remains from the Millville Site (47GT53), Grant County, Wisconsin. *The Wisconsin Archeologist* 50(2):93-108.

Pond, Alonzo W.
    1974   Wood Does Not Burn. *Field and Stream* 79(1):38-42.

Pond, Peter
    1933   The Narrative of Peter Pond. In *Five Fur Traders of the Northwest*, edited by Charles M. Gates, pp. 9-59. University of Minnesota Press, Minneapolis.

Quimby, George I.
    1961   Cord Marking Versus Fabric Impressing of Woodland Pottery. *American Antiquity* 26(3):426-28.

    1962   A Year with a Chippewa Family, 1763-1764. *Ethnohistory* 9(3):217-39.

Rachlin, Carol K.
    1955   The Rubber Mold Technique for the Study of Textile Impressed Pottery. *American Antiquity* 20(4):394-96.

Radin, Paul
    1923   The Winnebago Tribe. *Bureau of American Ethnology Annual Report* 37.

Ransom, A. Brian
  1966 Determining Age of White-tailed Deer from Layers in Cementum of Molars. *Journal of Wildlife Management* 30(1):197-99.

Renfew, Jane M.
  1973 *Paleoethnobotany.* Columbia University Press, New York.

Rose, J. N.
  1967 The Fossils and Rocks of Eastern Iowa. *Iowa Geological Survey Educational Series* 1.

Rostlund, Erhard
  1952 Freshwater Fish and Fishing in Native North America. *University of California Publications in Geography* 9.

Ruhe, R. V., W. P. Dietz, T. E. Fenton, and G. F. Hall
  1968 Iowan Drift Problem, Northeastern Iowa. *Iowa Geological Survey Reports of Investigations* 7:1-40.

Saxon, Andrew, and Charles Higham
  1969 A New Research Method for Economic Prehistorians. *American Antiquity* 34(3):303-311.

Schoenbeck, E.
  1946 Cord-Decorated Pottery in the General Peoria Region. *Illinois Academy of Science Transactions* 39:33-42.

Scholtz, James
  1960 The Kingston Site: A Hopewell Mound Group in Southeastern Iowa. *Journal of the Iowa Archeological Society* 10(1):20-35.

Schorger, A. W.
  1937 The Range of the Bison in Wisconsin. *Wisconsin Academy of Sciences, Arts and Letters Transactions* 30.

  1953 The White-tailed Deer in Early Wisconsin. *Wisconsin Academy of Sciences, Arts and Letters Transactions* 42.

  1954 The Elk in Early Wisconsin. *Wisconsin Academy of Sciences, Arts and Letters Transactions* 43.

  1966 *The Wild Turkey, Its History and Domestication.* University of Oklahoma Press, Norman, Oklahoma.

Schultz, Floyd, and Albert C. Spaulding
  1948 A Hopewellian Burial Site in the Lower Republican Valley, Kansas. *American Antiquity* 13(4):306-313.

Scott, Peter, and the Wildlife Trust
  1972 *The Swans.* Fletcher & Sons, Ltd., Norwick, England.

232

Semenov, S. A.
1970   *Prehistoric Technology*, translated by M. W. Thompson. Barth, Adams & Dart, London.

Severinghaus, C. W.
1949   Tooth Development and Wear as Criteria of Age in White-tailed Deer. *Journal of Wildlife Management* 13(2):195-216.

Shay, C. Thomas
1971   The Itasca Bison Kill Site: An Ecological Analysis. *Minnesota Historical Society, Minnesota Prehistoric Archaeology Series.*

Shelford, Victor E.
1963   *The Ecology of North America.* University of Illinois Press, Urbana.

Shepard, Anna O.
1961   Ceramics for the Archeologist. *Carnegie Institute of Washington Publications* 609.

Shippee, J. M.
1967   Archaeological Remains in the Area of Kansas City: The Woodland Period, Early, Middle, and Late. *Missouri Archaeological Society Research Series* 5.

Shotwell, J. Arnold
1955   An Approach to the Paleoecology of Mammals. *Ecology* 36(2):327-37.

Skinner, Alanson
1921   Material Culture of the Menomini. *Museum of the American Indian, Heye Foundation, Indian Notes and Monographs* 20.

       Observations on the Ethnology of the Sauk Indians. *Public Museum of the City of Milwaukee Bulletins*

1923   5(1):1-57 (Part I).

1925a 5(2):59-95 (Part II).

1925b 5(3):119-80 (Part III).

1926   Ethnology of the Ioway Indians. *Public Museum of the City of Milwaukee Bulletins* 5(4):181-354.

Smith, Bruce D.
1974a Middle Mississippian Exploitation of Animal Resources: A Predictive Model. *American Antiquity* 39(2):274-91.

1974b Predator-Prey Relationships in the Eastern Ozarks: AD 1300. *Human Ecology* 2(1):31-43.

Smith, Huron H.
  1923   Ethnobotany of the Menomini Indians. *Public Museum of the City of Milwaukee Bulletin* 4(1):1-174.

  1928   Ethnobotany of the Meskwaki Indians. *Public Museum of the City of Milwaukee Bulletin* 4(2):175-326.

  1932   Ethnobotany of the Ojibwa Indians. *Public Museum of the City of Milwaukee Bulletin* 4(3):327-525.

  1933   Ethnobotany of the Pottawattamie Indians. *Public Museum of the City of Milwaukee Bulletin* 7(1):1-230.

Spector, William S. (editor)
  1956   *Handbook of Biological Data.* Division of Biology and Agriculture, National Academy of Sciences—National Research Council. W.B. Saunders Company, Philadelphia.

Sprunt, Alexander, Jr.
  1955   *North American Birds of Prey.* Harper & Brothers, New York.

Starrett, William C.
  1971   A Survey of the Mussels (Unionacea) of the Illinois River: A Polluted Stream. *Illinois Natural History Survey Bulletin* 30.

Steel, Robert G. D., and James H. Torrie
  1960   *Principles and Procedures of Statistics.* McGraw-Hill Book Company, Inc., New York.

Steward, Julian H.
  1948   A Functional-Developmental Classification of American High Cultures. In A Reappraisal of Peruvian Archaeology, assembled by Wendell C. Bennett. *Society for American Archaeology Memoirs* 4:103-104.

Stoltman, James B.
  1973   The Laurel Culture in Minnesota. *Minnesota Historical Society Prehistoric Archaeology* Series 8.

Storck, Peter Ludlow
  1972   *The Archaeology of Mayland Cave, Parts I and II.* Ph.D. dissertation, Department of Anthropology, University of Wisconsin.

Straffin, Dean
  1971   Wolfe Havana Hopewell Site. In Prehistoric Investigations. *Office of the State Archaeologist of Iowa Reports* 3:53-65.

234

Struever, Stuart
  1964 The Hopewell Interaction Sphere in Riverine-Western Great Lakes Culture History. In Hopewellian Studies, edited by Joseph R. Caldwell and Robert L. Hall. *Illinois State Museum Scientific Papers* 7:85-106.

  1965 Middle Woodland Culture History in the Great Lakes Riverine Area. *American Antiquity* 31(2)Pt.1:211-23.

  1968a *A Re-examination of Hopewell in Eastern North America.* Ph.D. dissertation, University of Chicago.

  1968b Woodland Subsistence-Settlement Systems in the Lower Illinois. In *New Perspectives in Archaeology*, edite by Sally R. Binford and Lewis R. Binford, pp. 285-312. Aldine Publishing Company, Chicago.

Struever, Stuart, and Kent D. Vickery
  1973 The Beginnings of Cultivation in the Midwest-Riverine Area of the United States. *American Anthropologist* 75(5):1197-1220.

Struewer, F. W.
  1943 Raccoons: Their Habits and Management in Michigan. *Ecological Monographs* 13:203-258.

Swanton, John R.
  1946 The Indians of the Southeastern United States. *Bureau of American Ethnology Bulletin* 137.

Thomas, David H.
  1969 Great Basin Hunting Patterns: A Quantitative Method for Treating Faunal Remains. *American Antiquity* 34(4):392-401.

Tiffany, Joseph A.
  1974 An Application of Eigenvector Techniques to the Seed Analysis of the Brogley Rockshelter (47GT156). *The Wisconsin Archeologist* 55(1):2-41.

Tolstoy, Paul
  1953 Some Amerasian Pottery Traits in North Asian Prehistory. *American Antiquity* 19(1):25-39.

Trowbridge, A. C.
  1966 Glacial Drift in the 'Driftless Area' of Northeast Iowa. *Iowa Geological Survey Reports of Investigations* 2:1-28.

United States Department of Agriculture
  1941 *Climate and Man, Yearbook of Agriculture.* U.S. Government Printing Office, Washington, D.C.

United States Forest Service
  1948 Woody-Plant Seed Manual. *U.S. Department of Agriculture Miscellaneous Publication* 654.

Watt, Bernice K., and Annabel L. Merrill
  1963   Composition of Foods. *U.S. Department of Agriculture, Agriculture Handbook.*

Wedel, Mildred Mott
  1959   Oneota Sites on the Upper Iowa River. *The Missouri Archaeologist* 21(2-4).

Wedel, Waldo R.
  1938   Hopewellian Remains Near Kansas City, Missouri. *U.S. National Museum Proceedings* 86:99-106.

Wheeler, Richard P.
  1952   Plains Ceramic Analysis: A Check-list of Features and Descriptive Terms. *Plains Archaeological Conference Newsletter* 5:29-36.

White, Anta M.
  1963   Analytic Description of the Chipped-Stone Industry from Snyders Site, Calhoun County, Illinois. *University of Michigan, Museum of Anthropology Anthropological Papers* 19:1-70.

  1968   The Lithic Industries of the Illinois River Valley in the Early and Middle Woodland Period. *University of Michigan, Museum of Anthropology Anthropological Papers* 35.

White, Theodore E.
  1952   Observations on the Butchering Technique of Some Aboriginal Peoples: I. *American Antiquity* 17(4):337-38.

  1953   A Method of Calculating the Dietary Percentage of Various Food Animals Utilized by Aboriginal Peoples. *American Antiquity* 18(4):396-98.

  1954   Observations on the Butchering Technique of Some Aboriginal Peoples: Numbers 3, 4, 5, & 6. *American Antiquity* 19(3):254-64.

  1955   Observations on the Butchering Techniques of Some Aboriginal Peoples: Numbers 7, 8, & 9. *American Antiquity.* 21(2):170-78.

Will, G. F., and G. E. Hyde
  1917   *Corn Among the Indians of the Upper Missouri.* William Harvey Minor Co., Inc., St. Louis.

Willey, Gordon R., and Philip Phillips
  1958   *Method and Theory in American Archaeology.* University of Chicago Press, Chicago.

Williams, B. J.
  1974   A Model of Band Society. *American Antiquity, Society for American Archaeology Memoirs* 39(4)Pt.2.

236

Willoughby, Charles C.
  1952   Textile Fabrics from the Spiro Mound. In The Spiro Mound, by
          Henry W. Hamilton. *Missouri Archaeologist* 14:107-118.

Wilson, Gilbert Livingston
  1917   Agriculture of the Hidatsa Indians: An Indian Interpretation. In
          Studies in the Social Sciences. *University of Minnesota Bulletin*
          9.

  1924   The Horse and Dog in Hidatsa Culture. *American Museum of
          Natural History Anthropological Papers* 15:Pt.2.

Winters, Howard D.
  1967   An Archaeological Survey of the Wabash Valley in Illinois,
          (revised). *Illinois State Museum Reports of Investigations* 10.

  1969   The Riverton Culture: A Second Millenium Occupation in the
          Central Wabash Valley. *Illinois State Museum Reports of
          Investigations* 13.

Witthoft, John
  1949   Green Corn Ceremonialism in the Eastern Woodlands.
          *University of Michigan, Museum of Anthropology Occasional
          Contributions* 13.

Wittry, Warren L.
  1956   Kolterman Mound 18 Radiocarbon Dates. *The Wisconsin
          Archeologist* 37(4):133-34.

  1959a   The Raddatz Rockshelter, SK5, Wisconsin. *The Wisconsin
          Archeologist* 40(2):33-69.

  1959b   Archeological Studies of Four Wisconsin Rock Shelters. *The
          Wisconsin Archeologist* 40(4).

Wittry, Warren L., and E. G. Bruder
  1955   Salvage Operations at the Kolterman Mound Group, Dodge
          County. *The Wisconsin Archeologist* 36(1):3-12.

Wray, Donald E., and Richard S. MacNeish
  1961   The Hopewellian and Weaver Occupations of the Weaver Site,
          Fulton County, Illinois. *Illinois State Museum Scientific Papers*
          7(2).

Yarnell, Richard A.
  1964   Aboriginal Relationships between Culture and Plant Life in the
          Upper Great Lakes Region. *University of Michigan, Museum of
          Anthropology Anthropological Papers* 23.

  1965   Early Woodland Plant Remains and the Question of Cultivation.
          The Florida Anthropologist 18(2):77-82.

Zawacki, April Allison, and Glenn Hausfater
　1969　Early Vegetation of the Lower Illinois Valley. *Illinois State Museum Reports of Investigations* 17.

Zimmerman, Earl G.
　1965　A Comparison of Habitat and Food of Two Species of *Microtus*. *Journal of Mammology* 46(4):605-612.

Series Titles

Established in 1959, the Office of State Archaeologist has the primary responsibility for the discovery, excavation, and preservation of antiquities (Iowa Laws 305A). The State Archaeologist is appointed by the Board of Regents and serves on the faculty in Anthropology. Headquarters are at Eastlawn Building, The University of Iowa, Iowa City. Beginning in 1970, a series of reports and books has been issued on various investigations, describing and interpreting the discoveries. These studies should be ordered from the University of Iowa Department of Publications, Iowa City 52242. The prices include postage.

The Davenport Conspiracy by Marshall McKusick. 1970, report 1. (Out of print.)

The Kingston Oneota Site by Dean F. Straffin. 1971, report 2, cloth $5, paperback (out of print).

Prehistoric Investigations by Adrian Anderson, David Baerreis, Jerry Clark, Dale R. Henning, William M. Hurley, Marshall McKusick, Holmes A. Semken, Dean F. Straffin, and Larry J. Zimmerman. 1971, report 3. (Out of print.)

The Grant Oneota Village by Marshall McKusick, Appendix by Holmes A. Semken. *Commentary* by David S. Brose, Alfred W. Bowers, David Baerreis, Hester A. Davis, Henry P. Field, Elizabeth J. Glenn, Dale R. Henning, William M. Hurley, Floyd G. Lounsbury, and G. Richard Peske. 1973, report 4, paperback $3.

Post-Conquest Developments in the Teotihuacan Valley, Mexico: Part 1, Excavations by Thomas H. Charlton. 1972, report 5, cloth $5, paperback $3.

Silver Creek Woodland Sites, Southwestern Wisconsin by William Hurley. 1975, report 5, paperback $4.

Physical Affiliations of the Oneota Peoples by Elizabeth J. Glenn. 1975, report 7, paperback $4.

The Iowa Northern Border Brigade by Marshall McKusick. 1975, report 8, cloth $5.50.

The Iowa Effigy Mound Manifestation: An Interpretive Model by R. Clark Mallam. 1976, report 9, paperback $4.

Prehistoric Locational Behavior: A Computer Simulation by Larry J. Zimmerman. 1977, report 10, paperback $4.

The Central Plains Tradition: Internal Development and External Relationships by Donald J. Blakeslee. 1978, report 11, paperback $5.

Oneota Culture in Northwestern Iowa by Amy E. Harvey. 1979, report 12, paperback $8.

Hadfields Cave: A Perspective on Late Woodland Culture in Northeastern Iowa by David W. Benn. 1980, report 13, paperback $6.

HADFIELDS CAVE: A PERSPECTIVE ON LATE
WOODLAND CULTURE IN NORTHEASTERN IOWA
DAVID W. BENN   APPENDICES A–F
CARD NO. 1
DATE: 1980